SOME BRIGHT MORNING, I'LL FLY AWAY

SOME
BRIGHT
MORNING,
I'LL FLY
AWAY

A MEMOIR

ALICE ANDERSON

ST. MARTIN'S PRESS ❧ NEW YORK

SOME BRIGHT MORNING, I'LL FLY AWAY. Copyright © 2017 by Alice Anderson. All rights reserved. Printed in the United States of America. For information, address St. Martin's Press, 175 Fifth Avenue, New York, N.Y. 10010.

www.stmartins.com

Designed by Anna Gorovoy

The Library of Congress Cataloging-in-Publication Data is available upon request.

ISBN 978-1-250-09496-4 (hardcover)
ISBN 978-1-250-11185-2 (ebook)

Our books may be purchased in bulk for promotional, educational, or business use. Please contact your local bookseller or the Macmillan Corporate and Premium Sales Department at 1-800-221-7945, extension 5442, or by email at MacmillanSpecialMarkets@macmillan.com.

First Edition: August 2017

10 9 8 7 6 5 4 3 2 1

This book is dedicated to my sweet three, Avery, Grayson, and Aidan, without whom I would not have been able to fly away to such sweet "finally."

ACKNOWLEDGMENTS

I would like to express my profound gratitude to Jen Gates at Avevitas Creative Management, who saw this book from the first fifty pages to final draft and championed me every step of the way; to Nichole Argyres at St. Martin's Press, who believed without wavering in this memoir and the poet who wrote it; and to Mira Bartok, Jo-Ann Mapson, Barry Goldstein, Daniel Jensen, the late Stormé Delarverie, the late Norris and Norman Mailer, Stephen King and the Haven Foundation, PEN America, Caroline Leavitt, Luis Alberto Urrea, Lidia Yuknavich, my writing teachers Mark Doty, Jean Valentine, Sharon Olds, Dennis Schmitz, and especially the late Thomas Lux, my mother, Mary Anderson, and, of course, Avery, Grayson and Aidan Anderson.

PROLOGUE

We make chapels of our scars.

They cross our skin and soul, a topographic map of the past. Our scars are built on the delicate yet dazzling scaffolding holding our weary, ragtag hearts aloft. I have in me a scar where my childhood sits, made up of playground songs and the raised-red slap of despair, inside the slate-blue cloudless empty spot between my ribs. In me there is a scar made of Paris nights so bright, plumblack and terrifying, my legs striding cobbled streets toward something, anything, that doesn't look like disaster. In me I have a wedding scar, pasted on with disappointment, made of that sinking feeling of not knowing if you do, the moment before the moment you are required to say *I do*, and do. There is a childbirth scar, born of the one who came and left at once in blood and tears—too soon, too soon. There is a father scar, made of terrible nights and resolution and a line of still green trees standing ornate as lace in a grove outside a medical school, where my father gave his body, saying *my body for yours*: a kind of atonement by tree. And I must admit in me there is a terror scar—it snakes so gingerly around my life entire, barbed and impossible to escape, a battered paper sack of oblivion I carry with me everywhere I go. But there are love scars, too, the most jagged of them all—where one child and another and another and another were born in fire and bliss; where the one whose eyes shone like promise embraced you night after night, sharp kisses holding impossible daylight at bay. Every one of them is a chapel. Every one of them becomes the religion of your life.

We all make chapels of our scars.

PART ONE

SMITHEREENS

HOW I LEARNED

TO SHOOT A GUN

Extraordinary things always happen on ordinary days. It was another quiet Mississippi morning, with the acrid scent of debris-pile fires sharp in the humid air. The kids and I were making trips back and forth between the FEMA trailer perched in Mr. Manning's backyard and the Land Rover when his daughters, Lana and Shelby, showed up and asked the kids if they wanted to go to town for some errands and a treat. Lana was my best friend; Liam had always hated her. With porcelain skin devoid of makeup, a wild head of black curly hair, jeans so tight and tank tops so small, Lana was more '80s Nagel poster come to life than proper Southern gal.

The kids loved her, and so did I.

These days my sweet three were attached to me like sequins on an opera diva, but Lana and Shelby mentioned going to Tato-Nut (the local doughnut shop in downtown Ocean Springs, where the sinfully hand-fried doughnuts were made of a mashed potato dough), and so the kids eagerly hopped in her van, and it pulled away down the long, red dirt drive.

Mr. Manning, otherwise known to all as "Daddy," took one look at me standing there in my vintage Wranglers and sleeveless plaid shirt, cocked his eyebrow, and gave me "the look."

You know: *the look.* The one your daddy gives before he shoves you off the lake cliff, or guns the boat motor, or buys you your first shot in a dive bar down to Bayou La Batre. Like there's about to be trouble.

"Welp," he said, watching the van disappear between the scorched towers of salt pine savanna on either side of Poticaw Bayou Road. "Might as well learn you a bit of something while they're gone," he called over his shoulder, heading off in the direction of Lana's house.

We walked the three or four houses down the street to Lana's, went through the back door into the mudroom, then the kitchen, where he went about removing all the cereal boxes from the cabinet above the fridge.

"Are we supposed to—?" I started to ask.

"Hush up, now! You think I need permission to be in my own girl's kitchen?" He laughed.

Then he went about setting four, five, then six, finally nine pistols on Lana's kitchen counter, all in a row. Now, I'd never touched a gun before, let alone had a row of them lined up before me like new pocketbooks down to the Gautier mall out on Highway 90. We stood there, on opposite sides of Lana's periwinkle speckled kitchen counter, silent, staring down at the guns. Finally, Daddy broke the ice.

"Which one y'like?" he asked.

I stood looking at them for a bit, momentarily speechless.

"Well?"

"I don't even, I mean, I've never, I guess. Well, are these? I don't, you know, where did these? Um, did they? I just, it's just that, I couldn't, I mean, I can. I just haven't, or shouldn't, or, well, you know, I have kids! But I do want to, well, you know. Shoot."

Daddy laughed at me—hand slappin' his thighs, turning around in circles, wiping tears from his eyes, trying to speak but falling apart in squawking sounds of total conniption, stomping his boots, and finally (mercifully) resting his head on his arms on the Formica countertop and letting out a big, long, high-pitched sigh.

"Whew, girl! That was the best damn laugh I had since George Bush was on the WLOX changing a porch bulb with that Gautier doctor!"

Well, that got me.

See, after the storm, George Bush caught a lot of grief for being virtually absent from the disaster. He was off doing God knows what all while people tried to rise up from the mud and get their dead cool enough to bury. So before you could drag your party barge off your grandma's roof, Bush finally decided to do a flyby, past New Orleans, and on down the coast to Mississippi, where it seemed the whole world could not give a good goddamn we'd suffered a direct hit. Grayson and I were folding another load of our neighbor's clothes we'd done running the washing machine off the generator one day when we heard the unmistakable *whap whap whap whap* of a helicopter's propeller cutting through the wet air. We ran out just as it broke across the line of our roof behind us and passed above our heads: I stooped to scoop up Grayson instinctually, all the while hunched over like those blades would cut me down. But to my disappointment, Marine One passed right over us and landed another block down on the lawn of Dr. Jim Bullinger.

Bush stepped out, proceeded to shake hands, survey the swanky, mostly untouched-by-the-storm-surge yard, then stepped up on his porch, media clamoring, to change a bulb.

One damn bulb.

Meanwhile, folks were waiting for the earth to dry to bury their dead.

"Are you waiting for Jesus' Second Coming?"

Daddy knocked me back into the reality of that kitchen, and the guns, and how quickly I'd come from there to here.

"I can't," I finally announced.

"Yes, you can. And you will. And I'm going to teach you. Pick one."

There was a big black one that looked heavy as hell; a fancy little one with what appeared to be actual mother-of-pearl inlay that had my name all over it. There was a useful-looking metal number that looked either very professional or as if it were purchased in the "as seen on TV" section. Another had an old-fashioned, tooled Western handle. One was black, one flat gray, nondescript: shiny or not shiny, with smooth surfaces or textured shells.

"Where did y'all get all these?" I asked finally.

"That, my dear, ain't none of your business," Daddy scolded, then went about telling me where each and every gun came from and why it would never be able to be traced.

One came from his buddy down the road who bought it from his nephew's teammate on the football team at Ole Miss. One came from a gun show, where he got a guy to throw it in for free when he made a substantial purchase of a hunting rifle and other various items, after much bargaining. Another came from one of the ladies down to Mac's Ladies' Circle Bible Study. One someone in the family got in their stocking from Santa.

"You pick one, whichever one you want. If ever you fire it— provided you hit your man—ain't nobody ever going to know where the gun come from unless you see fit to say so. And if you do snitch like a damned fool, then I'm going to side with your snake-ass-soon-to-be-ex-husband and say you're just a Little Miss Nutcase. Got it?"

"Yes, sir," I whispered, heart beating loudly in my ears like a panicked bird in dark eaves.

"Now, don't go looking at me like that; y'all know you and your brood are family now, and we're behind you all the way, and that motherfucker ain't going to get away with any of this crap, and he sure as shit ain't going to come back and take up where he left off, and I wouldn't be here if I didn't trust you enough not to sell me down south to the fuzz."

I picked up one of the all-black guns that wasn't too big, wasn't too small, and looked like I might be able to handle it. With it cradled in my hands like a scented bouquet, I found myself unable to speak.

"And let me congratulate you, Miss Alice, for havin' the good sense to pass over that pretty mother-of-pearl pistol that's got you all aflutter because, A, it can't shoot worth a damn, and B, it shows you've got some jalapeño hush puppies hidden in those Yankee dungarees," he said, chuckling. "Now, let's go shoot."

"Yes, sir," I whispered, and I followed him out the door.

We walked down the road to the little white house, and he led me about fifty yards northeast of the house, to his shed—a squat, shanty-like structure.

I call it a shed for lack of a better term.

A shed brings to mind a structure for storing a riding mower, or tools, or an old pickup. A shed is a place you shove all your crap in when your garage is full up to the rafters. A shed is where boys go to set things on fire and smoke things their mamas told them not to. A shed is where a girl stashes letters from her secret boyfriend and where a man keeps a lockbox of cash he don't want his wife to know about.

This was less of a shed, more of a bunker. The walls were made of odd bits of cast-off materials. One wall was the ever-present corrugated tin. Another seemed to be patched-together pieces of an old railroad car or dumpster, with E-N-S-A-C-O-L-A in rusting two-foot-high blue letters stamped across the top. The third was clearly made from wooden privacy fencing. The fourth wall, the one that held the door, was simply a patchwork of varying, mystery rough-hewn odds and ends. The cciling was low, and Daddy had to stoop a bit as he made his way around in there. Every inch of space was crammed full up with all manner of industrial gadgets and tools, a virtual museum of country manhood.

I'd never been inside there before—never pondered the notion. But I tell you—that place was organized like you wouldn't believe. There must have been two hundred baby jar lids nailed to one wall, and that many jars again filled with every kind of thing you can (and can't) imagine a man might have in a shed screwed tight to each lid.

"Now, I've had my boys in here and my grandsons once or twice, but none of the girls, not a one, so you're sworn to silence, hear?" He lowered his eyes at me.

"Right," I agreed, pretty much along for the ride.

I had the medium-sized, midnight-black, not-too-heavy pistol in my skirt pocket, and I was keenly aware of that side of my body. I felt as if I were standing in one of those trick rooms at an amusement park, the kind that makes you feel like you're a freakish giant and that the whole earth is tipping and you're the only thing straining to stand up straight.

"Mac tells me you're a poet. A *real* poet," he said, one ragged eyebrow raised.

I nodded, not sure what he was getting at.

"Well, I didn't know people could be a real poet anymore, but I guess if there's still boys that choose to be a priest, there's likely some crazy girl who'd choose to be a poet, though I don't know what all kind of job you'd get with that kind of learnin'," he bantered, almost to himself.

"Yes, sir. I'm not known for my practical side."

"No matter, girl. Probably the world needs poets, and anyway, that's what made me decide to bring you in here and show you my bullets."

"Your bullets, sir?"

"My bullets." He smiled, that same eyebrow cocked high, nearly raising off the top of his head.

He was enjoying this.

There was a long pause. Dust motes sank in the humid air in the slash of jade light coming through a long stretch of green plastic standing in for a window.

"I make them myself."

Now, I should say that at this point, I was a girl covered in bruises and knife wounds living in an abandoned FEMA trailer, about to move back into her big, fancy house, whose husband had just been thrown out of his own house by the Jackson County sheriff. I don't know why standing in a makeshift shed with Daddy about to show me his homemade bullets brought me such an overwhelming sense of serenity, but it did.

In the back corner of the shed were two big drums full of what looked like broken-up pieces of metal about the size of cheese snack crackers. Dirty, grease-smeared metal pieces by the hundreds, maybe thousands. Daddy took a handful from one barrel, walked it back over to me, and threw the pieces down across his worktop like a fistful of dice.

"Any idea what these might be?" he asked.

I picked one up. They were heavy. Cold. Pale silver, with a bit of patina. Rough at the edges where they'd been broken up in chunks.

"Look closer," he urged.

I had no idea.

"C'mon, girl! Take a guess!" he urged.

I picked up a few more, held them up in the bottle-green, tropical air. Each piece had what looked like a reversed word or part of a word on it, raised metal text. Daddy chuckled when he saw me starting to figure it out.

"Typewriters?" I ventured.

"Do typewriters come with whole words on the keys, Miss

Smarty Poet Yankee Doodle Girl College?" Apparently, news had gone around I'd gone to Sarah Lawrence.

"No, sir," I mumbled, trying to read the words, having figured out at this point that most of the words were broken into pieces but that a few of the little metal chunks held at least one complete word or two, such as *the following d* or *rd and hen day* if you could remember to read them backward.

"Printing press, girl! It's from a printing damn press!" he shouted.

Then he told me where he had gotten these drums of printing press pieces, and he also explained to me how he heated them up, mixed them with Lord knows what all else, mashed them into little bullet molds, and turned them into his very own, homemade bullets, but in all honesty, I can barely remember a word of that part of the story.

I was having a moment—one of those destinations in time where you arrive and it seems the world is made for you. Some call it fate, others coincidence. To me, it's poetry: something I recognize in the world and feel in my soul.

Here I was, a girl whose husband had nearly killed her, a husband who had forbidden her years before from ever writing another poem, standing in a shed in unincorporated Latimer, Mississippi, with an untraceable pistol in her pocket and a barrel of broken-up stories sitting ready to be transformed into ammunition in the corner, waiting on getting her first lesson on how to shoot a gun.

He gave me a handful of bullets for my other pocket.

"C'mon," he said, "there's only so many Tato-Nuts them little rug rats can scarf."

We went through the garden patch and cut north toward the pond to a stand of trees in an otherwise elegant, silent clearing. There was a battered folding table out there, and a pile of newspapers underneath with a big rock on top to keep them from taking flight like seabirds. Daddy took a paper off the stack, walked into the grove, opened up the paper, folded it back again to expose a page with a big picture of some smiling politician with his hand up in the air in a sign of victory. Daddy brought a small hammer and a tack out of his pocket, nailed the page to a tree, and walked back to me.

"Hold it up like this," he said, coming behind me, grabbing my arms, putting me in place to shoot the gun. "Choose a target in the picture, find it, mark it, take a deep breath. And when you're ready—shoot," he whispered, his breath hot in my ear.

It was quiet.

About three seconds passed.

I pulled the trigger.

The sound was a shock. I didn't fall back; didn't drop the gun. The paper fluttered.

"Damn!" yelled Daddy, running across the field to the paper, still tacked to the tree. "Woo-hoo, girlie! You hit it, pre'near almost hit the target! You hit his hand."

I yelled, "Get out of the way, Daddy! His hand was what I was aimin' at!"

I found my mark again, made sure Daddy was a good bit off to the side and out of range, and shot again, this time hitting FEMA head Michael Brown right between the eyes.

Daddy ripped the paper from the tree and came running back to me, waving the paper above his head in a circle like a victory flag. He wrapped me up in his long arms and took my head in his hand, practically smashing it to his bony chest.

"You're a natural, girl. You gonna be okay."

I fell into his chest that smelled like chocolate and gunpowder and grease, laid my hand over his heart, felt it beat.

My other hand still held that pistol, scorching hot next to my thigh, with four more story bullets ready at the waiting.

CALAMITY

I sang the names of storms. When Hurricane Katrina barreled full force like a furious auntie breaking down a locked bedroom door into Ocean Springs, Mississippi, I never imagined the complete devastation of my town as I knew it would be the least of my troubles. A storm like that hits and you think you're going to have to go about rebuilding a life, a house, a town. What you don't expect is that your whole life—marriage, body, soul—will be blown to such ornate shreds that you will have to, if you hope to survive, resurrect your life entire. We'd evacuated so many times that season—with each named storm. I had been singing the named storms of 2005 with Avery to the tune of the alphabet song, and knew every one.

Arlene, Bret, Cindy, Dennis, Emily, Franklin, Gert, Harvey, Irene. Irene toppled three of our trees, one of which barely missed our house. We thought ourselves lucky.

Then *Jose*: scot-free.

And then *Katrina*.

We'd entered the long, slow procession east in a last-minute mandatory evacuation when the storm turned overnight in its path and headed straight for us. What I didn't know as I woke up blinking against harsh light in a tacky Tallahassee motel room with my sweet three lying against me—all of them sweaty, arms akimbo, their diapers puffed up with pee—was that the devastation I was about to endure wasn't to my beloved Mississippi coast as I knew it but to my life entire.

Because this is the story of my unraveling.

Like a strange ball of ribbon dropped from the sky in a storm—random, out of control—my life unfurled in a series of disastrous, love-soaked, sometimes dazzling, sometimes devastating events marked by a doomed love, by babies born, by a once-in-a-lifetime hurricane, by brutal domestic violence, by a night of the soul so long it seemed that daylight might never come. All of it complicated by a Gothic legal battle, a traumatic brain injury, and affairs of the heart both sweetly maternal and wildly romantic.

But on this day, I was in a scratchy motel bed with three babies, and I didn't know if I had a house or town or pot to stir in.

This is also the story of redemption found within a storm and how some things hold true, no matter what. There's one true thing about a hurricane: it doesn't change people, it exposes them. And yet how extraordinary circumstances led me to slip so slowly yet effortlessly, disastrously, down into the dark, silky, shameful corners of abuse over unchecked time.

Because abuse doesn't arrive with a neon light.

A neon light flashing DIRTY, UGLY, DIRTY, UGLY.

Instead, abuse comes in an exquisitely carved box, a boxful of secrets I thought (as every abuse victim does) only I was equipped enough—special enough—to acquire, to transform.

Abuse is a secret. A pact. A seduction.

Like a hurricane, it comes without warning.

Red flags blow in the storm, always there, often ignored.

Ignored because disaster fatigue and a kind of resigned tolerance to destruction of the heart led me to ignore all the warnings.

Abuse is quiet.

Abuse is seductive.

Abuse is a fucking liar.

But this is not a story about finding myself, but of finding my way back—back from the edge of a place where who I was was nearly erased. There's a pure white page that sits at the seat of my soul, and typed in black raised letters are the things that make me: poet, mama, woman, fighter. I walk through fire after fire, the flames threatening to burn that page at the center of my soul, to turn me to ash. This is how I fought the flames. This is how, even when I was ankle-deep in the ashes of personal tragedy, I rose.

And so I pulled myself out from under the sleeping heap of that lopsided motel bed and flipped on the TV set to see what I could see.

Most of the coverage was of New Orleans, where the levees broke. People perched on roofs they'd hacked out of, folks wading through water, pulling babies propped up in floating beer coolers, whole bridges of stunned folks from the jail wandering the expanse of a highway bridge, suddenly set another barely kind of free.

All of that was awful. I held my fingers over my mouth and watched, waiting. About five minutes of every hour of coverage focused on the Mississippi Gulf Coast. There were wide helicopter shots, showing what looked like scraped earth and ruin. Every floating Biloxi casino ripped from its moors and crashed, thrown upcoast, destroying everything in the way. The frozen chicken shipping containers in Gulfport Harbor had broken free and covered miles and miles of land with raw, now-rotting chicken carcasses. I saw the oceanfront mausoleum, the caskets ripped clean out, littering the beaches, the structure itself like one of those

Connect Four children's games where you dropped your coins in the slots, with the sunlight now streaming straight through.

I watched, desperate for a glimpse of my town. Finally, another helicopter shot flew to the east end of Biloxi and panned over the Biloxi Bay Bridge, what we locals call the Ocean Springs–Biloxi bridge, which was collapsed bit by bit, broken triangles of concrete and steel littering the bay. The newscaster said, "That looks to be the town of Ocean Springs ahead—likely more of the same destruction found there." Then the copter shot panned back westward, without even a glimpse of my town.

It was then I noticed he was gone.

My husband, Liam, was not in the room. His bag was gone from the closet, his wallet from the table, his toiletries gathered and vanished from the bathroom counter. I found a note propped up against the little coffeemaker:

Gone back to see if I can help. Left you the car. Buy supplies.

On the lid of the coffee carafe: a Visa card.

For just a few minutes it was silent. I whispered to myself as I put some water on for tea and to make the baby a bottle: *Don't cry. Don't cry. You ain't got time to cry. Crying's for pussies and cowards, and you are neither. Get it together, Alice. Get going. Generators will sell out before noon, diapers soon after. Don't you fucking cry.*

"Who you talkin' to, Mama?" Avery asked behind me.

"I guess myself, baby."

"You said bad words, Mama."

"I know, shuggie, I'm sorry. It's a bad day."

I realized then she was standing staring at the TV, her eyes wide. She looked at me, tears filling her eyes.

"We still got our house, Mama?"

"I don't know, baby, but I'm trying to find out. Wake up your brothers; we fixin' to leave."

"Okay, Mama. But you know what?" she asked, her hair a tangled mess.

"What, baby?"

"I ain't gonna cry neither."

We got the boys up and their diapers changed. When Avery started to open our suitcases, I stopped her. We all put on the clothes we'd had on the night before. Who knew when we'd be able to wash clothes again? What we had on the day before was fine enough. As I threw our bags out into the hall at the top of the motel stairs, my babies stood in the motel room, light coming in behind them. Aidan, just a toddler, his sandy hair brushed to the side as always, chubby brown legs in a sumo stance, smiled around the thumb he sucked, his big green eyes smiling, too. Avery, in her little cotton dress and pink rider boots with the hand-tooled butterfly detail, held one hand reflexively on her brothers' hips, holding them back from running out the door, was somehow in motion even in her stillness. Her hair, wild and dark blond, was almost to her waist, her huge eyes peering out from the tiny features of her face, full of earnest concern. And Grayson, always the thinker, the quiet one, stood with his tiny head bowed, platinum hair shorn almost to his skull, eyes staring at the floor. People often confused his quiet for shy, but I knew that even at three years old, there was a world of thought behind those sky-blue eyes.

At checkout, I asked to use the computer and logged into my e-mail. There were more than twenty e-mails from family and friends asking if we'd made it. I wrote back the same to each one: *Alive. Be in touch soon.*

I loaded our bags into the car and headed for Home Depot, knowing it would already be a zoo. When I got there, I got the last two generators they had—huge ones, about a thousand bucks each—and a kind young man loaded them for us into the back of the Land Rover. I put down all the seats except the front and moved the baby's car seat up by me. The other two car seats I left in the parking lot of Home Depot and drove away.

After a storm that big, all bets (and rules of law) are off.

At Costco, I filled whatever room was left in the back of the car with cases of diapers, flats of soup and chili, crackers, enormous jars of peanut butter, eight cases of bottled water. Right before I got to the checkout, I grabbed a pack of plain white men's T-shirts and a pair of white rubber shrimper boots my size. Across the parking lot was a chain Mexican restaurant, with a field behind it where what looked like hundreds of big white electrical trucks were staged, like white Arabians all in a line, about to take off. I put Aidan on one hip, Grayson on the other, told Avery to hold my skirt, and walked to the restaurant. Inside, every table was filled with truck drivers. We stood waiting a good while for a table. Finally, a couple of guys sitting at a six top motioned us over.

"Hey—y'all can sit with us," one said, motioning to the four empty seats at their table.

We sat down, the waitress swapping out wooden high chairs for both boys. Grayson was so tiny he was often mistaken for an infant, even though he was three. Avery sat up close to me, didn't look at the men.

"I'm Dave, and this here's LaRoy. Y'all from the coast?"

"Yes, sir, I got our truck loaded up and was thinking of heading back in."

"It's still mandatory evacuation," LaRoy said.

"I know, but I don't know what else to do. I got my truck loaded full up with generators and supplies, and if I leave it anywhere too long, it's gonna get jacked."

"Ain't you got no husband?" LaRoy interrupted, a skeptical look on his face.

"I do, but I woke up this morning and he's gone! Left a note on the coffeepot saying he went back to try to help. He's a doctor."

"Well, how'd he get in? Y'all bring two cars?"

"No, sir, just the one. I don't know how. I don't know anything."
Don't cry, don't cry, don't cry, crying's for pussies and cowards.
Dave and LaRoy exchanged glances, nodded.

"That settles it; y'all going in with us, girl," LaRoy announced. "Y'all got people once you got there?"

"Yes, sir," I lied. I had my girlfriends and my church friends, but I'm pretty sure that's not the "people" he meant. But I wasn't taking a chance he'd change his mind.

"Eat up quick now—we fixin' to leave."

So that's how I ended up sneaking back into the mandatory evacuation zone, my puny-in-comparison Land Rover about twentieth in a caravan of what looked to be a hundred-odd trucks. I felt like a silly little girl riding a streamer-bedecked trike in the middle of a formal funeral procession. I felt ridiculous. I felt small.

I was also born to fight, brought up on dark nights where survival was the only choice. Fight was a part of me, a reflex; I could shut down or rev up whatever resource of the soul needed to make it through hell. I had the scars to prove it.

If only I'd known what was coming, I might not have been so cocky.

We squared our bills, went out, and I pulled the Land Rover into the long line of electric trucks like a white procession into the heart of it all.

We headed west. The closer we got, the worse things looked. Across the long bridge over Mobile Bay, I saw the first hint of destruction. The seafood joints at the ends of long piers, the bars, the wholesale shrimp shacks—all gone. We kept driving. Just past Mobile, I noticed all the trees were red—a deep umber color, leaves burned off by saltwater surge. It was unfathomable how my world could be drowned and scorched at once, but that's how destruction often goes.

As soon as we crossed the border off Alabama into Mississippi, it was hell on earth.

At Pascagoula, every building stood in ruins, roofs ripped off, doorways blown open, empty shells of structures with debris rammed up sometimes ten feet or more high against the southern walls. Most trees were down, but those that stood, mostly oaks, were free of leaves and tangled thick with every odd manner of thing—sheets and curtains, trousers, purple lengths of silver-backed insulation, fishing nets and lace tablecloths and sodden fancy great room rugs.

At the Pascagoula Bridge the caravan stopped. A guy came banging one by one on each truck driver's window, yelling, "Back it up, half the bridge's down, we goin' on the wrong side over." We all backed up probably half a mile and then slowly headed the wrong way, west, on the east-going side of the bridge. The baby slept in his car seat. Avery was next to me with Grayson in her lap. I felt like an outlaw with the kids up front like that, but they were excited; both Avery and Grayson kept standing up and pointing at each new sight to see.

I spotted up ahead a body to the side of the bridge and told the kids to sit down and close their eyes, *now.*

As we traveled the last few trepidatious lengths of bridge into the town of Gautier, a single tree stood next to the now-still gulf, full up entirely with enormous vultures, like a skinny old man in a too-big, shiny, black raincoat. Ahead, the electric trucks turned one by one onto the Jackson County Fairgrounds in Pascagoula, their next staging area.

Little did I know that I'd spend the better part of the next couple of years of my life at those fairgrounds.

LaRoy and Dave stopped in front of me before turning in. LaRoy hopped out, ran back, and I rolled down my window.

"Damn, it's bad, girl. Your house far from here?" he asked.

"If I even have a house. But, no, sir, just about ten minutes up ahead. I'm going forward."

Don't cry, don't cry, crying's for pussies and cowards.

He leaned in and kissed me on the cheek then, real hard. "You come back and find me if you need me, girl, hear?"

I nodded, my mouth set in the ugly, turned-down pre-cry, stubborn line. We drove on, along Bienville Boulevard, otherwise known as Highway 49, through the undeveloped salt pine savanna woods between Gautier and Ocean Springs, now like a long, flat, endless pelt of a giant porcupine thrown down across miles of earth, the trees broken off sharply at the top like quills, burned black from salt water, devoid of green. Everything was silent. What birds remained were pushed and buried into pockets of ruin: silent, never to sing again.

We hit town, and I passed a line of Coast Guard trucks. I worried they'd stop me, but they just raised their hands in acknowledgment as I passed. As is the case in every Southern town, at the far end border of the city limits, as distant from the original downtown as could be, sat the Walmart. So that's what I saw first, and it was half-gone, a gaping hole where the grocery side of the store used to be. There was debris everywhere— downed fridges in the middle of the road, gutters full of every known thing, all mixed up and muddy, dead dogs pushed up against curbs, their still bodies shining with oil-like fur, dark casements of formerly loved pets reposed in the sunlight like onyx sculptures. And splintered wood everywhere. Piles upon piles of it, what remained of every house that ever was, jumbled up, all kinds of colors, broken, rammed up against any buildings that remained.

"No more pizza, Mama," said Grayson.

"Look! The steeple fell down," said Avery, eyes wide.

I made my way through the streets, driving over and around overturned cars, pieces of houses, boat halves, and deep freezes with tops blown off, bent-up bicycles and beer coolers every- where. The beer coolers floated out of every Gulf Coast garage, rode out the storm, then sank and landed where they may when the surge went back to sea. A silence hung in the air: the trees devoid of birdsong, structures plunged into the dark, dark hush.

I turned down our street.

"Oh no, Mama," Avery whispered. "Oh no, oh no, oh no."

"I know, baby, I know," I whispered. "It'll be okay."

Most houses were still standing on Bayou Sauvage but had been blown straight through by the storm. Our neighborhood, a single winding street, like a small peninsula, was mostly doctors and lawyers and judges, the most expensive houses in town. The homes on the left were backed up to deepwater bayou, half a mile from open gulf; the homes on the right were backed up to the Davis Bayou Area, part of Gulf Islands National Seashore, thick woods dotted with savannas and bayous and, again, about half a mile to open gulf. Every house so far: destroyed.

And then we took that slight turn in the road and saw our house.

You know how, on the news, after a tornado, they always have that helicopter footage? And the helicopter dips low and the camera angle is askew, revealing inconceivable destruction? And you can't believe your eyes how someplace where life existed just a day before was now such a jumble of ruin, edging into decay? And then the helicopter turns ever so slightly and you see it? That one house that somehow just missed the wrath of the twister? When we turned that bend in our road, that was our house.

It stood, two stories tall, the brick thick with mud, the black wooden shutters still latched tight. Trees down, two feet of finish worn off clean from the formal double front doors where the water lapped up against them for hours. The camellia bushes were barren. The fifty-gallon front porch flowerpots too heavy to move before we left were gone, but otherwise?

It was just as we'd left it.

Perfect. Nearly pristine. Lucky.

I didn't yet know the end of world had already started.

When we entered the house through the garage, it was dark and hot and damp. The windows, even under the clamped-tight shutters, were covered in mud. Inside it was silent. As I walked into the great room, I kicked an empty wine bottle that went careening in arcs across the dark, hardwood floor. The big candles on the coffee table were burned all the way down, and wax was drizzled all over the room like snail trails. My heart started beating hard. All the covers from my bed had been brought down to the great room, a messy bed made across the massive coffee table.

He wasn't here alone.

On the floor, next to the makeshift bed, a black pistol.

He doesn't own a gun.

I picked it up, slid it into the waist of my skirt, grabbed two wine bottles in my knuckles.

This is why he left.

The kids were toddling up the stairs to their rooms, even the baby scrambling up in a crawl step by step with Avery holding her hands up behind him in case he fell.

"What the fuck are you doing here?"

I turned, and in the doorway was my husband, Dr. Liam Rivers, staring at me.

"I snuck back in."

"You did, did you? I didn't tell you to come back."

"Daddy!" the kids went running to him, grabbing his legs.

"We sneaked back in with a whole bunch of men!" Avery announced.

"A bunch of men, huh?" he asked, looking at me. "I bet."

"Go check out the backyard for me, babies, will ya?" I asked, and they unlatched the back door and went out. I could see them through the mud-filmed windows walking across the trunks of overturned trees.

I stood looking at Liam and he at me. For a minute I thought he was going to embrace me.

"Clean this fucking mess up," he whispered, left the room, went out to the drive, got in his car, and pulled away.

HECK ON WHEELS

There was a time that Liam would have respected that I could score two generators, months of food and supplies, then finagle my way back into a mandatory evacuation area all on my own within a span of twenty-four hours. It was that badassness in me he'd found so sexy in the first place.

We were cut from the same cloth: two broken people born to families with expectations so low in life anything above "not a dropout" or "not in jail" was a wild success. Families who played it by ear and kept what happened in the dark a secret come daylight. Families that didn't even show up to our graduations. Histories of drink and violence and despair. What we had, we got from scraping the very back corners of our own dark hearts.

We started, both of us, from scratch.

I spent my first two years after high school at the local community college in South Sacramento. My family had relocated from Mississippi. Mama told Papa if he didn't get her out of Jackson she'd leave him. So there we were, picked up from one Delta town to another: night and day. And all the other "smart kids" at John F. Kennedy High had long since shipped off to four-year institutions, but my parents had made no plans whatsoever for my college education. Never spoke of it: never considered it. Cosumnes River College was my start, and while high school had mostly bored me silly (outside of show choir and jazz choir and dancing with the Hawaiiana Revue), college inspired me in a way that was soul-deep, exhilarating.

I wrote essays on Emerson that bled off the page. I choreographed a modern dance solo to a recording of Audre Lorde reading a poem. I loved how I could take a history class that fed into my art class that fed into my lit class that fed into my music class. Education was everything to me suddenly.

Days in class, nights downtown at cafés or the clubs, dance classes. I got everywhere on my little sky-blue scooter.

I was riding down Riverside Boulevard, which runs below the levee next to the Sacramento River all the way from South Sac to midtown. My girlfriend Ava was riding behind me. There is a turn in the road where Riverside crosses under Interstate 5, and for a moment you can't see the traffic coming from the other direction, and so when we banked, it was only at the very last second that we saw her: the lady with the stiff white beehive behind the wheel of the impossibly large, shiny yellow Cadillac DeVille, a cigarette perched artfully in her right hand off the steering wheel. Passing into the shade under the overpass, I sped up to miss her, and the front wheel of the scooter hit the curb, tipping up. Everything went slow motion as I watched Ava fly up and over me, into the ivy that lined the levee.

"Oh, fuck," I said, and I saw her face turn toward mine as she passed me in the air, her short platinum hair around her like a punk halo.

Then I flew through the air, too, following her, a graceful hurl halted in a dreadful jolt by the solid, six-inch steel bus stop pole.

The pole bent: I broke.

Ava rose from the bank of ivy with barely a scratch.

On the sidewalk, the EMTs split my jeans up the center, and my shirt, but there wasn't a scratch on me. They loaded me in the ambulance. Even so, I was going down fast. Like the rest of my life, the damage was all inside.

When I wrapped around that pole, my rib cage had shattered, and my shattered ribs had punctured both lungs, and those jagged ribs had lacerated my liver into several separate pieces, and the impact was so severe that my common bile duct was not just impacted—it was gone. *Poof.* No longer existed. It took the trauma surgeons a good bit of time and several experimental surgeries in the first few days to figure out how to sew me back together and give me back a life.

That summer was spent in the hospital, with surgery after surgery. My gallbladder was sewn, experimentally, to my duodenum. I disappeared to seventy-eight pounds, at five foot eight inches tall, a skeletal version of my former self. They fed me through a tube for months, trying to get my insides back in order. The white, silky lipids would snake down from the tube and into me, filling me with a flash of heat: I got used to it. When finally they wanted me to eat real food, it was a revolting task. Mama would bring me french fries, begging me to eat.

"I already ate *three!*" I'd screech, frustrated.

"It's okay, Alice, just do what you can," Mama would assure me, the love in her voice the only thing I could count on for sure.

Mama nearly lived at the hospital, spending easily nineteen hours a day there. At first I had lots of visitors, but as the months wore on, usually it was just family. Papa would come nearly every day, but he couldn't stay in my room longer than a few minutes without breaking down.

"I'm so sorry, babe. I'm sorry, I'm sorry," he'd repeat over and over, until Mama would quietly shoo him out of the room and he'd go back to being mayor of the waiting room, bolstering all the other families on in, as it was called, the motorcycle trauma wing. Papa was like that, the king of everything, the most popular, the hand-shaking, back-slapping everyman head of every board and club and industry in which he traveled. King of everything, that is, except his own family, where he was sort of the exiled dictator who came back occasionally—impotent yet raging—as we moved around him with equal parts pity and dismay.

Lying in my hospital bed with the feeding tube under my clavicle and the drainage tube coiling out my side and the oxygen hooked in to my nose and the IV pumping in the top of my right foot because the veins in both hands had been shot months before, I was helpless. A little pitiful. Gone was the alpha girl always at the head of the class, the jazz singer off to the South of France at fifteen, the skater chick keeping up with the hard-core boys at the Mile High Skate Halfpipe up in Tahoe, the Littlest Princess dancing (at five years old) with the Los Angeles Ballet. I was fragile—near death, in fact, on several occasions.

The first day I'd come in, they'd taken me straight to an OR. I remember sliding away on the table, not sure if it was consciousness or anesthesia, but I remember a nurse taking off my nail polish, and I had the thought, *Too late, too late.*

It's too late to worry about my nail polish. I'm gone.

Then everything in the room slid around backward like through a fish-eye lens, and I saw myself crucified there on the OR table, and I saw the nurse taking off my nail polish, and I saw Dr. James Holcroft slice me straight down the middle from breast to pelvis, and out of that wound I saw my whole life rise up, all of it, the blood and the guts of it, the shit and the flower petals from my parents' wedding raining down on me the first time I fucked a girl and me dropping into a half-pipe and a wave breaking over me in the ocean like the way my father's hand went over my mouth so easily the first time he entered me, and I heard myself sing an aria in the fourth grade—that's the first time I discovered I had a voice—and black birds sprang out of my mouth and into a sky filled with stars the shape of every moment of shame I'd ever swallowed and then they fell to the ground, beautiful, shooting jade, exploding into laughter.

Everything was silent.

I didn't see God.

"Alice? Alice?"

I opened my eyes.

Dr. Holcroft smiled down at me.

"It's too late for my nail polish," I said.

He smiled.

"You made it," he said.

I looked down, my belly swollen up the size of a basketball.

"How long have I been asleep?"

He laughed. "Not long enough for that kind of trouble—about twelve hours."

I had four more surgeries in the next week.

I was in four months that first stay.

Once, when fluid had built up in my lungs, they rolled me down to the bowels of the hospital and sent me into the sterile white tube of the MRI.

"Okay now, Alice, hold your breath until we say you can let it out," came a disembodied voice from the tech, as I slid into the white tube, cold and silent.

"Breathe now," said the voice.

The table moved me slightly out of the tube.

"One more time, Alice, take a deep breath and hold it in."

Again, into the tube, out.

Then a long pause, nothing.

I was feverish in a way I'd never felt before. It seemed that everything inside me was boiling over, and I felt the heat surround me, too, almost sitting off my body a half an inch or so, scalding and suffocating. *Why am I so hot?*

"Alice," said a familiar voice, Dr. Holcroft, "try not to move at all; we're going to do a little surgery right there on the MRI table."

My drainage tube had somehow backed up, and a lung was so full up it was in danger of bursting: too dangerous to move me now.

They came in, put up a tent in front of my face so I couldn't watch them cutting into me, piercing the abscess, inserting yet another drain in between two rib bones straight into my liver.

I'd just come back from this surgery on the MRI table when Papa came in, standing at the end of my bed, holding on to my foot, crying. Papa wore very thick glasses in a square shape, and the tears pooled up in the bottoms of the frames before spilling down on his red, rough cheeks. "I'm so sorry, babe. I'm sorry, I'm really sorry," he'd say. And I'd look away and let my eyelids fall slowly closed, feigning sleep. I needed sleep, anyway, and besides, I couldn't stand to see him cry, and I wasn't anywhere near close to telling him, "It's okay," when we both knew that his apology wasn't for my sickness but for something sicker still.

Aside from the patients from Folsom State Prison, whose doors remained closed with full-time guards standing at the ready, there were a lot of guys with head injuries on the motorcycle wing. One would yell, "Waitress!" every ten minutes, when he needed his nurse. Another routinely escaped his room, ripped off his gown, and came running into my room, yelling, "Fuck me, waitress! I love you!" Fake sleep was a defense I knew well and used often.

I started to ease myself out of bed every morning before the sun came up. I convinced Mama to bring me regular clothes, and when the doctors and their gaggle of med students would arrive about five, I'd be sitting in the visitor's chair in my room, the hospital bed made, asking to go home. This ritual continued for about three weeks before they finally relented.

After nearly four months, I was finally released from the hospital. I had a drain in my side where a gaping hole oozed bile and liquids from my inner swelling; I could barely stand straight from my stomach muscles being cut down the middle in so many surgeries; and I was still less than eighty pounds. But I was out, and alive, and ready to get back to school. I remember the ride back to my parents' house (my apartment had been packed up and moved out of months before) noticing that the leaves were changing on the trees. The highway runs adjacent to the treetops in Sacramento, which is known as the City of Trees, and I remember thinking that the burnt orange treetops were the exact same color as the carpet in my parents' den.

School started three weeks later, and even though I'd missed the application deadlines, I met with an admissions counselor, my perfect transcripts from community college and my thick stack of medical records bound up with a thick rubber band. She let me in.

I started as a junior at Sac State in the fall semester. I was like every other student, marching around campus in my Levi's and Docs. Everything seemed as if it might return to normal. But doors were too heavy for me to pull open; chairs hurt the bones of my scrawny behind. My hair was falling out in patches, a classic body-trauma response. When I raised my hand to speak in class, the wrinkly sound the drainage bag at my waist made me cringe each time. More seriously, I kept falling ill again—passing out in public or uncontrollably vomiting or spiking a wild fever—and being readmitted a day here or two days there. Finally, the doctors convinced me to stay home and do nothing but rest and work on increasing my strength.

I dropped out of college, dejected.

Now my days were spent in my childhood bedroom, watching daytime TV, reading fashion magazines, letting Mama change my dressings and my drainage bag, pretending to eat the cream-laden food she brought in on trays.

One evening, I convinced Mama I was strong enough to bathe on my own. She had a lawn chair in the bathtub for me to sit in, and usually she'd undress me, help me get in the chair, then wash my hair and the rest of me, get me out, towel me off, dress me, and put me back to bed. But this time I wanted to do it myself. I went in the bathroom and shut the door. I took off my clothes that Mama had bought from me from the girls' department, peeling them off and stepping out of them where they fell. Just as I went to step into the tub, I looked over at myself in the mirror. A ragged girl, her hair missing in clumps and white and fuzzy like cotton where it remained, eyes sunken in and dark, lifeless. My body—truly skeletal, covered with ragged, raised red scars up and down the stomach, the dreaded drain protruding from the side of my waist, every rib and clavicle standing out like sharp twigs—was a shock. I fainted.

Mama got me back to bed, and I stayed there. And stayed. Nothing could rouse me. I hit a funk so hard I couldn't drag myself out. So what did Mama do? Signed me up for modeling school.

The Mannequin Manor on Howe Avenue was a suite of offices outfitted with mirrored makeup rooms, several practice runways, an on-camera studio, and other classrooms. My first week there, they declared me a "spring." I didn't know if I should laugh or cry, but I could see—after the careful application of makeup by my slinky, gorgeous, elegant teacher, Zara—that the girl I thought I'd lost was still in there somewhere.

After the eight-week course was finished, the head of the modeling school showed us a video about a modeling convention in New York. And because it was my normal mode to follow everything through to the extreme, I convinced Mama and Papa to pay. A few weeks later I went to New York.

It was a silly thing, the convention. Models aren't taught in schools, and stars are found in midwestern malls and Southern Friday-night football rallies, not the Hyatt Centric Times Square.

There were three parts to the competition: runway, commercial, and print. I'd gone and taken my photos beforehand with a photographer in San Francisco and some shots of me, wholesome in a cropped Guess jeans jacket, won first place. I also won first place for my rendition, on camera, of a L'Oréal "Because I'm worth it" commercial.

On the last day of the convention, a room was set up with scouts from various agencies for the girls to take their books around. I woke up the morning of the scouting session thinking, *I don't want to be a model, I want to be a poet,* but I dragged myself around anyway. I was signed by two agencies—McDonald Richards in New York, a big commercial talent agency who thought I had a future in shampoo commercials and foot modeling, and Maxi International, a Paris agency I'd never heard of.

The owner of Maxi International, Sabine, sat at the table alone, looking like a cross between a Chanel model and a middle-aged math teacher, her dirty blond hair pulled back in a strict long braid down her back, with a pink grosgrain ribbon to match her suit. She flipped through my book, saying, "*Oui,*" and "*Oui,*" and "*Oui,*" with each glossy page that passed.

"We'll be in touch, *oui?*" she said.

And that was the end of the convention. I flew home, ready to get back to school.

Two days later the phone on the wet bar in my parents' house in Sacramento rang; it was Sabine, offering to send me a ticket to Paris. She suggested I go to the office in San Francisco, get a "hurry visa," and arrive in ten days.

I said yes.

I wasn't nearly well enough to be moving to Paris to model, but with school off the table for a while, I had nothing else to do and— heck on wheels—I was skinny.

THE MAXI PAD

All I knew was that someone would pick me up.

When I arrived at the airport on a sharply cold, slate-gray day, I had the faint feeling that I'd taken a wrong turn. I'd spent the last six months in the hospital or in a twin bed in my childhood bedroom, and suddenly here I was, standing on a curb at Charles de Gaulle, with an enormous suitcase filled with stacks of Levi's, a dozen white T-shirts, one tiny black spandex dress, three pairs of Western boots, a pair of biker boots, a pair of red fishnet stockings, and a black leather biker jacket. There was no one there to greet me, no hired driver with ANDERSON scrawled across a white sign the way I'd expected. I dug through my bag for the agency address, and, finding it, held up my hand for a taxi, the long purple fringe of my suede coat fanning out behind me in the wind. Just then, a burly young man roared up on a motorbike and said, "Alice?"

I nodded, wondering how this stranger knew my name.

"Hugo," he announced as if this would mean something to me. "I will take you to Maxi," he continued, tipping his head to indicate I should hop on.

"But my bag?" I asked, looking down at the impossibly large, black suitcase.

"Leave there," Hugo barked.

Confused, I did what seemed the only thing to do—I hopped on the back of his bike, wrapped my hands around his thick chest, and held on as he roared into traffic, darting between cars and buses and vans. Glancing back just in time, I saw a gentleman loading my abandoned suitcase into an older-model sedan.

Riding into the city on the back of that bike, holding dear to this surly, slightly dangerous-seeming stranger, my platinum hair wild, tangling with the purple fringe of my coat, I felt perhaps I had not taken a wrong turn after all but had barreled down the right path, toward something that would revive my aching soul.

Though I'd been to Paris twice before, once on a middle school field trip with the French club and again in high school touring with the jazz band, I wasn't entirely familiar with its neighborhoods, noted streets, and landmarks beyond those you visit as a tourist.

"Almost there!" Hugo shouted over his shoulder as we turned onto a very swanky street.

"Almost where?" Was he taking me to the agency? To the models' apartment?

"To Sabine."

The day opened into brilliance, the kind of sunlight only a Paris day affords, every shop window glinting promises, every impossibly thin new *maman* pushing a polished pram formal as an impeccable dark chocolate petit four, every couple squeezed into each tiny café table up to the edge of any avenue holding deep claret glasses of simple house wine, dark and decadent nonetheless.

And as we zipped closer and closer to our destination, we weren't traveling down a back road, through a forgotten alley, a dusty *rue* lined with packing stores, but down one of the finest streets in all of Paris—the Rue de la Paix. Passing the Ritz, Tiffany, an endless row of tony shops, finally Hugo hopped the curb right across the street from Cartier, left the bike in the middle of the sidewalk, and nodded for me to follow.

He pressed a bell and was buzzed through an unmarked door next to a *salon de parfums*, and we walked up five flights of stairs and into the agency, entering a large pink room with a wall of windows looking out onto the avenue below. There was a small runway at one end, an office at the other, and some desks where regular, secretary-looking girls sat at desks in the middle of the room. Zed cards were organized in a shelf on the wall behind them, a hundred pretty faces staring back at me.

"Alice! Alice! Alice, baby! My blond baby! My California girl!" cooed Sabine, rushing toward me, out of her office, wrapping me in an embrace.

She was much dowdier than I remembered from New York. She was, for lack of a better word, motherly. I hugged her back. Soaked in Chanel N°5, she wore (of course) a pink knit Chanel suit with cream trim, a cream blouse, and her long blond hair pulled back harshly into that same braid that went all the way to her waist, a schoolgirl's ribbon tied at the top.

"Come zeez way, let's zee you," she said, leading me to another part of the main room, where a partial wall divided the room and mirrors surrounded the area. "Take eet all off, my sweet."

"Everything?" I asked with a nervous giggle, glancing at Hugo, still leaning against a wall, smoking, pulling at the various zippers of his leather jacket.

"Yes, darling, everyzing. Zis is Paris. Don't be see-lee."

And so I did, stripped it all off—my purple-fringed suede jacket, my white Fruit of the Loom T-shirt, my little black lace bra, my cowboy boots, my beat up 501's, my black lace G-string, my white tube socks with the red stripes around the top, and stood there totally naked.

Sabine looked at me, her eyes taking me in from head to toe, slowly. I was by now, at five foot eight, about ninety pounds. She took each of my breasts in her fingertips, lifted them up a bit, gave them a little shake, said, "Nice ones!"

We all laughed, even Hugo.

"The scars, why you did not tell me of the scars?" she asked.

I had a scar that ran from between my breasts all the way down my torso, making a little detour around my belly button, disappearing into my pubic hair. Another one crisscrossed my ribs on my right side, my liver tucked underneath. There was a big gash on my right waist where the terrible drain had been and a raised, red notch above my clavicle where the feeding tube had pumped the thick white lipids in like clockwork every night.

"Um, well, I guess you didn't ask?" I said, starting to feel a kind of panic raise.

Why didn't *I tell her? How stupid could I be?*

"I mean, if it's a problem, I can go home. I mean, I didn't think I'd be doing swimsuits or anything, and so—"

"Well, in Paris, anything, possible, will be a problem. Blond, will want lingerie. We will have to make you more fashion, cut hair, make more hard, maybe change name."

"Okay. I'm sorry, Sabine, I didn't mean to—" I started.

"It is problem," she said, "but Sabine smart, can fix problem."

Sabine had a way of talking in these halted sentences as a way to bridge the language barrier, even with those of us who spoke fluent French.

"Just no more lies, and you don't work, you pay back every money, you understand?" she scolded, looking me square in the eye, her double chin quivering unflatteringly.

"Yes, of course."

"So pretty," she switched tone, running her hand down my waist.

"Can I get dressed now?" I asked.

"First, you walk," she challenged.

"Okay," I said, strutting over to the little runway, hopping up and walking back and forth, nude, gliding to the quiet house music playing in the background, making use of the seventeen years of ballet I'd studied before my scooter accident.

The secretaries stopped their phone calls and watched.

Hugo's cigarette gathered a long cylinder of soot at the end.

Sabine stood with her arms folded in front of her ample chest and smiled.

I forgot I was nude. If there was one thing I was comfortable with, it was being on stage, it was performing, it was—if I had to admit it—pretending.

I could step outside of myself in any situation and become whatever you needed me to be.

This was a talent I gleaned from terror but used for mostly my own good.

My father started abusing me sexually when I was four, coming into my room at night just after I fell asleep. I'd long since written it all off as something I'd "survived." I ran groups for survivors, I was a mentor for survivors. But here's the thing about abuse—surviving it doesn't mean that at any moment, a turn of the corner or a lover's bite of your lip or a stranger's touch can't rock your soul in a way that shatters your entire sense of the safety of the universe. No one escapes abuse unscathed.

The damage to my soul was something I thought I could repair with sheer will. Most of the time, I could.

Transforming the pain of abuse into my own sort of power was my rebellion, my power. It made me fearless. It made me reckless, too. There was nothing that scared me, because I had this inner sense that no matter what happened to me, I controlled the outcome.

So even though walking naked on a rickety runway in a tacky pink room in front of a wall of windows in Paris with hundreds of people walking by outside and a heavy-lidded young man staring at me felt like shit, I was able to embrace it—even enjoy it. This is something every survivor knows: you hate it and you love it. Because you know it. There is a power in knowing you can go further than another girl can; you can be reckless, you can push the boundary, you can say *fuck you* or *fuck me* with your face or your ass because that's what you've been trained to do. Because you give them way more than they ask for, you make them squirm.

So up on that runway, even though it wasn't where I wanted to be, even though it wasn't *who* I wanted to be, I called the shots. And when the song morphed into a new one, I walked off, picked up my clothes, dressed, walked past Hugo, swung through the door and down the stairs. It was time to check out my new digs.

Model apartments are famous for being ten rungs down from sweatshop dorms. Agencies rent tiny studio apartments, fill them with multiple bunk beds, and cram in as many girls as they can at once. It's often a shock to new girls in the business, arriving to find that they'll be stacked like sardines with up to twenty other girls in an apartment meant for perhaps four. Model apartments were usually in parts of town where rents were cheap, public transit was close, and grit was the name of the game.

The ride to the Maxi apartment with Hugo was another exercise is surrealism. I half wondered if he was taking me on an obligatory sightseeing tour, past the Tuileries, L'Opéra, le Tour Eiffel, the neighborhoods becoming swankier, the apartments becoming statelier, lined with flower boxes, wrought iron balconies, the miniature Statue de la Liberté rising from the Île aux Cygnes in the river Seine, until we arrived at the Maxi Pad, at 15 Avenue de Versailles.

He handed me the key and said, "Penthouse, choose empty room."

And 15 Avenue de Versailles was an impeccable, white Paris apartment building, tall and stately, square, with gleaming rectangular windows and terraces in mathematical precision across its flawless façade. The double doors were gleaming glass with a swirling wrought iron pattern overlay, more ornate than whimsical. I slid the key in, turned it, and pushed the heavy door open into the large foyer, the door dragging the deep pile of the deep red carpeting, my suitcase right inside the door standing off to one side against a curved, flocked papered wall.

The ceiling stretched up endless floors, and the lighting was muted. Off to one side, a small elevator was tucked behind two folding wrought iron doors, and ahead of me was an enormous red winding staircase twisting into silty sunlight from somewhere far above. I hefted my suitcase, dragged it to the elevator, fought open the wrought iron doors, and shoved the behemoth in. I tried to sneak in with it but got hit with the door twice before finally holding the door open with one foot while backing into the elevator, then letting the gate shut behind me.

There were only two buttons: one arrow pointing up, one arrow pointing down. I pressed the arrow pointing up. The elevator did nothing. I pressed the pointing up arrow again. The elevator suddenly fell about two feet and then slowly, very slowly, with a horrible screeching noise, started to inch up, back up to the level of the lobby and then up past it, then to the interior of the building in between the lobby and the first floor, then to the interior hall of the apartment on the first floor, and then kept going and then a little more and then suddenly fell about two feet back down to the first-floor hall with a big shudder and thud.

I thought my heart had fallen straight through to the lobby.

I pried open the elevator gates and yanked the behemoth out of there so fast you'd think the elevator was on fire. In doing so, I fell on my ass and found myself sitting on the floor of a very pretty foyer with a telephone table on which a baby-blue rotary phone sat by a pad of paper and a cup of sharpened pencils. I heard tiny laughing behind me. On the bottom step, a girl in red cowboy boots and a puppy costume said, "You're a new one."

"Yes, I am, apparently. Who are you?" I asked.

"I'm your neighbor, but don't tell Mama, because I'm not supposed to talk to all a y'all. She's a magazine editor."

"Oh, well, it's always a good idea to avoid 'all a y'all,'" I said, breaking into my Mississippi drawl from my childhood days in Mississippi, "'cause all a y'all are always gonna git ya into some kind of trouble."

Giggle.

"Can I ask ya a question that would require no talkin' whatsoever, do you think?" I asked.

Nodding.

"If a girl who found her fool self movin' to Paris tryin' to be a model was tryin' to find her apartment but seemed to end up in some pretty little puppy dog's hallway instead, would you think she should get back in a really *scary* elevator or should she go up some great big red stairs instead?"

Silence.

"Oh, that's a question, huh?"

Nod.

"I should take the stairs."

Nod.

"All the way up."

Big nod.

And so I nudged the puppy dog's curly black hair and dragged the behemoth up six more flights of very wide, winding, rosy carpeted stairs until I arrived at what was known far and wide around Paris as the Maxi Pad: three penthouse floors of luxury apartment, eight bedrooms overlooking a single three-level great room, two kitchens, three bathrooms, and a sunny roof deck overlooking the better part of Paris, right on the Seine. It would be several weeks before I would figure out why the models of Maxi International enjoyed such luxury.

When I arrived, the place was empty. Midday, all the girls were out on go-sees or working. I poked around from room to room; despite the luxury of the apartment, it wasn't overly furnished.

Most rooms looked comfortably lived in, with twin beds and scratched wardrobes. There were a couple of Day-Glo fuchsia and orange hippie futons in the living room and beat-up tables with mismatched chairs in the kitchens.

The least-private bedroom, on the lower floor next to the great room with only a curtain dividing it from the main room, was the only available room. A twin bed was propped up behind the door, with a set of sheets and a big old quilt folded atop a painted desk. I figured the desk was a good sign for me. I pushed the bed into a corner near the window, where a wrought iron balcony overlooked the wide avenue, made the bed, peeled off my jeans, fell into bed, and dropped into a deep sleep.

FOR WHOM THE

BELLE TOLLS

I don't know how many hours later it was when I heard, from the depths of dreams, voices above me, laughing, talking.

"Bet she's Swedish! Look at her hair!"

"No, New Yorker, everything in her suitcase is black!"

"Get out of her stuff, Blue, that's so rude!"

"God, I hope she speaks English at least."

"Wake her up already!"

"What in the helicopter is wrong with y'all?" I asked, opening my eyes to see five stunningly gorgeous girls lolling around my room in various stages of disrobe. "I mean, besides being way too fucking pretty?"

One, a Hemingway-esque brunette, sat at the edge of my bed smiling at me. "Hi, I'm Wendy." She was very tall and very thin, with a strong jaw, a perfectly upturned nose, blue eyes, and the cheekbones of a Siamese cat.

"I'm Alice." I yawned, feeling like hell on wheels.

"Ha, that's funny. Sabine told us you were 'Aleché.'"

"Oh, yeah, she says she needs to unpretty me and harden me up, so now I'm a teenager from Milan instead of a twentysomething from California."

"Works for me. I'm a 'teenager' too!" Wendy laughed. "Well, get up, there's a Madonna concert tonight, and my friend Barry might be able to get us backstage," she said in a slight Florida drawl.

"Cool." I smiled. This was my kind of first day. "I need to get ready, though."

"You got a little black dress and boots?" she asked.

"Are ya new here? Have you met me?" I smiled.

"I'm going to like you just fine."

An hour later, Wendy and the pixied Texas gamine named Blue and I headed out to meet Barry and his buddies near the Arc de Triomphe to get the passes. Climbing the Métro steps, one of three models dressed in black in the early evening emerging onto that famous avenue, I felt as if I were in a scene from a movie. All the hours in the hospital slipped away, all the hopelessness and pall of sickness fell from my body like a coat lost running in a crowd, and my sense of self came rushing back.

We loitered around waiting for Barry, watching people pass, the great rush of Paris humanity surging around us. He didn't show up.

"I'm starved; let's eat," Wendy suggested.

The next thing I knew, I was in line in McDonald's. My first night in Paris and I was standing in line for Le Big Mac? *Shouldn't I be ordering steak au poivre in a smoky café?* Besides, the music was deafening.

Who knew in the McDonald's on the Champs-Élysées they'd pump house music like you can't believe? Or that there would be dudes in line that break out in moves and grab you to dance and, funny, they'd expect you to be able to keep up! But, stranger yet, what those dudes would not expect (and neither would your new model roommates) is that you've been hanging out with skaters the last four years of high school, have been going to punk shows and raves and house shows, and so it turns out you can keep up, and so you end up making a big scene.

Which is to say, you are break-dancing with Madonna's backup dancers in McDonald's on your first day in Paris.

Shabba Doo, who basically invented break dancing, is some-one I was very familiar with, though I don't let on. He is enter-tained by this ski-slope-nosed blonde who can pop and lock. And the little boy on Madonna's tour, the one in the fedora? He can't believe his luck at having run into a bevy of models two heads taller than he is at, of all places, McDonald's in Paris. He doesn't know we are fresh-off-the-bus models with crappy tear sheets and a questionable agency. He is just a kid on tour with a pop star. Regardless, he is charmingly starry-eyed.

We ended up going to the show with them, going backstage, causing all kinds of trouble, convincing everyone we were an up-and-coming girls' country-and-western hip-hop group called For Whom the Belle Tolls. At the end of the evening, we all headed from the outskirts of Paris (where the concert took place) to town again, ending the evening dancing at Le Bains Douches, and from that night on, Paris was in the palms of our hands.

At first I believed that Paris was ours simply because of this lucky, wondrous, silly start. But I came to know that we held an-other quiet power simply by being models, specifically models with the Agence Maxi, and all that the owner of the agency rep-resented. But I lived and worked a few carefree months before I discovered the secret, simply enjoying being the toast of Paris.

GO OMAN OR
GO HOME

I have a few test shoots right away, and though I've never liked having my picture made, they aren't really bad. They're quite good, actually, to build my book. As Sabine suggests, they paint me as a fashion girl, much more "hard" than the early tear sheets, which show me as a sunny, blond, cheery, wholesome California girl. Frankly, I like my Paris persona better. It feels like the true me.

I am Aleché.

I don't have any trouble navigating go-sees or test shoots, as I've taken French for six years in school. Everyone buys the Italian thing, as my French teacher was Mrs. Beatrice Tournabene, and it turns out I speak French with an impeccable Sicilian accent.

It's true that my heart isn't entirely in it. I'd rather be in school. I'd rather be writing. I'd rather be doing anything but model, but every day I see the go-sees and gigs as my dues for living in Paris.

I never wanted to be a model, and being immersed directly into this world of Paris fashion leaves me cold. It's not the high you'd expect. Sure, it's intriguing, even sexy, but it doesn't call to any of the important parts of me—it doesn't shake me or make me want to cry with relief or run down avenues or fuck until the sun rises. I envy the kids I see streaming in and out of the Sorbonne, their fingers stained with paint, their lips bitten raw. One day, coming out of a casting, I come across Shakespeare and Company.

I go inside. I talk to George Whitman about why I'm in Paris and how I hate it and love it and how I climb down the bridge and drop down on the island every day I can, and he is willing to let me take as many books as I want out at a time. I take them and read them without paying, careful not to break the spine, and return them back to the shelves for paying customers. Sometimes I shove money at him, but he refuses it, shoving it back. George smiles at me as I sit within the aisles of the store for hours when I am supposed to be at go-sees, and he lets me take naps in the bed below the bulletin board. He feels bad for me that I am in Paris for modeling.

I'd like to move into the apartment above, but I already have a sweet place, so I don't.

"Take advantage of it. Don't waste time on guilt!"

The more I talk to George, the less I audition, the more I take books and peaches to my favorite spot. I begin to write: first on the paper bags, then in a spiral notebook I bought at the grocery.

Just behind the Maxi Pad, the Île aux Cygnes sits in the middle of the Seine with the replica of the Statue of Liberty rising up in the sunlight. I like to fill my messenger bag with the diaries of Anaïs Nin and the notebook and sharpened pencils and ripe peaches and slip over the guardrail of the Grenelle Bridge down onto the island and sit in the sun all day, reading and nibbling on the peaches I can never really eat and writing letters and poems. The tourist barges pass like lazy hippos floating, and sometimes tourists take photos of me, the Paris girl. At least that's what I imagine.

I bring George bags of peaches with poems I'd penned on the outside of plain brown paper sacks. He tears the poems from the bags and walks around the store while we talk, tucking them into random books that people later, I presume, would purchase.

"I hate modeling," I tell George. "I hate it."

"Go to Deux Magots, not Bains Douches," he scolds.

One day, George gives me a copy of Anaïs Nin's *Little Birds*, and I read it again and again and wish I had a lover.

I want a lover, but I'm too wounded. From my childhood, from my accident. I want to be a writer, but I'm writing poems on paper bags and my life is go-sees and nightclubs. After the clubs, I go with wandering, still-drunk groups of models and musicians and artists and I watch as couples peel off into the gloaming of pink skies two by two, and even when someone wraps their fingers in my hair, tangling it, even when they kiss me hard on the mouth, the stain of my dark lips smearing while mothers push prams in the early morning light, I pull back.

Gather myself.

Make excuses.

Hold back.

Drop myself neatly into a sack of my own making: like ripe peaches rotting in a paper sack, sweet and uneaten, wild poetry scrawled on the outside, useless, anonymous, a decoration.

I look for human connection in the most desperate, small places.

On the dance floor: a body next to mine.

At a fitting: the kindness of a pretty seamstress running her hand the length of my waist.

In the Métro: packed tight, the whole car shifting as one.

Sometimes at night I wake up in such acute, exquisite pain I take the scary elevator down to the street, catch a cab to the American hospital where a terribly kind, young doctor starts a morphine drip for a few hours—until I stabilize.

Sometimes I imagine that this doctor, whose name I do not know, is my lover.

Sometimes I think I should go home.

But still I want to make enough money to pay for a year of college, and I want to make enough to pay for my stay. I go to a little runway workshop with an ancient woman from Chanel who is there to ridicule girls who cannot walk.

I walk last.

I strut the two lengths of the runway, and the little old lady takes Sabine immediately and with some force by the arm, marches her to her office, slams the door. All of us look at each other, shrug. I wonder if I'm about to get sent home.

Instead, I'm then booked for the Chanel runway during fashion week. That's enough to pay my way, and I am even lazier after that. I wonder how many go-sees I can skip before Sabine realizes I'm not going instead of just not getting the job. I'm either reading on the island, napping at George's, sunbathing nude on the roof of the Maxi Pad, or drinking too much at the Bains Douches.

One shoot I actually make it to instead of blowing off is with a photographer everyone raves about named Baptiste Devaux. He's a bit of a legend, and his studio is impossible to find, on the outskirts near the train tracks, a warehouse with enormous windows on one wall that let in a gritty white light the color of broken mornings. We start out on the tracks and eventually move back into his studio. My hair is wild and my eyes black and my lips red and my skirt short, a kind of Debbie Harry look, and it all falls into place the way a poem does when you just know it's working. It's the first time I've ever felt that "click" in modeling, like I might be making something real. He has me climb up onto a short ladder in front of the window, and he is shooting me from below and says, "Take off your top."

And there it is.

I'm in Paris and I don't know anyone who hasn't taken topless shots. Not a single girl.

Kate Moss and her bee-stung tits are on billboards everywhere, and I'm nobody in a warehouse by the tracks, and who am I to say no?

"I'm not your little bird."

He laughs.

"Take it off."

"Fuck you."

That's when he yanks at my ankle, tries to pull me off the ladder. Now he's furious.

It all happens so fast. I'm off the ladder and we're circling each other and he's yelling and I'm yelling and I'm gathering up my stuff, my makeup and my book and the clothes I came in, stuffing it in my messenger bag, and he stalks me around the studio, screaming that he's going to destroy all the film from today.

I tell him I'm going to tell Sabine not to work with him anymore. He calls me a cunt and grabs my hair. I kick him in the balls and he doubles over and immediately pops back up and punches me smack in the left eye.

I'm so shocked I just stand there, crying.

He's laughing at me, actually cracking up, pointing at me, mocking me, with the camera in one hand. I don't know what comes over me, but with one swift move I reach out and grab his camera and put it in my bag and run toward the door. He runs in front of me, pushing me aside, down the long hall of his studio and locks the door. He turns, stamps his foot at me, the way you do to scare off a dog, and I back up, all the way to the back wall.

It's a standoff.

He's pacing up and down the hall, laughing. He finds it funny, this skinny model girl who won't take off her top, who has his camera in her bag. He's a big guy. He's talking to himself under his breath now, saying how he could do anything the fuck he wanted to. He could take off my top himself.

He could take his camera back.

He could make sure I don't work again.

He could tell Sabine anything.

This girl is nothing, just some fucking everyday ordinary girl.

He could do things to me and take pictures of it.

He'd like to take pictures of me with the black eye—that would be fucking brilliant in my book if I had any fucking guts.

Pacing, pacing.

He could tell Sabine, this fucking girl, she never showed up.

He could fucking kill me.

Fucking little cunt, he's muttering, laughing, back and forth, pacing, back and forth, his thighs straining his black wool trousers.

What a little cunt baby, doesn't she know who I am?

I could get any girl to do any single thing I want.

And I'm standing there on the concrete floor of his studio, in front of a big plate glass window, watching him. Watching him with my big messenger bag linked over my shoulder with my book in it and his bulky camera in it and I have on my jeans and my motorcycle boots and over that the Debbie Harry miniskirt and impossibly red lipstick and heavy makeup and wild white hair, and what Baptiste Devaux does not know is that I am not just any ordinary girl, because the next time he turns away from me in his pacing, in his rant, I turn, too, away from him, and I jump, full force, through the big plate glass window.

Glass erupts everywhere, falling in shards, splintering all over the place and behind me as I run. I run and run and run, until I get to Shakespeare and Company, where there is a reading going on.

I walk in as quietly as is possible, but George sees me with my black getup and my black messenger bag bulging and my black eye growing more swollen by the moment.

"Give me your boots," he says.

And I take off each boot, hand them to George. He knows if he has my boots, I'm less likely to sneak away and leave.

My boots are my promise.

"Now, go get into your bed and sleep."

I crawl up the ladder to the little bed above the bookcase with the bulletin board above it. I put the bag with Baptiste Devaux's camera underneath the blanket with me. I can hear the reading going on, and I fall asleep reading the little notes posted to the bulletin board, wondering what I'd post if I were to write one tonight.

Little Bird seeks oblivion.

The next morning, I wake up to find a coffee, croissant, a copy of Hemingway's *The Garden of Eden*, and my boots at the end of my bed. I gather my stuff and head straight to Maxi.

At the agency, I take Baptiste Devaux's camera out of my bag and drop it on Sabine's desk.

"Hugo!" Sabine barks, and he comes and takes the camera away, the film still inside.

"Sabine, Baptiste—" I start to tell her what happened, but she raises her hand in a warning, saying what in English would mean "Not a word, you."

She says, "Ah, ah!"

I take the Métro back to the Maxi Pad, shower, change, and head back to Maxi in the late afternoon. The glossies from my shoot with Baptiste Devaux are there, and they are fucking spectacular. She wants to send them everywhere and print new zed cards with this photo on the front.

"Zeez," she declares, "is my Aleché!"

"But what about the photo credit?"

"We leave it off," she says.

No one ever hears his name again.

"I have a job for you," Sabine says. "Runway, but it is out of the country."

"Really? What is it?" I ask.

"You go on Friday, and you don't ask too many questions. Are you okay with zeez?" Sabine asks.

"Are you kidding?" I ask her.

"I never kidding," she says.

"Uh, yeah, I don't think I'm okay with that," I say, laughing.

"I will take you to lunch today, then," she says, "with a friend. Dress nice."

Now this has me intrigued. "Am I in some kind of trouble, Sabine?"

"No, no, no, my dear, no trouble, at all." She laughs. "You are smart girl, brave girl. Just meet me at the Ritz Bar, one o'clock."

"Well, then, okay. See you then."

I wear a dress they gave me when I walked for Chanel. They'd fitted it to me and let me have it in the end. It was cream with a weighted hem, a little black tie at the neck, and butterfly sleeves. I wear it with my black cowboy boots, pear-shaped rhinestone earrings, and red lipstick.

Walking into the Ritz Bar, I spot Sabine right away, the braid giving her away from behind. I am surprised to see Hugo sitting next to her, slumped like a brooding gangster. In the third seat at the table is an impeccably dressed gentleman, handsome and erudite—something about the way he moves, slowly, the very air around him charged with a kind of quiet energy, as if everyone in his presence is waiting for his cue—engaging the waitress in what appears to be a spirited and intimate conversation. When I go to the table, he stands.

"You must be Aleché," he says in a strange accent I can't quite place.

"Well, yes, as a matter of fact, I am. Pleasure to meet you," I say, my Southern accent coming back the way it does any time good manners are required.

"I'm Max, and you are as lovely as your photographs, even lovelier."

"Well, thank you," I say. "I do what I can."

"Ah! Modest, too!" He laughs.

"A realist, sir," I deadpan.

"Hardly, my dear."

"And what agency are you with?" I ask.

He roars with laughter. First, let me say it is clear that he is no model. He is a middle-aged businessman of very great means. A deep, jagged scar runs from the corner of his right eye down his face, etching his jawline. Now, if you've never spent time with a certain kind of Southern woman who loves to flirt, you'll likely assume my comment to be crass, even cruel. To the contrary, a Southern girl knows how to take the unspoken in the room and turn it into the sexiest, funniest detail in mixed conversation.

"Well, now that you ask, I am with Agence Maxi Internationale," he declares.

"You are?" I say, acting surprised. "Me, too!"

"I own it."

"Uh-oh."

"Uh-oh?"

"I'll tell you later," I whisper, leaning in, as if it is our secret alone.

"Sabine, this one is a keeper," says Max, and we continue with lunch. While Sabine and Hugo fall mostly silent, Max and I talk literature and politics, art and oil rigs and travel, one subject falling into the next the way they do in any great conversation. By the end of the lunch, he knows that I have no interest in being a model, and I know that he has no interest in owning a modeling agency. Nonetheless, by the end of the meal, I've been invited to a "modeling engagement"—a fashion show in the Middle East—and it sounds like the best idea in the world.

At the time.

Sabine calls later in the day to tell me to be ready to fly to Oman Friday and that I will not need to bring anything but a small bag of toiletries. After I hang up, an unsettled feeling in my stomach starts inching up the way the cream did in the milk bottles that were delivered at my granny's every Saturday at her place before sunrise, and I wander up to Wendy's room on the second level of the Maxi Pad.

"Wendy, do you know Max, the agency owner?" I ask.

"Oh, my gosh, you met Max?" she asks, surprised.

"Yeah, Sabine took me out to lunch to meet him."

"How'd you like the Ritz?" she asks, smiling. "I love Max. I know him really well. He's great."

"Well, who is he?" I ask. "I mean, besides owning the agency?"

"Oh, yeah, you got that, huh?" She laughs. "He's huge. He's Max Berg. He's a big oil trader. His manor house got blown up by some South African revolutionary group."

"Come again?" I ask. "I mean, what the living fuck? Seriously?"

"Seriously."

"Goddamn. And that doesn't seem a little, I don't know, down the bayou of batshit of crazy?" I ask.

"Not if you know him," she says. "He is the best guy, the kindest. He will do absolutely anything for you if you need him."

I wonder what kind of absolutely anything I could or would need from a man like Max Berg, and what the purpose is for him owning a modeling agency in Paris if his business is doing oil deals in the Middle East.

I can think of about twenty different reasons off the top of my head. And then I think about Baptiste Devaux, and suddenly I realize that a few topless photographs will likely be the least of my concerns.

I have two choices—go Oman or go home.

DIVING

INTO THE WRECK

I came to explore the wreck.
—ADRIENNE RICH

I went home.

After six months in Paris, I was determined never to model again. I wanted to write and study. I wanted to be who'd I'd always planned to be, not some bizarre dolled-up version of the real me. The accident had thrown me way off course. I got wrapped around the pole, and the subsequent surgeries and resulting illness had whittled me down to a poor excuse of myself. A skinny shell: a pretty decoration but nothing more. I'd been running around Paris writing poems on paper sacks while people judged me for what I looked like.

Not tall enough.

Too blond.

Too skinny.

Not skinny enough.

Droopy eye.

Scars.

Strange face.

Druggy.

Ugly.

Typical.

Fat.

Proportions off.

Hideous.

Commercial.

Too sweet.

Too slutty.

Too nice.

Too pretty.

Not pretty enough.

Something about it made me feel used up, consumed, like I was the little girl my father gobbled up all over again, his sexual abuse consuming in a drunken, hungry rage all the best parts of me until I was nothing but a pretty, performing doll. How I'd endure it time and time again, night after night, and every day I'd wake up and pretend I was fine, how I'd polish up my little soul. How I'd smile and keep on marching through my days like I was just another ordinary, happy little girl. Everything in Paris somehow felt like I'd stirred up the dirty pond of my childhood and wore it like a party dress.

So I went back to school and left modeling behind.

At least I planned to. As it turned out, modeling was a much better way to earn cash that the usual college opportunities. It was also a great way for a girl like me to travel and write and be in the world. So, I would go back (to Japan, to Milan, to Geneva, even to do some commercials in New York) in the fall semesters, save up the cash, then take a double load in the spring. But by then I knew it was a means to an end, not the other way around.

And then I met Liam.

It was the last semester of my senior year of undergrad in Sacramento. After living through my accident, then Paris, I decided

I was tired of chasing things that meant nothing to me. I scrapped my law school plans and applied to three master of fine art programs in poetry.

So much for practical.

My application to Sarah Lawrence had been so last minute (I'd never heard of it until my poetry professor, Dennis Schmitz, suggested it) that it was written longhand on five unlined pages. There was nothing to do now but wait.

I was feeling nostalgic and wanted to frequent all my favorite Sacramento spots before leaving town forever.

Sam's Hof Brau was the kind of place that lived up to everything promised in its blinking, golden, beer-suds-popping-like-tiny-fireworks neon sign. On the corner of Tenth and J Streets in downtown Sacramento, it was one of many dive bars visited on weekends by Sac State students. Inside, the light was warm and hazy, as if you were submerged in a gleaming glass of beer. Behind a steamy window, sturdy spits turned with fat turkeys and dripping hams, while charred tri-tip rested on battered carving boards. There were great interchangeable metal pans of greasy sides, and fluffy white rolls in enormous brown paper sacks, torn open at the top. The dimmed light was golden; the battered bar was long. The tables were in the back room, and the main room had the bar along one side, some skinny bar tables against the other wall, and way down adjacent to the swinging front doors was a raised, square stage.

That night, the Beer Dawgs were playing in all their rough, honky-tonk glory, while a mix of midtown hipsters, old hippies, and college kids filled the cramped dance floor under glittering domes of light. I went out three nights a week in those semesters I was home from abroad. No matter that my final semester I was— with special permission from the dean of humanities—taking an entire year's worth of courses in one semester, I was full blown on the lookout for love. Moving back and forth every semester left me feeling, while thrilled, always a bit lonely, displaced, never able to maintain the deep friendships and love affairs hallmark to college life.

I was just home from Osaka, my last semester abroad modeling before I graduated, when we met. Liam was sitting at the bar at Sam's, wearing ripped-up Levi's, a pair of cowboy boots, and a threadbare vintage yellow cowboy shirt with abalone snaps. His hair, sandy blond and wavy, reached just below his shoulders, soft and thick, not wild but feral nonetheless. He didn't have a classically handsome face—his chin was weak, his nose a little big, his skin not that of a fresh-faced college boy but of a laborer who spent long hours in punishing sun. Somehow all the rough added up to handsome, though. Mostly, because he had those eyes—deep set, almond shaped, so big, and the palest color of blue-green you've ever seen. Like aqua with diamonds shot through. He was slight, lanky, about my height. I'd seen him a few times before—at the Zebra Club, and the VFW Post, and the Press Club. I pulled up a barstool next to him, said, "Hey, I'm Alice."

"I'm Liam," he said, too quiet for me to hear.

"Arron?" I asked.

"Liam," he said, louder.

"Wow, that's a nice name."

"Yeah, my mom thought it sounded like someone on a soap opera." He laughed.

"Was your mom into soap operas?" I asked.

"No, she just wanted to sound like she wasn't a fifteen-year-old, white-trash, high school dropout," he said, the smile spreading all the way to those dazzlingly morning-blue eyes.

"Ah, well, fancy names for your kids will cure a lack of education every time, right?" I answered. "I suppose you have a brother named Ashton and a sister named Blaire?"

He laughed. "Hardly! Two sisters, Sandy and Brandy, and a brother, Huck. I guess they got ripped off."

"I guess so!" I laughed. I was halfway through my Diet Coke, and he was ordering another beer.

"How'd you end up with a name like Alice?" he asked.

"I was left on the doorstep of an old-folks home in a basket, and the old folks named me before the news crews arrived."

"No," he said.

"No," I said, "both my grandmothers were named Alice; it was fate."

"Would you think I'm crazy if I told you that sitting next to you here feels a little bit like fate?" he asked, only half smiling now.

"You're teasing me."

"I might be." He smiled. "I've been watching you for months."

"Where?" I balked.

"All over town, all the clubs, at school."

"You go to State?" I said, shocked. I'd never seen him there.

"Yeah, I'm premed."

"Ah," I said, nodding. "That explains it. I have science-geek blindness," I teased.

"Very funny."

"I'm only kidding. You're going to med school, then?" I asked.

"Yeah, I've always wanted to, my whole life," he said, growing serious.

"How come? I couldn't imagine being a doctor," I added.

"Growing up, we had nothing. I mean, nothing. Less than nothing. Most of the time we were homeless. If someone was sick, there was nothing we could do about it but just endure it, you know? As a kid, I always thought that I was missing out on something. That if we had the money to go to the doctor, that we'd be getting some sort of powerful medicine that would make us better. I don't know, I felt more than sick. When one of us got sick, and we were always sick, I felt like it was our fault we were sick. We were dirty, you know. Somehow in my kid brain I got it in my mind not only that if we had money to go to the doctor we'd be well but that also we'd be clean and we'd be, I don't know, somehow, as good as all the other kids, like, worthy. Whatever, it doesn't make any sense," he trailed off.

"It makes a lot of sense, actually," I said, putting my hand on his arm, a sensation like a ferocious wave running down my body at the place where our skin met.

"I just want to help people, do something meaningful," he said.

"That's amazing."

We sat in silence for a while, side by side at the bar. The Beer Dawgs went through a couple of songs while people danced and talked and laughed above the music. From the next room, silverware clinked while couples feasted on their roasts and fowl. Liam ordered us another round, Diet Coke for me and a dark brew for him, and we drank it slowly, his hand on the small of my back while we sat in the gentle light of Sam's, content in our silence. Eventually, my girlfriend Lark Noble, who I'd come with, came to get me to dance with her. She tried to pull Liam along, too, but he refused. As Lark pulled me away from him, he called out to me, "Hey, what are you going to be when you grow up?"

"A poet!"

I danced, grooving and losing myself in the hard blues on the little dance floor under the big arts-and-crafts chandelier, the now-muted light dropping a soft yellow ease over the throbbing mass. Liam joined up with the buddy he'd come with, but he watched me for over an hour from the bar. I saw him standing there at the edges of the crowd, and I thought how different we were—me at the center of the action, him at the fringe. But there at the bar, side by side, it felt like we were the same kind of person. Like we could sit there for a long time and never run out of things to say. Like we could unzip our chests and the same pile of wounds would fall out. Somewhere toward the end of the evening, he came and shoved a little piece of paper with his name and number in a terrible scrawl in the pocket of my jeans and left. He told me later, much later, that he announced to his friend that night, "That's the girl I'm going to marry."

THE "I"S HAVE IT

I called Liam the very next day. On the phone, his voice was soft, with a happy lilt, as if everything he said was the penultimate line of a joke. Turns out he didn't live far from me.

I had a flat in midtown on Twenty-third Street in the heart of the city, a gorgeous white Victorian that had been chopped up into seven flats, all with polished hardwood floors, odd angles, and big, sunny, wobbly windows looking out on the church across the street. Liam rented a converted garage in the statelier environs of East Sacramento's Fabulous Forties neighborhood, not far from where Ron and Nancy played house in Sacramento for the governorship.

Despite Sacramento having the reputation of a cow town, those were heady days for a twentysomething college kid in school there. People were forever asking me why on God's green earth I went back to Sac between modeling assignments. The truth was cheap rent, being a big fish in a small pond, and a pretty thriving scene to keep me entertained when I wasn't in Paris or Milan or Osaka or New York kept me coming back.

On any given weekend, you could see a hard-core punk band in an abandoned warehouse in a back alley on Friday, a very-young Nirvana at the Cattle Club on Folsom Boulevard on Saturday, and Cake in a friend's backyard on a Sunday afternoon. Chi Cheng from Deftones was in my poetry-writing seminar, and I was taking Intro to Native Art from Frank LaPena. Besides, I had neither the grades nor the cash to get into a better school. I was making the best of Sac State, and—even taking a year's worth of classes each spring—I was still clearing a near 4.0.

Everyone knew everyone. My teenage crowd of skaters and punkers became artists and journalists and rock stars and chefs. My parents were pretty liberal when I was in high school, and we always had a homeless skater or two crashing in the poolroom. Mama'd deloused and supplied pancake feasts to more than her fair share of tweakers and lost boys. Junior year, I donned a vintage strapless black Betty dress and went to prom with Chico Garcia—who promptly got drunk and drove Mama's white Lincoln Continental up the curve and almost into one of the lakes in William Land Park. I'd had my first fuck with my boyfriend's best friend in her Dodge Charger after band practice. The point being that despite the fact that I was nerd when it came to making the grades and had never touched so much as a single joint in my life, I knew from boys and butch girls and troublemakers. From the stories Liam told, it sounded as if he had been around the block and halfway back, and yet I'd never so much as heard his name. I found it strange we'd never crossed paths, but I brushed the thought away.

Who needs red flags when you've got red tap pants instead?

Perhaps that was part of my downfall—I liked to play awful dirty, but I liked to keep my dresses pristine. While everyone else was rolling out of bed the next day at noon, I was sitting in the front of the class, raising my hand like a guileless fool. I do have the hindsight to realize now this was, quite literally, a near-fatal flaw.

We talked for hours the first few days after our night at Sam's, exchanging stories about our childhoods: mine Southern and wretchedly storied, his decadently horrific, both abusive to the utmost extreme. Between us there was a lot of "past" to cover—not only our childhoods but our college years, too. Nothing was off limits; secrets were a sharp tool of seduction we'd both honed well.

We were both just about to go into our last semester. He'd applied to six or seven medical schools, and I'd applied to exactly three MFA programs in poetry—Iowa, Columbia, and Sarah Lawrence. Meanwhile, his applications were not quite due, and he asked me to "take a peek" at the personal statement part of his applications. A few days after we met at Hof Brau, we made plans for Liam to come over to my house the following night at six.

It was raining and dark. I was wearing one of my favorite outfits; no one around Sacramento wore anything like it. That's why I thought I was cool. In other words: I was young, arrogant, and trying mighty hard to be sexy. Everything came from a thrift store: the men's XL tuxedo shirt with the extra-wide cuffs, little woven knobby links instead of buttons, perfectly pleated bib front, and tiny stand-up collar; black lace bustier underneath; waist-high, lace-edged satin tap pants, red; big woven tooled cowboy belt slung low on the waist; knee-high tube socks with black stripes around the top; vintage cowgirl boots with inlaid roses; tons of turquoise jewelry. My blond hair was pulled back more severely than one of the girls in Robert Palmer's "Addicted to Love" video, and my face was bare except for a dark, deep-red stain of lipstick.

Fucking ridiculous.

This look might—and I emphasize *might*—fit in perfectly were I, say, sitting backstage waiting for hair and makeup at Chanel in

Paris. In Sacramento, I looked like I had not only forgotten my pants but my makeup and my hairstyle, too. If I had a mama who ever gave a decent slip of advice to what made for a decent young lady, I'd have known better. Not that I'd have listened. But good Lord and Savior, what was I thinking? Not much other than what was going to happen the minute he walked through the door. I checked my lipstick one last time in the mirror above my cassette deck. The rain came down hard. I was ready.

He was late.

First, just a few minutes: no big deal, really. Though I must say, I've always been a bit of a stickler for promptness. Instead of behaving like a normal college chick and having beer in the fridge and a bag of chips on the counter, I had an inlaid lacquered tray of hors d'oeuvres set out on a battered wooded trunk between the two love seats in my main room with tiny pieces of soft cheese and broken unraised bread and tsukemono and hard meats, a couple of bottles of good sake, and two perfect tiny little sake cups at the ready. I had a book of Ono no Komachi poems that just happened to be there on the trunk, too—*just in case.*

Outside, the rain fell like rice grains poured into a silk sack. I reapplied my lip stain. I had a mixtape playing on the boom box— shakuhachi, Mazzy Star, Nirvana, K. D. Lang, Cowboy Junkies, and Jane's Addiction.

Twenty minutes passed.

I milled around in front of the window, watching a steady stream of people leave through a side door of the church into the rainy night. They were all dressed normally, not dressed up. Not like anyone in Sacramento dressed up for church—I hadn't seen finery for church since my childhood days in Jackson. It was a Wednesday, and it didn't look like they were coming from a service. Some held a little blue book. Some had papers or coats they held over their heads against the rain as they dashed to their cars or down the sidewalk into the night. Every few feet a streetlight shone a soft, bright, almost white illuminated waterfall unto itself.

I stepped away from the window and backed into my ruined book-case.

A few weeks previously, just before I'd come back from what would be my last semester away, there was a hard freeze in Sacramento, and the pipes burst in our building. The burst in general was a big disaster in the building, with people moving in and out, floors being pulled up, people staying in hotels, and mammoth old industrial fans whirling, whirring, day and night. Unfortunately, during the hoopla, no one thought to look in on my little flat, and so no one realized that there was water damage inside until I came home.

As soon as I turned the key in the lock and pushed open the heavy door, the smell of rot hit me. Stepping in, I encountered my one bookcase, half-decayed, expanded, the books engorged, the deckled edges of beloved books dotted with spotty green mold, the solid wood of the case split up the sides. That was the extent of the water damage, other than an ugly spot on the roof—the books had slowly soaked up all the water as it came down. The floor could have use a bit of sanding underneath where the book-case sat, but nothing disastrous. Despite the smell, I hadn't had the heart to do anything about it yet, almost a month now. The bookcase stood in ruin between the main living area and my bed. Every now and then, I'd try to pry one of my favorite volumes of poetry—maybe the first edition Whitman Daddy had given Mama for Christmas one year, maybe my beloved clothbound copy of *Tikki Tikki Tembo* Mama had read to me 4,327 times at bedtime growing up—from the expanse, with no luck. It was heartbreaking and somehow haunting to me, the perished bookshelf.

I must have been standing there pawing at the rot factory like an absurd librarian for some time, because when my buzzer finally went off and I checked my vintage men's Rolex, it showed 7:17!

Almost an hour and twenty minutes late?

Buzzzzzzzzz.

In one movement, I ducked as low as I could, then stuck my hands in front of me like a synchronized swimmer and dove through midair as far as I could across the main room, sliding a good distance on the slick hardwood, then slither-slunk-slither-slunk-slither-slunking a little farther behind the more beige of the two beige love seats, heart galloping.

My first instinct was this: *hide.*

What in the helicopter is that man thinking showing up an hour and a half late? I hissed very loudly in my most infuriated inner voice.

And why am I still waiting? And don't I have a paper due tomorrow? Oh, Lord, oh, Lord, oh, Lord oh, Lord, please don't let him have seen me sweet Jesus in the camellia bush, I prayed.

Buzzzzzzzzzz.

"Alice? You okay? Did you fall?" he called out, sounding concerned.

"Uh, fall? Fall? Um, no . . . just trying to, hold on a second, I wasn't expecting you, I was . . . ," I stammered.

"I know. Sorry I'm so late. It's the weirdest thing. I was going to call you, but I thought you saw me with the guy in front of your house?" he yelled out, sounding apologetic, hopeful.

"Guy? Um, no."

"Yeah, you were standing in the window, I waved at you?"

This sounded like, pardon my French, a crock of shit.

"Yeah, I'm pretty sure that didn't happen," I sang out.

"You were standing there, kinda looking out at the rain?"

Am I actually buying this? I mean, I have had about fourteen Cokes with this guy and talked to him on the phone seven (very entertaining) times, and though he may be kind of weirdly cute in an outsider/hobo sort of way, what do I really know about him?

"There was a bunch of people walking out of the church, and I was right in front of your house, by the gutter, with an old man? Does any of this ring a bell?"

"Oh, well, yeah," I called out. "I mean, some. The church

people do. I mean, anyway," I said, getting up, rearranging my shirt, adjusting my belt, going to the door, inching it open. "I'm sorry, come in."

I opened the door and there he was, in ripped-up Levi's and old brown pointy-toed cowboy boots and a mother-of-pearl snap-front Western shirt, his long hair loose to his shoulders.

"Oh, my stars, you're wet!" I screamed.

"I know!" he said, laughing, looking down at his jeans clinging to his legs like paint. He was beyond soaked; he was positively sopping.

"What am I thinking? Please, come in!" I said, leading him into my place. "Do you want to dry off? Let me show you the bathroom. It's right back here, through the kitchen, well, of course you can see for yourself this is the kitchen, it's a pretty tacky one, but as you can see unlike some college girls I do use it and anyway all the way back here's my little bathroom it's really a closet but it has all the working parts and it's all yours and you can feel free to use those towels on the rack there, they aren't just for show or guest towels or what have you, well, they are, but they're for times like this, because, well, you're the guest I guess, that is to say they're clean, and you're wet, you know? Anyway, um," I sighed, winding down.

He was really wet.

"Would you happen to have a hair dryer?" he asked.

"Oh, gosh, no, I don't. Sorry! That's totally abnormal, especially for a girl, right?" I said, stammering. "But my hair's stick straight, and I just wash it and let it dry and that's it, give or take a tube of gel and the ponytail du jour, that is," I blathered. "One time I got a perm, and it plum washed right out the first time I took a shower. Mama'd like to have kill me. I think she paid nearly two hundred dollars for it or something, isn't that just something? Mama didn't think so! Anyway, I just never use a blow-dryer, to tell you the God's honest truth."

Why could I not just shut my mouth?

"It's okay, really," he said, leaning on the door.

"Are you sure?"

"I'm sure."

"Okay," I said, "but, oh! Maybe I could borrow one from my neighbor?"

"No, that's fine," he said, hanging off the door, holding on now to one of my good, white towels.

"Okay. I'm really sorry."

"It's okay."

"Don't worry about it."

"Okay."

"Alice?"

"Yeah?"

"I'm going to shut the door now, okay?" he asked, smiling.

"Oh, good Lord, of course. Just pull me down from the noose when you come out."

"Will do," he said, laughing, and shut the door. I heard the lock click in the knob.

I went into the main room.

Sat on the love seat.

Moved to the other love seat.

Took my hair out of the ponytail.

Put it back in.

Sat on the floor.

Noticed the soft cheeses were hardened; the charcuterie was curly around the edges.

I took Ono no Komachi and slid her under the love seat.

Breathe, Alice, breathe! Why was I getting so asinine about some loner science geek with a significant height impediment and a crucial promptness impairment? *When that gentleman is finished soiling the good linens, you are going to promptly show him the door, missy!* I admonished myself.

Twenty minutes later, Liam came out with sexy, curly hair on his collarbones and a very damp V-neck Fruit of the Loom T-shirt untucked from his wrinkled Levi's, his soggy boots squeezed between two fingertips. "What'd I miss?" He laughed.

"Well, about an hour and a half, to start," I quipped.

"About that," he started, and then told me what happened. "First, I shouldn't tell you this, but I changed clothes about twenty times before coming over here, like some kind of freak. I mean, guys aren't supposed to care, right? Then, speaking of blow-dryers, you'll love this: I have to blow-dry my hair for, like forty minutes to get it right, because it gets all curly when it's rainy and it looks horrible, so I have to dry it and dry and dry it like a motherfucker so I don't look like a girl. My dad always told me I looked like a girl when I was growing up. His favorite thing was to call me 'girlie.' Drove me nuts. Anyway, so then finally get out of my place, but I leave the piece of paper with your address on it at my house, but I'm already late and I'm pretty sure I remember the street, so I just keep driving, and I figure I'll see your car since it's so memorably hideous—no offense! Where'd you get that thing? The pinstripes alone will blind a person. Anyway, I'm speeding like a bat outta hell, and I practically spin out at that intersection by AM/PM, you know the one, right? That place is Grand Central Crackhead-ville. Anyway, this guy pulling out of AM/PM gets all pissed at me and flips me the bird and starts following me down P Street and wanting to start some road rage drag race or something. Crazy, right?"

In no point in this story was there a moment for me to interrupt, comment, or so much as reply to a question. I simply listened, nodding, looking back and forth between his pale, pale eyes and the rain streaming down the window, my green eyes like the automated peepers on a Japanese cat clock.

"Finally I just slam on my brakes, turn down an alley, and totally lose him, but by then, I'm halfway to downtown, and then I have to circle back up to midtown, and then I'm fucking beyond the beyond late, if you know how that feels, and so finally I get here, and sure enough, your car is parked right out in front of your place, which I couldn't miss if I wanted to—seriously, what the hell is that? That car is some funny shit! Anyway, now I'm thinking I've got it made, that probably you live in this house because A, your car's in front, and B, it's a pretty white Victorian and it looks like the kind of place you'd live in and, C, there's all those ferns hanging from the porch and you're from Mississippi and the ferns remind me of some house in the Deep South and then *bam!* I see you standing in the window like some *goddamned* Scarlett O'Hara waiting for my arrival, and I'm thinking, *Damn, this is your lucky day, Liam!*"

Good thing he thought it was his lucky day, as it clearly was not going to be his lucky night. By that time, I was starting to regret opening the door. His hair was still curled around his collarbones in the most appealing way, but his mouth was moving in a way that reminded me of those hungry baby birds, blind still, gulping for food, who don't care if they get it from their mother or an upturned trash can. They're just hungry.

"So *then*, I get my statement paper and the flowers and I hop outta the truck and I see all those people coming out of the church, and one of them, this stick-up-the-ass lady, asks me, 'Are you here to pick him up? He said his son was coming to pick him up.' And I look down and there's this old dude and he's just lyin' in the gutter right in front of your house! You didn't see him? No? Really? No? He was just lyin' there, old white dude, jeans and boots and Pendleton? Nice Pendleton, too. My dad used to wear that kind. You know the plaid kind that's kind of blended together, not the real sharp plaid? That kind. So anyway, he's lyin' there with his GD hat on his chest like he's takin' a nap! But, man, you could smell him a mile away. Whooooeee! I know that smell like, well, not like the back of my hand, 'cause that don't make no sense, but like something—I can't think of right now, 'cause that's a smell I know. The old dude reeks of whiskey. Like he's sweating it. Like he's breathing it, you know? Like he pisses it and bleeds it. Whiskey's something you can't mix up with other smells, you know? No? I know whiskey. I could smell whiskey from a mile away. I could smell whiskey in a field of three hundred angry skunks. I could smell whiskey if I was lying down face-first in fresh tar. I could smell whiskey, well, you get the idea. Anyway, there's this old dude. You really didn't see him? That's weird. Do you wear glasses? Anyway, this lady, she's just plowin' right ahead, sure I'm this old dude's son, and she's insisting that I take him home *right now*. She doesn't even let me get a word in edgewise. Don't you hate it when people do that? And she also says that he is, *quote unquote*, not getting credit for attending the meeting because he *did not* attend the *meeting*; she was there the whole time and he did nothing but come in and sign his name and walk right out and apparently drain the contents of a cheap bottle of his, *quote unquote*, preference. Can you believe that? She says, 'His preference.' Like she's talking about his favorite food or his favorite side of the bed. I'm telling you, I was not a fan of this lady. She's just like the person in school who sits in the front of the class and raises their hand every goddamned time, even when the teacher has already called on them."

That person would be me, I thought.

"Well, hell, I tried to tell her a few times that I was not this old dude's son, but after a while—get this! The old guy, he starts puttin' his hand on my arm, 'cause by now I got him sitting up on the curb by my truck. He starts sayin' to me, 'Son, son, thank you for coming, son!' Crazy shit! But kind of sad, too. Because, you know, I really felt sorry for the guy. I mean, he wasn't a bad guy or anything, he was just really, really drunk. We've all been there, right? So I figured I'd start off slow—I asked him if he knew where he lived. I asked him if he could walk home. The lady— she was kind of hanging around with a few other people from the meeting—she came back over and asked me straight out if I was going to take him home. I told her, 'Yes, I will take care of it.' But even that wasn't good enough for her! She told me she was going to stay there to, *quote unquote*, see that I took my father home or she was calling the police! Man, I didn't know what to do. I mean, who knows what this old dude did to these people. Probably nothing. Though they were seriously something pissed at him. But he didn't seem like a bad guy to me, really he didn't."

I had nothing to say, it seemed. I wondered why he hadn't simply walked the ten steps to my door to at least let me know he was preoccupied with saving a drunk.

"Let me tell you a story, okay? You don't mind, right? I remember once when I was about ten, my dad didn't come home one night. Now, this was not an unusual occurrence. My dad didn't come home lots of nights. Sometimes he didn't come home for weeks at a time. My mom just did what she could until he showed up again, and she never asked questions, you know? But she got a phone call this time. I remember it was real early in the morning. She told me, 'Liam, you got to go downtown and get your dad.' Now, this was in Laynesville, Missouri, a tiny little town in the middle of nowhere. There was one little nothing hotel, and I can't think of any reason my dad would be at the hotel. I mean, what do I know? I'm, like, ten or something. Did I say that already? No? So I got dressed and walked into town, wondering the whole way what I was going to find when I got there. It was a long walk. The day was starting by then and people were starting to go to work, or get off night shifts, head to school, open up the café, the postman starting on his rounds, you know, everybody and anybody. And I'm walking into town to go get my dad. And the hotel is right in the middle of town. It's an old-fashioned building, just like every other building in Laynesville, with a low brick front and a big glass front with LAYNESVILLE HOTEL printed across. And underneath the printing is a kind of wooden bench under the window, and on that bench is my dad, tattooed as he is to high heaven, in—get this—only his tighty-whities and his cowboy boots, with his pistol stuck in one boot, snoring away, shit drunk."

Liam started laughing, almost uncontrollably, tears welling up in his eyes, his face going red. I laughed right along with him, but inside I felt like someone kicked me right in the middle of my chest.

"And I gotta go inside the hotel, into the lobby, wake him up, get him up on his feet. That was no easy thing, let me tell you! Because believe me, he's as drunk as he was when he passed out there, whenever the hell that was. My dad's missing clothes are nowhere in sight, and no one is offering anything to spare. I'm ten and I'm wearing polyester slacks and a polyester rainbow striped polo shirt, so nothing I'm wearing is fit to be shared. But that's not even the worst part. The worst part is that I have to prop him up, staggering all the way back home, in the light of day, back through town, back through the rich neighborhoods, across the proverbial tracks, past not one but two buggies full of shocked Amish, back down the country road, back to bumfuck nowhere to where we live in someone's rented basement with a hose coming in through a tiny window above the kitchen sink as our only running water. Just like that, with my dead-drunk dad, in his boots and undershorts, I gotta walk all the way home. How humiliating, right? I remember one of the Amish men saying something nasty to me, and I got all pissed off and started throwing handfuls of rocks from the side of the road at the back of the buggy. My dad thought that was the funniest thing he ever saw. It all seems funny now, actually. But it's not."

He stopped talking then, drawing his knees up to his chest, resting his chin on them, suddenly looking about ten years old. I wanted to touch him but didn't dare. Mama taught me—don't lay a hand on a man in tears. Mama was like that. She didn't mother me much. You could say I was an unmothered girl—she didn't keep me from being devoured by Papa, she didn't mind laying all the weight of her personal crisis at my tiny feet, but every now and then she'd tell me a thing or two, like "Never touch a crying man; just leave him be."

And so in a moment like this, when Liam was crying, I held back. I knew a man broke open could mean one of two things: too tender, too mean.

I wanted to touch him. I knew the wounds were falling out of him right there in front of me, but I didn't know yet that I was willing to pick them up and put them in my mouth, that I was willing to devour them one by one until he was free and I was holding down all the pain for the both of us.

He took a deep, shuddering breath, poured himself a glass of sake, and continued what somehow felt now like a confession, like a long-winded, tenderhearted apology.

When he spoke again, his voice was so quiet I had to lean it to hear him, the rain falling hard enough now to drain out the strange, velvety sound of his sorrowful voice.

"To tell you the truth, that old dude tonight reminded me of a hell-of-a-lot-more-decent version of my dad, and I didn't want that snotty lady to call the police on him, and he just kept telling me, 'You're a good son, son. Thank you, son.' So I just folded him into my truck and took off. Did you hear me tear out? It turns out he was at least halfway sober enough to direct me to where he lives, which turns out to be a halfway house in Alkali Flats. I thought about going home after that and just calling you, and I probably would've if I'd realized how much time had passed, but I *really* wanted to see you. It's all I could think about, all night long. Oh shit, the flowers!"

He ran back out to his truck then and brought in a bouquet of delicate purple wildflowers mixed with sage and rosemary that I stuck in one of the now-empty sake bottles.

We sat on the floor and talked for what seemed hours about the things that people who are going to be lovers talk about—the best and the worst of themselves. We told one another all the pretty stories: all the details that painted us in our best, shining glory. We told one another all the terrible stories: all the details that revealed the most fragile, damaged corners of our wounded souls. I turned the mixtape over two or three times.

"That's quite a tragedy," he said, looking up at the bookcase.

"Indeed," I agreed.

"You're the only girl I know who uses the word *indeed* in regular conversation, you know that?" he asked, brushing his thumb across my lower lip, which was just a tiny bit chapped from all the lip stain.

I may have nodded.

"It must break your heart, huh?" he asked.

"What?"

"The books," he said in an almost whisper.

"Indeed," I said, smiling, then started to cry.

In the wide world of people roaming their lives, looking for love and answers, there are certain people—people who have been to hell and back, lived to tell the tale—who recognize in one another at once someone who has survived brutality, who wears that same scrappy oblivion disguised as survival on their sleeve. When you live through a childhood made out of cruelty, a childhood of raised skin, of hungry nights and the tender, awful ache between the thighs, you cannot help but display it: the mark. We both had it: Liam recognized it in me and I in him.

I tried to hide my face, screwed up with tears. Liam turned my chin, kissed me.

I turned, kissed back. We rose and walked across to my bed. And I even reminded myself, during that first heavy breath, that fall to the bed: *do not close your eyes.*

But Liam was long-limbed and long-haired and kissed like a house afire, and I forgot my promise, and I closed my eyes. And that's when I saw him—a figure, moving form, enormous shadow appearing somewhere between my eyes and the air. I felt again how easy it was to be that small—how my chin fit in a mouth, my buttocks in the crook of a hip, how easy it was then to be filled.

Behind closed eyes, I was six again, turning cartwheels out on the sidewalk, with my mother in the kitchen window, calling, "Be careful not to turn into the road!" But I kept turning, windmilling from asphalt to sky, asphalt to sky. I smelled the beefsteak on the barbecue, where my father called over the fence to the neighbor, saying, "This is the life." But when I hear his voice—my father's—it is enough to send me sideways. I fall into the street. My knees are scraped and filled with rocks, but I'm almost me again, knees wide open, panties pushed to the side. I'm gone now from the wavy windows covered with falling rain: someone else has taken my place. I'm cloud now. Blue sky. I'm gone. Liam is there, but I can't see him anymore.

And then.

He bites my lip. I bite back. Pain is what I know. We move together like we've known one another all along. And when finally it happens, I realize that it isn't my father filling me this time; he is only making me fall. My eyes are open and staring at Liam, who looks back and almost seems to know. And when finally it happens, Liam filling me, I open my eyes and I'm back.

And Liam says, "Isn't sex amazing?"

And I say, "Yes."

It takes only that one time for Liam to recognize what was in my childhood, how I was a girl marked in the way so many girls are marked—keeping the terrible secret from everyone, except those who themselves carried the undeniable mark.

After, we got up. He put his jeans and T-shirt back on.

"You're leaving?" I asked, putting on my tuxedo shirt and sounding like a college girl who just got fucked on a first non-date.

"Oh no, but . . . my personal statement. Do you mind?" he asked.

"No, not at all," I said, blinking. I'd completely forgotten. He was out the door to his truck and back in an instant, a crumpled little stack of white paper filled with three pages of single-spaced, typed material, PERSONAL STATEMENT OF MR. LIAM RIVERS blazing across the top of the first page in Baskerville Old Face font.

I sat down on one love seat with it and began to read. He stood looking at the ruined bookshelf, reaching up from time to time just as I often did to try to pry one book or another out from the expanded wreck.

The books wouldn't budge.

He tilted the shelf toward him, balanced it on his knees, tried to bang the separated frame of it back together with his palms. His statement paper was pretty straightforward—about his impoverished childhood, his alcoholic father, and how as a child he'd vowed that if he ever found a way to get to college, he promised himself he'd go to medical school so he could help the disadvantaged. It was spectacularly poorly written, but I didn't want to tell him that. I wasn't sure what to say. I sat staring at the page long after I'd finished reading.

"Well, what do you think?" he asked, a look of hope in his bloodshot eyes.

"When do you have to send this off?" I asked.

"Tomorrow," he said apologetically. "I have to work on it when I get home. Actually, I have to get going in a minute here."

"In that case, there's just one thing I can tell you."

"What's that?"

"Maybe try not to start every single sentence with the word *I*."

SO MUCH
CALAMITY SMOKE

Not long after we started squatting in the FEMA trailer they wouldn't take away, I realized that in the very near future we were going to have to go back home. My black eyes were still dark as the tree trunks in the salt-water-scorched piney woods surrounding us. It had been only four days since that wretched night, but I'd left the next morning and had already filed for divorce. My attorney, one Miss Addison McClanahan, was making swift work on a motion to have Liam removed from what was now referred to as the "marital residence."

I didn't know Addison McClanahan from a hole in an altar guild cloth before the attack. She went to St. John's Episcopal and sat behind me and my babies in the old wooden pew with her tall, handsome husband and sweet little girl, her gravelly voice raising in perfect alto harmony with the old hymns. She was one of those perfect Old Ocean Springs gals who made me a little nervous. It wasn't that I didn't like her, not at all—it was just that I was slightly intimidated by her perfect blond coif, deep connections in the community, and seemingly perfect family. Not only that, but she had a big billboard out to the entrance of the I-10 advertising, "Addison McClanahan, Attorney at Law," her smile wide, her eyes steely, her suit crimson and sharp-shouldered.

I had spent the first night in the Gulf Coast Women's Center for Nonviolence, awake till dawn, huddled in a bunk bed with all three kids, singing "Don't You Worry 'Bout a Thing" over and over to my babies until some lady down the hall hollered, "Shut up, stupid!"

The next morning, Lana called the secret cell phone Mama'd sent me from California months earlier, after Liam had forbidden me to have a phone, and said to pack up our stuff and come out to Latimer, a little town north of the coast, where she lived with the extended Manning clan entire. Her brother was in possession of "one bona fide deluxe FEMA trailer" in which we could—for the time being—hide out. For now, my residence was that borrowed FEMA trailer, and I was glad of it.

If I was going to leave that little tin haven of security, my husband was going to have to be long gone from the marital residence before I'd go. Liam (said soon-to-be ex-husband) was still rattling around the immaculate behemoth of a house, drinking and carrying on pretty much as he always did, as if life itself hadn't gone up in so much calamity smoke. Tragedy and violence were realities he was unwilling to entertain: as far as he was concerned, life was just fine and I'd return to my senses and be home shortly. About the only thing different in the days following that wretched night was his new mission as drunken telephone harasser, leaving threatening messages for me at my mama's house in Sacramento.

Liam was sure I was camped out in Mama's rickety parsonage house next door to the church in Sacramento, where she'd been the janitor for twenty-odd years, and so he called her landline repeatedly, on the hour. He'd leave beseeching messages one minute about how I was only making things worse and how we could still put things back together, then immediately call back and read—in a muddy, deepwater-bayou-bottom slur—verbatim, the interstate kidnapping law he'd found who knows where the next.

"Interstate child abduction by a parent is a felony offense, punishable by permanent loss of custody and federal prison time, plus a fine of up to . . ." He faded off, belching under his breath. "Up to, up to, well, a fine, punishable, felony, baby, you better . . ."

This was his official drunk voice, a kind of oratory desperation he affected when he wanted to make a point while ruthlessly obliterated.

I was used to it; Mama was not.

"I feel sort of sad for him, really," Mama started, her gentle voice lilting, forgiving.

"Mama."

"But he sounds so sad . . ."

"Mama."

I knew better. Mama hadn't seen me yet, hadn't witnessed the ravages of his marks on my skin; she couldn't quite accept what he'd become. I knew he was getting to her, and I begged her not to answer his calls, no matter what.

"He really used to be a nice young man," she started.

"Mama."

"Maybe I could talk to him."

"I'm serious, Mama. No. Matter. What."

"I could call *his* mama."

"Mama."

"Maybe I could answer when he's not drunk?"

"Mama. He tried to kill me. He stabbed me. He strangled me."

"I know, okay."

It reminded me of all the times I'd gone to my mama about Daddy going after me at night and she'd said, "He must have had too much to drink." I'd lost count at some point. Those conversations echoed in my head like a hymnal refrain.

Mama, Papa touched me.

He's a good man.
Mama, Papa touched me.
Be good, sweetie.
Mama, Papa touched me.
He must have had too much to drink.
Mama, Papa touched me.
Your papa does a lot of good in this world.
Mama, Papa touched me.
You want us to be homeless?
Mama, Papa touched me.
Hush up, young lady.
Mama, Papa touched me.
Nice young ladies don't talk like that.

"Where are you staying?"

"What, Mama?"

"Where are you staying? Did you get a nice hotel?"

"No, Mama. We're with friends."

"I just hate that this happened. I really do. For all of you."

I knew she meant him, too. In other moments, later, she'd get mad at him. It was her way. She was codependent to the brutal end, but there was no changing her now. She was the only mama I had.

"How are the babies?"

"They're okay. We're all okay, Mama. Just promise me you won't talk to him."

I couldn't trust she wouldn't let slip the fact I was not hiding out in Sacramento but was instead right there on the Gulf Coast of Mississippi, within Liam's easy, angry reach.

"Well, I'll sure try not to."

The minute Liam found out I was still within hair-pulling range, any flimsy scrap of security I had would go up in flames like so much crumpled wrapping paper in a roaring-hot Christmas morning hearth. So Liam stayed put in our house in Ocean Springs's swankiest planned deepwater bayou subdivision, the

Bayou Sauvage, while the brood and I lay low in our hijacked FEMA trailer on the Mannings' burned-out ancestral seat.

The fanatical, rambling messages continued—official declarations that the Ocean Springs Police, the Jackson County Sheriff, the Mississippi Highway Patrol, even the goddamned FBI had been informed.

Mama'd call me on my secret cell to keep me updated.

One message really scared her in a way that only a professional, chief of medicine, bank board member voice droning on in dulcet tones could.

"Hello, this message is for Mary Anderson, or for any members of the Anderson family related to Alice Mary Anderson, or any known parties willfully related to the interstate abduction of the minor children known respectively as child one, Avery Macen Anderson Rivers, child two, Grayson Layne Anderson Rivers, and child three, Aidan Lake Anderson Rivers. The FBI will be in direct contact with you within the next forty-eight hours regarding the felony offense of interstate kidnapping and your criminal involvement with said offense—just thought you'd like to know. You're really screwing yourself."

When Mama called to tell me, half whispering the relayed message, which she failed to realize was irrelevant, as I'd not taken the children to California and she was, therefore, not involved in a felony kidnapping conspiracy, Mama substituted the words *screwing yourself* with *you-know-what-ing yourself*, the tone of her voice rising in an almost panic that told me she was getting to the end of her rope of being involved.

There was nothing I could do about it; one hour Liam would leave menacing threats of bodily harm, holier-than-thou proclamations of God's wrath by first light the next.

Mama's answering machine sounded like a broken record of the last sixteen years of my life.

I tried my God's honest to keep the brood entertained until we had our next day in court. At this point, Liam didn't know I'd been to court at all. It was a grace period of sorts—not only a time before he was involved in the whole mess of family court but a window in which I still held dear to my early-days Pollyanna notion that the court of the great state of Mississippi was going to be an absolute victory of justice for me.

That there'd be justice at all.

I was a great wife and mother, right? Everyone in town knew it, I reasoned to myself as I spent sleepless hours squeezed between five-year-old Avery on one side, the thumb-sucking boys on the other, atop the rock-hard, bug spray–scented, full-sized mattress of the trailer each night.

Never mind the candy necklace of bruises around my neck, never mind the scabby gashes where I'd clawed his hands from my neck, never mind the raw raised scrapes across my belly from the menacing tip of our kitchen butcher knife. Never mind the punctured pink T-shirt and white tank top and carefully wrapped butcher knife I had in a handbag hidden on the top shelf of the trailer fridge, the blood surrounding a hole in the same shape as the puncture wound above my heart.

Honestly, by that time in my life, I wasn't used to being right on any occasion, which is why I ticked off a desperate list of reasons I was entitled to protection from a husband who seemed to be—at least from the outside, the way my father did my whole life growing up—ideal.

Our home was run like an immaculate island resort.

Our little slice of extravagant unreal estate, finished just a few months before the storm, was a cross between a coastal estate and a Paris flat, spare and clean and ocean-influenced and filled with books.

I had the mantel around the custom-designed eight-foot fireplace fitted with the same glittery mercury glass tiles that graced the backsplash of our plantation chic country kitchen. Chandeliers lit every room, including the powder room off the study, baby pink and cobalt and savanna green and glinting jet crystals hanging like miniature sugared fruit. I'd had the ceilings built to twelve feet and, downstairs, each one to the last was painted a blameless, true sky blue.

The first time Liam's hardscrabble parents came to visit, his mama looked up at that ceiling and sang, "Blue skies, nothing but blue skies, nothing but blue skies, from now on," the contempt dripping off her unmistakable in a way that sounded like a warning more than anything else.

I should have taken heed.

But the blue skies of our life, of our nine-year marriage, were a little cloudy, and had been getting cloudier by the day ever since the storm. In Ocean Springs—in fact, everywhere along the Gulf Coast—we didn't refer to the havoc that came in like a drunken vixen to our lives as "Hurricane Katrina." In social halls and parking lots, in the blacked-out freezer section down at the Walmart, on roadsides next to sky-high debris piles, what we talked about, the way we named that wanton destruction was simply "the storm."

And night after night, in that wretched, toxic trailer bed, as my babies snored next to me like baby doves, my midnight musing— a kind of desperate conjuring—continued.

Surely, it'd be clear I was a good mother, with our well-behaved children spit-shined within an inch of their pristine lives. My girlfriends called me the Baby Whisperer with not even a teensy trace of irony or disdain. I had a secret for maintaining the flawless silence of infants through endless Sunday services; a knack for achieving a baby's full night sleep like clockwork at eight weeks old; a gift for being the one woman at garden club into whose arms you could plop any baby and be assured no fit would ensue.

My children's birthday parties were extravaganzas of organic culinary delights, wholesome yet gratuitous entertainment of circus-like proportions. Castle bounce house for the girls, monster truck bounce house for the boys, with ponies circling the kitchen garden like moody unicorns, glittered and ashamed.

Of course, these parties took place under the carnival paintings of horror hanging from every wall. Except for my closest girl-friends, no one invited me back in return.

Dinner parties were executed with a flawless devotion to elegant precision. Each bathroom stocked with baskets of fanned-out hand towels in the shaped of elaborate seashell conchs. The floors glistened to a fare-thee-well; the Schonbek New Orleans crystal chandeliers in every room glistened like starlight from every high ceiling. Honestly, I don't know how in the helicopter I managed to live up to Liam's ever-rising standards, but I did. Everything in our little small-town, traditional, pitch-perfect life was flawless—everything, that is, but the man of the house, my "sweets," Daddy, the man.

Everything went right until everything went wrong.

I'd been working for years to get Liam help for his drinking and, as he called it, his "crazy." He always laughed a maniacal laugh when he referred to "my crazy" and used it often as an excuse for poor behavior.

He'd been diagnosed with a severe case of obsessive-compulsive disorder when I was pregnant with Avery, after a wild night in which he happened to hear a Cake song on the radio and, knowing that I had dated the lead singer, screamed at me about a "secret affair" and how I was "carrying the Cake baby," and finally he chased me out of the house until I escaped in my little red Honda Prelude. He chased me down the street, with my driver's door open and him holding on to the door, until finally I could pull away and go to Mama's.

As yet unmarried, I called the next morning and vowed I'd live a separate life altogether with my baby girl unless he got his increasingly bizarre behaviors in order and quick. And he did. He got a diagnosis, stopped drinking, started going to AA nearly every night.

I bought one of those god-awful silk slips of a wedding dress that I thought was Carolyn Bessette-Kennedy–esque but in pictures just looks like I was wearing, well, a slip, and married him.

He took his high-dose Fluvoxamine, and soon the hand washing, the superstitious touching of doorknobs and faucets, the equation of death with elaborate patterns of dimes he would not allow me to pick up from windowsills faded.

Over the years, he went on and off various drugs—mostly off. As soon as he'd get it all under control, he'd decide he was fine and didn't need the medicine anymore. Then when things would start to spiral out of control, he'd self-medicate with samples from work and yet more alcohol. You'd think, as an internist, he'd know better. But the mind is sometimes stronger than common sense, and doctors are notorious for being their own worst caretakers. As the chief of medicine at Ocean Springs Hospital, he was devoted as a newlywed to his mental health vow of secrecy.

Despite my best effort to make sure everything was as he needed, his OCD ruled every part of our life. This was a man who put on surgical gloves and cleaned not just the rims but also the black rubber tires of his car every single night upon arriving in the twice-weekly pressure-washed circular drive.

In our second-to-last house before the storm, he'd ordered me relentlessly to spend the better part of three weeks first bleaching (with a cup and toothbrush) and then painting, meticulously, the grout on our tile kitchen floor. The tile was a sparkling quartz white, but the grout, a dove-gray color surely meant to hide dirt, instead proved for him evidence of "filth."

I must say, my housecleaning was extraordinary—daily wiping down of baseboards, washing windows, dusting fan blades, polishing toilets into oblivion. Pantry alphabetized. Laundry room like a scene from a magazine, with big apothecary jars full of powered soap and pure silver scoops.

It was a passion fueled by panic. With every new household imperfection was an equal cruelty: verbal, emotional, increasingly sexual.

Every inch of our home, despite three babies and the constant creep of bayou soddenness at every windowpane, was pristine.

Even so, Liam met and registered evidence of dirt everywhere, every day, in every last corner of the place.

No, he wasn't a neat freak when I met him. We had apartments a few miles from one another after I'd finished grad school and he was doing his residency, and his bathroom was so filthy there was green mold growing on the shower ceiling.

But Liam had grown up in what can only be characterized as chaos.

The youngest of four children born to a speed-freak truck driver father and his middle school–dropout teenage bride, Liam—along with his siblings—spent his formative years being dragged from flat brick projects to unfinished basements to KOA campgrounds of rural Missouri, stealing and selling feed corn to pay for clothes and food. Family lore held that little Liam refused to wear jeans and would only wear "soft slacks," no matter how small or how short they got.

He said he used to save the empty generic breakfast cereal boxes—he said with four children they'd go through three or four a week—and meticulously take them apart, turn them inside out, and use the back side to draw elaborate cartoons. In the cartoons, squat, happy, well-fed children lived in a jungle paradise where hams grew on trees and flowers were made from every kind of candy you'd imagine. I guess he thought to draw himself out of his real life and into something sweet.

In high school, Liam's daddy, Wayne, got thinking he could make some folding money off that skill for drawing and set up Liam in one of those drive-through Fotomat parking lot booths, giving tattoos for cash. People would drive on up to the Fotomat, stick out their arm or leg, and Liam would give a tattoo through the window.

People came from all the other towns around, and for a good while, Wayne tried to convince Liam to quit high school and "franchise" the TattooMat. But Liam kept on going to school and would usually find Wayne dead drunk, slumped on the high red stool, by the time he arrived at the TattooMat after school. Finding his daddy drunk was a theme in Liam's stories.

Why did I never see, even for an instant, that those stories could become my story?

Liam told this one story about how he and Huck went out to the country with Wayne and his buddies, and they somehow were all so drunk Liam had to drive back and he was only maybe ten or eleven. Somebody in the back seat had a gun that went off, and the men thought it was hilarious, and Liam said he just kept on driving. I always thought of that, of Liam, how small he must have been, peering over the wheel, the smell of gunshot in the car, rocking along, soaring through the night, toward another shitty basement they'd back out of before the rent was due, and how he came all the way from there to here. And yeah, maybe he was a drunk. But he was not the same kind of drunk. He was a doctor, and he was trying to help people, and even his OCD? That was a kind of sad way his brain had of trying to gather up the chaos of his childhood, scoop it all up in a neat pile and make it less ugly, less wild. Liam could put on a white coat and walk away from that car where Wayne's buddy pissed the seat and shot off his gun. Every morning he could put on a white coat and walk away from a thousand nights like that. He might be hungover, and he might have called his wife a fucking cunt through snarled teeth, but it was something, this white coat and this disease: it was all he had.

And I could love him for it. One more day. And the day after that. And I could see him looking over that dash and driving any way, each time he fucked up, and each time he was cruel to me.

That story was one of the reasons I loved him. He had a million of them. They were like party favors he handed out to me each time he struck a blow. And the blows came harder. First they were just demands, then obsessions, then jealousies, then insults. All of it smoothed over with more and more perfection—nicer house, nicer clothes, nicer cars. The ante was constantly upped.

But no amount of pretty or money could erase the heart-heavy disarray of his violent, vagabond childhood. It became a kind of fanatical pastime, erasing this past and proving his worth. Likewise, erasing everything about me that didn't relate to him would become a ruthless, dreadful necessity.

Every day, after he shined the tires, he'd walk in the side door to the kitchen. I'd be there waiting for him, everything ready for dinner, in order.

"Didn't finish that grout yet, sweets?" he'd ask, tiptoeing from one tile to another.

And we'd start dinner—the same level of formality night after night, lemons on the water glasses, linen napkins, bubble bath–sweet kids in their starched pajamas silent until spoken to, the courses all of an ethnic theme, cuisine-specific background music lilting from the great room, and drinks to match.

There were a lot of drinks, once they started. At least for Liam. He'd pour me a drink to equal his every one, but I am a miserable drinker. No, *miserable* isn't the word. *Failed*. I can't even finish half a beer without getting a headache. I'd pour each of mine down the sink drain while he was talking. It's not that I was secretly disposing of them, but by eight or so he'd be drunk enough and so stuck on the merry-go-round of his obsessive thoughts about who'd crossed him or one of my myriad failings that I could pour the drinks out right in front of him.

Our nights consisted of the dignified dinner, a few hours of the drinking-and-rehashing session, and then early to bed. In the world according to Liam, only "trashy, lazy" people woke up after five, and so bedtime was never past nine, no matter what I wanted. Despite the drunkenness and early to bed, there was sex. Lots of sex.

My papa was this kind of drunk—the professionals call it "high functioning," but I'm more partial to "high miserable."

No break allowed by a passed-out husband. Ever the overachiever, Liam managed to be sexually insatiable. I didn't get pregnant four times in five years by coincidence, I'll tell you that.

Part of my "job" as perfect wife included a huge lingerie and high-heels collection, mixed in with elbow-length gloves and leather collars and Mardi Gras masks and various wigs—his favorite being a severe black *Pulp Fiction* bob. He had what can only be described as cruel intentions in bed. Rough sex was easy for me; I could meet him in that, match him in that. Sometimes I could even beat him in that. Sometimes I enjoyed it; more often it disgusted me. When it was playful and sexy, I liked it. When it was a requirement demanded by a drunken husband, I loathed it.

And myself.

Like most women, I would have liked a little bit of sweetness here and there, a little kindness. I found myself begging, to his delight, for even one tiny scrap of tender. Instead, he'd whisper all kind of nastiness in my ear as if it were a love poem.

As he got closer to finishing, slapping my skin in places generally saved for street fights and not sex, he'd whisper, "You're a good wife who will do whatever I say. Now, come."

And I would. There were serious repercussions for disobedience, and it was easier to comply. In the final two years, if I said no, I paid. He had access to drugs and wasn't afraid to use them.

I can't count the number of nights I lay, drugged and lifeless on our bed, while he fucked me. The next day, he'd accuse me of drinking too much. One time I was bleeding so much, he dragged me to the shower, pushed me in, and turned it on. Problem was, he went to bed while I was passed out on the shower floor. I woke up several hours later—half in the shower, half out—with ice-cold water raining down on my aching thighs.

I learned that saying yes was preferable to rape. Over the years, I rewrote this story to believe this sick, sexual dance was something we did together, and I tried to push deep down in my soul the idea I was being abused. I had written a book on abuse. I led survivor support groups for years. How could this happen to me? But it did, the way it can. To anyone.

Sometimes after sex, I'd forget, and think I might be allowed to drift off to sleep next to my man, legs entwined. And even though what happened next was part of the nightly ritual, I was never prepared for it. I must have been in a post-sex delusional haze to think that I was living in some kingdom of normal. I was not.

"Going to sleep all filthy like that, sweets?" he'd sneer, yanking my hair to wake me, rolling away.

I'd step into the shower, grateful at least to be there on my own accord, the water hot as I could stand, without turning on the light. I'd twist my hair into a bun atop my head, running my wet hands over it to make it seem as if I'd washed it. There was a big window in the shower, with a view of treetops stretching out over the Davis Bayou that backed up to our land. Those were lonely, pain-drenched showers.

After, I'd turn on my blow-dryer, setting it on a towel in the sink and slinking down to sit on the cool hardwood of the moonlit bathroom, back against the custom-made Shaker cabinets, rivulets of tears coursing down my stinging cheeks.

The children slept in their rooms down the hall, baby scrunched as usual into the corner of his crib, quiet and content. From the window, I watched sandhill cranes rise off the bayou surface, their lissome wings clattering in the damp air. I didn't allow myself to cry in front of Liam—he despised it and mocked me on the few occasions that I did break down. But every night, as the blow-dryer droned away in the sink, the sobs sprang up in me, cresting in soundless, salty surges.

When I returned to bed, Liam snored and reeked of Belgian ale.

And each morning dawned anew, as if life were ordered the way it was meant to be. But I was the duchess of hidden despair. I'd wake up before five, shower again, dress, apply makeup, good clothes, good Southern lady jewels. In the kitchen, I'd make Liam's coffee and breakfast, begin again.

Every night, the sick ritual.

Every day, begin again.

Bathrooms needed to be stocked with folded white hand tow-els, fifty or so in a basket on the counter, because one could not be expected to use a towel to dry one's hands more than once. Leather couches needed to be conditioned. Tables oiled. Windows shined. Pantries alphabetized. Flowers arranged. Floors hand-scrubbed. Groceries transferred into more acceptable receptacles—glass bottles for the milk, Fire-King containers of fresh fruit, yogurt parceled into individual tiny vintage Ball jars with silver lids.

Where the kids had thrown an impromptu picnic the day be-fore, dragging a velvet throw out onto the lawn, the grass had to be raked upright again. The yard-sullied throw already turned in the dryer.

These were the details I ticked off one by one in my mind, star-ing up at the paneled ceiling of the little trailer as raccoons hissed and whinnied in Mac and Daddy's compost ditch. I could make a list a mile long of everything I did to be a good wife, assuring my-self the court would be on my side. The court was there to help me, to keep me safe, or so I thought. In my mind, the court would force Liam to get the help he needed, even against his will. I be-lieved swift and firm justice would soon provide. Like I said, it was early in the process.

Very early.

Behind the FEMA trailer was Lana's brother's house. He'd stop over, very gently rap the "code" knock at our door, make sure we had all that we needed, that the power was still running and whatnot. On the other side of the trailer was Lana's sister's house.

Lana's parents bought this big plot of land forty-odd years ago, and as their kids had grown and married and had babies, they'd parceled it out and given it away. Pretty much the whole of Poti-caw Bayou Road was all Mannings', save a few lots where maybe someone might've split part of their land and sold a lot to outsiders when times was thin and wallets was flat. But there at the end of Poticaw Bayou was Mac and Daddy's white house, and that was something to be counted upon.

Mac was a petite lady, tough as nails, with a drawl more N'Awlins than Delta. Everyone calls her Mac, even her children. Ms. Mac, if she's your elder. She's the kind of lady, if you were to meet her on a train, you'd assume she'd just been living in her house in the small town of Latimer since the day before infinity, doing small-town stuff like getting married young and running fund-raisers down to the Catholic church and carrying her children to and from school and growing a garden. Hell, even I might have thought that (for a minute or two) when we first met. And then someone mentioned to Ms. Mac that I have a graduate degree in creative writing from Sarah Lawrence College.

After that, she asked for my e-mail address. Soon after, she'd fire off daily drafts of her frequent letters to the editor of *The Sun Herald* in Biloxi, supposedly for my "proofing." If anything, her letters needed only a little watering down. Whatever was the issue du jour—floating versus landlocked casinos, crooked judges with fat pockets, corporal punishment in the public schools, wetland redirection in the name of progress—Mac had an opinion. Her letters were full of fire and fiercely fluent. She'd traveled the world and back, knew history like a tenured professor, and did not set her opinion upon flighty whims but within the wingspan of history and wisdom.

We could tramp through the back of Lana's lot into her, Mac, and Daddy's vegetable garden and come out the other side at their house.

"Hey, y'all! Purdy day, ain't it?"

Mac more than likely would be inside but at the kitchen window, putting up some canning or cooking a covered dish to deliver to someone whose kin had passed away.

Daddy would be sitting on the porch swing more often than

not. If he wasn't on the porch swing, he was gone—in his shed, out fishing on the pond or in the creek, gone shooting, down the road visiting, helping someone mend a fence. I never once saw him in the house. But the sight of that house—oh, my. I'll never forget the first time I saw that house.

MAC DADDY

Of course I'd met Mac and Daddy before, being friends with Lana for years. But it'd always been at Lana's house, or at St. Alphonsus Catholic School, or in the hardware department down at the Walmart, or what have you. I'd never been invited to their home. Sweet bucket of peas, I'd never even seen their home until that morning we left the Gulf Coast Women's Center for Nonviolence and drove all the way to the end of Old Northwood Road.

There it was, at the end of the lane—the kind of modest square place you see in a Grandma Moses painting. It had no wrap-around porch or tall, stately columns or any of the usual hallmarks that brand a house "Southern."

In fact, the Manning homestead house boasted nothing at all.

But it was a Southern house if there ever was one. First, there was no front door. Forget about "friends come in the side door." The side door was the only door. And the side door was off the porch—a square ten-by-ten-foot slab of home-mixed concrete with a corrugated tin cover atop; a porch swing made from slats of wood and ordinary metal chain; a whole lot of broken-in, muddy boots; old rusty Community Coffee cans full of growing herbs and whatnot; and a cooler that could just as easily be full of ice and Barq's or a mess a' crawfish.

If he had been there, Daddy would have been sitting on the swing, his long legs stretched out, knees up high and feet planted on the porch, swinging slightly as a dawn breeze, his back to you. He needn't turn around to know who was there.

When we drove up that first day, after springing ourselves from the lice-infested shelter, I followed Lana's instructions to the very tea and cucumber square detail (turn left at the burnt-up tree trunk shaped like a vagina, right when the gravel turns red) and drove up to the house.

There was no mistaking I'd found the place.

About a year before Katrina, Mac and Daddy's house caught fire. All the kids in the family, the volunteer fire squad of Latimer, and just about every other able-bodied Jackson County South Mississippian of sound mind had come to put the fire out. But a good ten acres of salt pine savanna woods surrounding went up in flames, and Mac and Daddy's house burned not to the ground but pretty good straight through inside. After the fire, everyone got organized in shifts, stripped the place down to the studs and rebuilt the inside entire in just a few weeks (good practice, as it would turn out, for the coming storm). When we pulled up to it the first time, we saw a white house with dark green trim and smoke stains above each window same as above a hearth that's been collecting soot for about forty seasons without a good scrub. There were these great oval arcs of gray smoke stains above every window and that little side door, too, just in case you thought you were about to forget how close the place came to burning down. Once you stepped in off the little porch, you'd never know—save for a slight smoky scent—the house had been afire. But life is busy and Mac and Daddy had more pressing things, and no one ever got around to repainting the outside of the place.

We pulled around to the right of the house and, behind it, tucked our shiny white Land Rover in between the charbroiled homestead and a brand-spanking-new doublewide trailer.

In the storm, Meemaw's house flat-out floated away, and everyone agreed she was too old to tolerate the time and sweat it would take to haul it back from where it drifted or rebuild from scratch. At a post-storm family meeting, Meemaw herself made it clear that along with being too old to rebuild, she had too little time left on God's green earth to tolerate the dignity it would drain from her to have to live in the guest bedroom of someone else's home, even if they were family. So the family had gone in together and purchased outright the honkin', brand-new trailer that sat next door to Mac and Daddy's place.

When we pulled up, the metal door of Meemaw's trailer slapped open, and she leaned out like a lady waving on a departing train, shook her fresh perm at us in the Land Rover, and barked, "Back up! Y'all shadin' my light!"

"Yes, ma'am, sorry," I called back, putting it in reverse.

The door slammed shut again, and that was that.

Mac and Daddy were waiting on the porch swing for us. Mac was wearing a pair of clamdigger jeans and a flowered blouse, shelling a big bowl of peas. She had a smaller bowl for the shelled peas, and she was tossing the hulls in a pile on the concrete porch floor.

My children, bless their little OCD-brainwashed hearts, stood with their mouths hanging wide open big enough to catch a horsefly colony, staring at that pile of pea hulls on the porch floor as if it were a pile of soiled unmentionables from Mac's personal boudoir collection, they were so shocked and scandalized at the mess.

Daddy sat there wearing a pair of denim coveralls, no shirt, and the biggest pair of beat-up old boots (with no laces, and no socks) you ever saw. He had a sack of Hershey's Mixed Mini candy between his legs on the swing, and he picked up the sack, held it out to the kids.

"Hey, y'all want a candy?"

Their eyes shot to me in horror. With a false cheeriness, I blurted, "Yes, sir, they just love candy to the last one of them. Don't y'all?"

The kids stood there like a circus show of conjoined triplet deer stuck in blazing white blinking headlights, and I nudged them forward. "Go on, y'all can have some. Y'all remember Ms. Mac and Mr. Daddy, don't y'all? Be sweet now and say thank you!" I chirped like a fool.

They timidly took one each, then stood there eating their candy, each one to the last folding the wrapper into smaller after smaller tiny squares, not knowing what to do with their trash. Daddy noticed and laughed and said, "What kinda crazy children are y'all? Just throw them wrappers down there on the heap with the hulls."

They did, dropping the wrappers onto the hull pile as if they were dropping single long-stemmed roses into an open grave. And then it was silent. The children leaned in it seemed as one, like a gate listing toward muddy earth. You could hear their need to pick up the wrappers, feel the tension of their fear in the air. *Tick-tick-tick*, while we all stared at the pile of hulls and wrappers. And stared some more.

And then we laughed. Hard. We laughed and carried on until our sides nearly split and the kids had chocolate mustaches and chocolate fingertips and I'd nearly peed my panties and shed a bunch of crack-up tears that threatened to expose my two blue-black shiners and all the peas were hulled and the kids had left their saltwater sandals (although in a perfect little row, bless their hearts) at the edge of the porch and were running through the vegetable patch and picking random tomatoes and squash and who knows what all else and eating them—it would've been the death of them, had their father known it—directly off the plant!

These were children who'd taken two baths a day their life entire. Children who'd never been allowed to shake their own salt onto their organic steamed collard greens. Children who couldn't leave the house without a combed-sore straight pink part in their hair and fingernails groomed to the hilt; who weren't allowed to have their photograph taken if they had a scratch or a—Lawd forbid—filthy mosquito bite on a visible stretch of skin. Landing on that front porch was like giving a poor child a million dollars cash and setting 'em free at the gates of Walt Disney World Orlando.

With chocolate bars and a pile of pea hulls and candy wrappers, bare feet kicking up tufts of dust in a four-acre garden of fruits and vegetables free for the picking, dirty and delicious, this was their first taste of freedom, their first chance to jump under the rope, into a life double-dutching with happiness and abandon.

Only after all the candy and running and fun (after Mac filled our bellies good with some boiled peas smothered in butter and cooked with bacon and served with some leftover casserole and some deer steaks Daddy grilled out back, away from the house) did they walk us over to the trailer. Lana's brother's house sat on a lower patch of land and had flooded out in the storm. The slab from Meemaw's float-away house sat below his. Somehow, Lana's brother was lucky (or connected) enough to get one of the first FEMA trailers that came rolling into town on the trains.

FEMA trailers, if you have never been in one, are not anything close to what you think of when you think of a trailer you might borrow from a neighbor to go RV-ing.

FEMA trailers are thirty-foot boxes of chemical-scented ripe tin walls and roof—a formaldehyde palace on wheels. Lana's brother, being the handy type, with a big family and lots of good friends and support, got back into his house within about twelve weeks.

He tried to get FEMA to come get the trailer as soon as he was finished with it. And he tried. And he tried again. No luck.

He even tried to get them to at least let one of the families living in the tent city at D'Iberville High School or at the makeshift campground at the Biloxi Buddhist Temple to come out and live in the FEMA trailer where it was on his land, but that apparently broke some sort of official government emergency management bylaw.

So while scores of people scraped by in tents and in cars and in homes with no water or power or plumbing, that next-to-new FEMA trailer sat on his land without a fine how-do-you-do from FEMA. The Mannings were happy to set me up in it.

They simply jury-rigged the power back up, filled the tiny fridge with groceries, put sheets on the bed and toilet paper in the latrine, left a pile of picture books and playing cards on the table, and wished us sweet dreams. I couldn't help but feel that we were breaking the law. I'm sure we were. But frankly, I was happy to be somewhere that Liam couldn't—wouldn't—think to look. The one time I'd convinced him to come to Lana and Kurt's house for dinner, he'd nearly had a nervous breakdown in the germ-ridden environs outside of the city limits. And I was relieved to be out of the shelter, freeing up space for another family, happy to have a place to rest.

There really wasn't anywhere but the trailer to stay. The big casino hotels were all in ruins on the mainland, pulled off their pilings and thrown across the highway by the surge. The small motels were the kind with a front parking lot and doors that open straight to the highway; I was afraid to stay in one, terrified Liam would find me and I'd open the door and he'd finish what he started in a quick lick. Besides, every motel between Bayou La Batre, Alabama, and Natchitoches, Louisiana, was booked up with government officials, contractors, news folk, church volunteers, and upper-echelon coast trash waiting to get back into their storm-drenched McMansions.

Certainly none of our friends were willing to take us in. Most of my girlfriends did make a pilgrimage out to Latimer, bringing all kinds of entertainment for the kids and food for us to pile on every available surface of the trailer. They'd seen my too-thick makeup, my ever-present leopard scarf wrapped around the handprint-bruise-blossomed neck; I'd even lifted my shirt a few times to show the scrapes and puncture wounds where knife met skin. They were good girls, but no one wanted to put their own family in peril. As in every small town, word spread fast. Liam was at this point universally agreed upon to be a lunatic with high probability of danger spillover.

That night, when we broke through the barrier of the west end of the vegetable patch and the kids saw that FEMA trailer, a great cheer went up in the hush of an April night in Latimer, Mississippi. "Camping!" they screamed.

Aidan was literally—not figuratively, but in the absolute, bouncing sense of the word—jumping up and down, his by-now-heavy tee-tee-soaked diaper hanging low between his sweet, chubby thighs.

"Camp! Camp! Camp! Camp!" the three of them chanted. "Yaaaaaaay, camp!"

I'm not sure how they even had a notion of what camping was. Certainly the Anderson-Rivers family had never been on a camping vacation, unless the Ritz-Carlton offers a "Deluxe Ultimate Camping Package" complete with butler and two-bedroom linen tent suite. Maybe I'd explained, somewhere along the line, what campers are used for when they're put to use for temporary housing after a natural disaster? Maybe the cat family goes camping in one of the Richard Scarry books? I'm not sure, but the kids were beside themselves and three seats down when they saw that FEMA trailer waiting for us to move on in.

They didn't care that they'd left nearly everything they owned back at our house. They didn't worry that "Dada was going to get mad and get us" again. They didn't worry about a thing.

They stepped up on the metal step of the trailer and vaulted themselves into the wretched bed as if they were the luckiest children in all of Mississippi. Daddy handed me a scrap of paper with his cell phone number on it, barely uttering under his breath, "Use it if y'all need it. Comes to it, just holler loud; I'll hear ya."

And he was gone.

We had several days' reprieve, thanks to Mac and Daddy and the whole Manning clan, not to mention the stunningly inefficient workings of the Federal Emergency Management Agency. It was a moment in time to catch our breath, laugh, have our bellies filled, get good and spoiled, and rest.

We were safe.

Every day Lana would drive me to town for a meeting at Addison's office. As we got to town, I'd scrunch down in the seat and we'd pull around to the back door. You never knew who'd see me, and Liam had lots of friends'd mention in a hot minute that they saw me riding around with Lana Manning.

We'd go over Addison's latest legal documents, make corrections, change the wording, and prepare for court. We were filing a motion to extend the emergency motion for protection and temporary custody of the children. I knew from Addison that Liam had hired an attorney, and I was terrified at the thought he'd get word of our motion and show up to contest with Liam in tow.

Along with extending the order of protection and custody, we were asking that I be given sole use of the "marital residence" and that the Jackson County Sheriff forcibly remove Liam from the premises.

In other words, shit was getting real.

Addison explained that the judge would decide one way or the other and that the motion would be granted solely on my testimony. If the motion was granted, the first Liam would hear of it would be when the county sheriff showed up out our house on Magnolia Moonlight Drive, delivered all the court paperwork to him, and escorted him (immediately) off the premises.

Addison assured me this was business as usual in a divorce that initiated with a domestic violence incident, but I was terrified to imagine what Liam's response might be.

But nothing was usual. I imagined that I was likely in a very small club of women who leave their husbands after the first incidence of violence, and Addison said it was true. Each and every time I went to her office, she asked me the same question first.

I'd sit down, the ever-loving same leopard silk scarf around my neck to hide the handprint bruises, across from her at the desk. She'd look me in the eye; tap a pen on the desk.

"Do you still want a divorce?"

"I do."

It's funny how the same phrase that got me into this mess was about to get me out of it.

Because once was enough. I didn't believe I had the luxury to see what might happen the next time around. Maybe I'd have given him another chance if he'd have given me a single black eye. Or pushed me into a wall.

Still, it wasn't easy. He'd broken me down for so many years I was almost afraid to escape.

In a darker place in my heart I wouldn't admit to a soul, I didn't believe at that time that I deserved to live in that house on my own with the children with Liam paying for everything, no matter what horrendous act he'd committed. I didn't believe I deserved peace, or safety, or that Liam had a responsibility to take care of me—if not as his wife, then as the mother of his children.

He'd been telling me three things every single day of our marriage for the last nine years.

"You're stupid. You're fat. You're ugly."

Somewhere about the third year of hearing that daily mantra, I bought in.

Since the storm, it had become much worse. He had it in his

mind that I might be thinking of leaving, and so he'd included another lucky three daily pronouncements.

"If you leave, I'll take your children from you and you'll never see them again."

"If you leave, I'll have you locked up in a psych ward and you'll never see the light of day again."

"If you leave, I'll have you good ol' boy'd right out of Mississippi so fast you won't know if you should scratch your watch or wind your ass."

If ever I dared argue that his threats might not come to pass, he'd simply refer to plan B.

"Plan B?" I asked the first time.

"Plan B." He leveled his eyes at me, smiled.

"Which is?"

"Which is I'll kill you. Without one second thought."

From the first time he said it, and for the next six months, he told me every day he was going to kill me. That's why we'd started seeing the specialist in New Orleans. It was actually a fairly common thing for those suffering severe OCD to have obsessions about killing their loved ones.

But something inside me told me this was different.

I should have listened.

As the day of the motion grew near, I grew more and more quiet. The kids were transformed overnight into "normal" kids—going barefoot, making mud puddles, feeding chickens, building forts with sticks and old floral sheets, falling fast to sleep with contentment and slap-happy exhaustion the minute their heads hit the FEMA-issue mattress. With each day closer to the motion to remove Liam from the house, I grew more tense, more scared, a wounded bird with broken wings, backing up into the corner of an abandoned garage, shafts of light pouring in, providing not hope but instead exposure to every raw spot, shining a harsh light on my deepest fear, illuminating my shame-soaked soul.

SO HELP ME GOD

Finally, we had our day in court. Lana drove me down to the Waffle House, where we met Addison in her little cream-colored Mini Cooper. I was wearing the same clothes I had on when I left home days before.

We drove across the bridge in Gautier, to the Jackson County Fairgrounds, where the City of Pascagoula had set up headquarters in a series of plain white FEMA trailers scattered across the dusty grounds.

Inside the FEMA trailer Courthouse A, there was one folding table for the judge, one for the court reporter, and metal folding chairs in off-kilter rows. The Honorable Hank "Bubba" Taylor presided. Tall, with movie-star handsome looks, he had the face of a country preacher. In fact, Addison told me he'd once been one; he'd started his own congregation in Green County when he felt the Southern Baptists had fallen too far left from the Word.

That detail sent a shock of fear straight to my very soul.

I was sworn in, and Addison began to outline her motion to have Liam (referred to always as Dr. Rivers in court) removed from the family residence and the order of protection continued. She briefly referred to the violence inflicted on me and asked Judge Taylor if he would like to view my injuries in person or in photographs.

"No, Ms. McClanahan, I'd like to hear from your client, if that's okay?" he said.

"Yes, Your Honor. Mrs. Rivers is prepared to speak. What would you like her to speak to, Your Honor?"

"I'd like to hear," he said very gently, "in her own words, exactly what happened on the night in question. Can you do that, Mrs. Rivers?" he asked me with a kind of gentle coaxing.

"Yes, Your Honor, I can."

"Okay, Mrs. Rivers, you can start whenever you're ready."

I took a breath and began.

The night before I sat on the metal step of the FEMA trailer and whispered the whole story to the South Mississippi moon.

It was an ordinary night, really.

Liam, I mean Dr. Rivers, was coming home from work at his clinic—he comes home earlier now since there isn't much business because of the storm. I mean, with everyone evacuating and not coming back, you know. He drinks, my husband, and has been drinking more and more in these last months. He also has obsessive-compulsive disorder, so all the debris and dirt and disarray, well, it's really a nightmare for someone like him and stresses him out something terrible.

"Yes, Mrs. Rivers, I understand folks have been under a lot of stress, but can you stick to what happened that night?" Judge Taylor asked.

Yes, Your Honor, I'm sorry.

I took a deep breath, straightened my spine, and started over.

So, that night. Well, I was making dinner, like I said. I make a big dinner every night. We're pretty old-fashioned that way. We sit

*down to dinner every night. My husband tends to like ethnic foods
like Thai or Vietnamese or Italian or Indian, so that's what I usually make for him. But the kids just had been after me the way kids
do for fried chicken, so that night I made a big Southern dinner—
the fried chicken and coleslaw and baked beans and potato salad
and yeast rolls and snap beans. You know, the usual stuff. I had the
table all set with a cloth and dinner ready when he got home, even
though it was only four o'clock. I was waiting for him to come inside. He gets a beer or two from the fridge in the garage and cleans
his car every night when he gets home; that's part of his obsessive-
compulsive disorder. I don't think he's been taking his medicine
for it.*

"What happened next, Mrs. Rivers?"

*Well, he came in and right off he was unhappy about the din-
ner. He said it was "trashy" food and he wanted something different. I don't know what came over me, but I said that I wasn't going
to make anything different. It was all ready and the kids were hungry and there was a time, a while back, when Dr. Rivers would eat
that kind of dinner. I didn't think he'd mind it. But he's been on a
big health kick this last few years, going to the gym at 5:00 A.M.
every day. But one day shouldn't matter, right? I mean, it was just
one day. And the kids were all waiting to eat, and the baby, Aidan
Lake, was muddy, if you know what I mean, so I quick took him
upstairs to change him. When I came to come back down with the
baby, Dr. Rivers was at the top of the stairs. He was mad. He said
he was going out for dinner and he was taking the baby with him.
By that time, the other kids had come upstairs. And that's when it
started.*

I took a deep, sharp, ragtag breath, willing myself to go on.

*Well, I wouldn't let him take the baby. I just couldn't. He was
already drunk, and I told him so. I didn't want him to drive drunk
with the baby. Lately when he gets mad at me and storms out drunk,
he usually grabs one of the kids and takes them along. It's terrible
for me, worrying about him driving drunk with one of my babies in*

the car. I mean, I guess that's part my fault, but I can't stop him. But he told me the police are all his patients—he takes care of the whole Ocean Springs Police Department—so if I called them to arrest him for driving drunk with the kids, they'd just laugh at me and arrest me for making a false report. This time, I just couldn't let him do it. I decided to fight. We fought with Aidan between us at the top of the stairs, with him trying to pull Aidan out of my arms. I had a real bad feeling, though, and I fought hard. Liam was screaming, and the kids were crying.

"What happened then, Mrs. Rivers?"

Well, I guess I won. I mean, I didn't win, it wasn't a fight really, but Dr. Rivers gave up on taking the baby. He screamed at me something awful, and I asked him to stop, and he was scaring the kids. I showed Dr. Rivers where Aidan Lake's little thighs had gone red where Dr. Rivers had grabbed him. And he said I did that to the baby, not him. Aidan Lake was just flat-out howling by then. Grayson—that's our middle child, who's three—finally yelled, "Stop yelling at Mama!" and Dr. Rivers left, saying he was going to find his own dinner. When he was gone, I sat the kids down, and we all had the chicken dinner. It was really strange, sitting there without Dr. Rivers. It was a good dinner—the kids liked it and ate it right up.

"Mrs. Rivers, I'm going to have to ask you to get to the part where Dr. Rivers assaulted you," Judge Taylor intoned. "Can you talk about that, or would you rather Ms. McClanahan address it?"

I could feel myself rambling and not getting the story out in the way you probably should in a court of law, but I was nervous, and telling the story felt surreal, standing in that little trailer with the artificial lighting and the dust rising outside the cracked open windows behind me.

I can tell you, Your Honor. I'm sorry. Okay, first, Dr. Rivers came home after a little while—he wasn't gone that long—and cleaned his rims and his wheels like he always does but for a really long time. Grayson went outside to see what he was doing. I could see out the window that his daddy offered him some leftover pizza from the Magic Mushroom. I could see Grayson shake his head and start to talk about what looked like an explanation of everything he ate, as he was ticking off his fingers and smiling and holding his little tummy.

"Mrs. Rivers, don't tell me what other people said, only what you know firsthand, you understand?"

I nodded.

"So what happened next?"

Well, Dr. Rivers came in. I didn't talk to him. I was in the dining room, folding laundry on the table into piles and stacking it into a basket. He came in there and started yelling at me like he usually does. I didn't say anything, just finished and took the laundry basket and started to go up the stairs. We have steep, hardwood stairs. We built the house about a year before the storm. I had the ceilings raised to ten feet, but the builder didn't plan ahead well for how steep that would make our stairs. About halfway up, I felt something hit me in the back. He, I mean, Dr. Rivers, threw something at me— another laundry basket. I tripped but got back up and went into our bedroom. All of a sudden, he was behind me, shoving me real hard. I fell into our bedside table, which is how I got the big bruise and gash on my thigh.

"Did you fall on the ground, Mrs. Rivers?"

No, I kind of fell sideways and onto the bed. And then I started to get up, but Dr. Rivers shoved me, hard, so I fell back onto our bed. He was yelling at me the whole time—screaming, really—his face dark red, and shaking. The kids were all at the door watching, and I told them to go back downstairs and that everything was fine. I didn't want them to see it.

"And then what?"

And then, sir, then he climbed on top of me and put his hands around my neck and choked me. I tried to get him off me, grabbing his hands and scratching at my neck to pry his hands off.

"Your Honor," interjected Addison, "may I have my client show you her neck? She has hand-shaped bruises inflicted by Dr. Rivers as well as scratches from her own fingernails where she tried to pry his hands off."

"No, Ms. McClanahan. That's not necessary. I will take your word for it. Continue, Mrs. Rivers. What happened next? Did you pass out?" asked the judge.

Yes, I did. I remember everything starting to go dark and seeing stars, and the last thing I really saw was Grayson standing there, even though I'd told him to stay downstairs. He was just standing there, leaning on his daddy's leg as he choked me. He had his thumb in his mouth and he was holding his little blue blankie. I don't think Dr. Rivers even noticed he was there until he said something. He said, "What are you doing to Mama, Daddy?" The next thing I knew, Dr. Rivers was off me and was taking Grayson downstairs with him, telling him it was time for his bedtime snack. I was dizzy, kind of starry-eyed, if you know what I mean. I had blacked out, I suppose. I got up and went into the bathroom. In the mirror, I could see that my neck was very red, and it looked like I was getting black eyes.

"Did Dr. Rivers also strike you in the face?"

No, not yet. I think it was from his squeezing my neck so hard. I was in a panic now; I really didn't know what to do. I was in a kind of trance, if you can imagine that. I could hear Dr. Rivers downstairs getting the grapes and cheese out of the refrigerator and asking the kids to sit down to eat their snacks before bed. That's what they always have. He choked me and now he was acting like nothing happened.

The courtroom was silent a moment. I took a deep breath, continued.

Then Dr. Rivers came back up and started yelling at me again, telling me he was going to kill me. I was, I don't know if this makes sense, but I was trying to defuse the situation by not really responding. I told him I was going to go help the kids finish up and put them to bed. I was just a few steps down the stairs when I felt a really rough push on my back, and I went flying down the stairs.

Flying. In the air. Until I hit the landing in a hard thud on my knees and hit my head against the wall. At the landing, all the kids ran over to me to see if I was okay. I scrambled right up to my feet and acted like it didn't happen and told them to just finish up and it's time for bed. Liam came down and started screaming at me again.

"What was he saying?" asked Judge Taylor.

The usual stuff like that I'm fat and ugly and stupid and trashy and no one loves me, not even the kids. But he was also using very nasty language, and he kept saying, "I feel like I'm going to kill you." He's been saying that for the last year or so, Your Honor. I even went to a counselor and asked about it, if it was a normal part of OCD, because I read in a book that it could be. We took him over to Ochsner to get treatment for it. He has a serious sickness. Anyway, I told the kids to hurry up and go upstairs. My daughter, Avery, the oldest, started crying. She's five. I bent down and hugged her, told her it was going to be okay, asked her to try to stay away from Daddy and to keep the boys with her, that that was the safest thing to do and that Mama would try to calm Daddy down. The kids went upstairs then. It seemed like all this had been going on for a long time. It seemed like the whole night was happening in slow motion. I remember noticing that the night had turned dark and there were stars out and it was past the kid's bedtime. I tried to clean up after the kids' snacks, but Dr. Rivers kept yelling at me and shoving me, hard, against the counters and the cabinets. He'd push me down, and I'd get up again.

"You didn't try to run away?" asked Judge Taylor.

No, Your Honor, I didn't. I probably should have. I didn't know how I could get away and bring the three kids with me, and I didn't really know what to do. I wasn't going to leave them there with him. I was in shock, I think. Dr. Rivers kept hitting me, pushing me, yelling at me. Then the boys came back down.

"What did the boys do? Did they see their daddy hitting you?"

Yes, Your Honor. They did, and then they started screaming at him to stop, and screaming at me that they were going to save me.

"We'll save you, Mama!" I can still hear their voices in my head. I kept telling them, "No, no, no, go back upstairs." They had these big plastic dinosaurs that they like to play with and they were poking their daddy with them.

"Poking him?"

Yes, they were poking the sharp tails of the dinosaurs in their daddy's legs and backside, screaming, "Leave Mama alone! Leave Mama alone!" But Dr. Rivers was in such a rage I don't think he even noticed them. It was like they weren't even there. They were like little ghosts to him, invisible. He told me to get my fat you-know-what upstairs and he'd put the children to bed. Now, he never puts the children to bed. Never ever. That's my job. But I listened to him. I would have done just about anything to get him to calm down and stop hurting me, especially in front of the kids. He led the kids upstairs, and I followed as quietly as I could. I was kinda trying to just be invisible at that point, hoping it was over. I'd have done anything to be a ghost at that moment. I went into my master closet and started hanging up the clothes out of that laundry basket from before.

"And was that the end of it?"

I thought so—I was in there for a while. Every bit of me was aching, but I was just going on like it was life as usual, until Dr. Rivers came up behind me in the closet. He seemed like he was calmed down. He wasn't yelling anymore, and his face wasn't as red.

I stopped then, overwhelmed with memories of what came next. It had only been a few days.

"Mrs. Rivers, do you want Mrs. McClanahan to continue?" Judge Taylor asked, noticing the tears rolling quietly down my face.

No, thank you, Your Honor, I can tell you. Dr. Rivers turned me around to face him. He had a big butcher knife in his hand from our kitchen. He said he was going to kill me. I didn't say anything. He started to kind of swipe at me with it. He told me I was ugly and made me lift up my shirt and told me I was fat. He took the tip of the knife and scraped it back and forth across my belly skin, cutting me. I asked him not to kill me. "Please don't kill me," is what I said.

"Judge Taylor, I'd like to introduce into evidence the photographs of Mrs. Rivers's stomach and chest," interjected Addison.

"Mrs. McClanahan, I find your witness credible, and I don't think she wants those photos introduced into the public record."

"Yes, Your Honor," Addison agreed. "For the record, we also have the knife and the bloody shirts available to introduce as evidence."

"Noted. Not needed at this time. I think the visible injuries I can see are sufficient to support your client's account." He asked me to continue.

After he cut my stomach, Your Honor—or scraped it, really, scored it like you would a steak, you know? I begged him not to kill me. He told me I was a waste of a human being and that I was a heartless you-know-what, and he held the knife up to my heart and started to stab me. I could feel the tip of the knife going into my chest.

"And then what happened, Mrs. Rivers?"

Then Grayson came back.

"Could you repeat that, please?"

Then Grayson came back.

I was sobbing at this point, the thought of little Grayson, just three years old, trying to protect his mama.

"Grayson came into the closet with y'all?"

Yes, Grayson came back—he just kept coming back that night, over and over again—and he asked again, "What are you doing to Mama, Daddy?"

And Dr. Rivers turned to look at Grayson, who seemed calm as can be, still holding his little blue blanket, one thumb in his mouth, and Dr. Rivers, he said to him, plain as day in the creepiest, nasty voice, "Mama is trying to kill me. Here, take the knife."

"He gave the knife to your son who is . . . let's see, three?"

Yes, Your Honor. He handed the knife to Grayson. And Grayson took the knife and he walked downstairs and he laid it in the sink. I was moving like in a dream now, following Grayson down to the kitchen, seeing the knife in the sink there with my blood on it. It was like a dream—a bad dream. The kids were standing so silent in the kitchen by then, but at least Dr. Rivers finally seemed kind of, I don't know, out of steam. He gathered up all the kids, took them up the stairs and to the master bedroom, with me following real quiet-like behind, and he stood there in the door of our bedroom and told me, "I'm going to bed now, with my kids. If you even think of calling the police, my police, you won't have any kids to worry about by the time they get here." *And then he shut the door and locked it.*

"I'm sorry, Mrs. Rivers. What did you do next?" asked Judge Taylor.

Addison put her hand on my arm now and stepped forward, sensing my exhaustion, taking over. "She stayed up all night, listening to Dr. Rivers snore through the locked door," Addison announced. "She also called her mother in California, who had the good sense to tell her to call the women's shelter to ask for advice, which she did. The night counselor at the Gulf Coast Women's Center for Nonviolence advised her to refrain from any actions that would reescalate the situation and also that if she called police and Dr. Rivers pressed countercharges against her, the children would be removed to foster care until any criminal proceedings were resolved."

I couldn't let my children go to strangers! I said with a kind of wild panic, out of turn.

"Mrs. Rivers, please don't speak unless I ask you to, okay?"

"Your Honor, Mrs. Rivers has put the welfare and safety of her children ahead of both her own safety and any sense of justice that should have been served. She prays that the court, by way of the Jackson County Sheriff's Department, remove Dr. Rivers from the marital residence and extend the order of protection so that Mrs. Rivers may care for the children as she moves forward in this divorce, Your Honor."

"Is that all, Ms. McClanahan?" Judge Taylor asked.

"Yes, Your Honor."

"Mrs. Rivers, do you have anything else to add?"

Um, I wonder if the court could make Dr. Rivers get some kind of treatment for, you know, his problems? He wasn't always like this, and I don't want it to happen again and he used to be, you know, a good person.

"I don't doubt that, Mrs. Rivers. But the court in this state can't order that kind of treatment. We can make recommendations, of course. But let me give you a piece of advice. What you have been through has been terrible. You worry about taking care of your children and let the court worry about the rest."

Yes, sir.

Addison made a few closing remarks, reminding Judge Taylor of my master's degree from one of the most prestigious liberal art colleges in the country, my esteemed publishing record, my former illustrious career in the publishing industry, and how I'd willingly and in agreement left it all behind to be a wife and stay-at-home mama for my sweet three. She talked about how I had taken charge of working with the contractor to build the new house, choosing and approving every last detail, down to the metal color on the door hinges and the shelving in the nursery for the baby that I'd lost the spring before. She stressed that I had used my business savvy to start Dr. Rivers's two medical clinics and to promote them and keep them going, how his new clinic was indeed built on land that I (not he) owned, and that I was every bit as deserving and equal a partner in our marriage as was he. I think she was trying to counteract the miserable little injured mouse I'd portrayed myself as.

"Mrs. Rivers, is everything you've said today true and honest to the best of your abilities?"

"Yes, Your Honor," I managed to shriek out in a small voice.

And then, just like that, the Honorable Hank "Bubba" Taylor granted the order.

"What happens next?" I asked Addison as we got back into her Mini Cooper to drive back over the Pascagoula Bridge and back to the Sonic across the street from the Gautier mall, where Lana would meet us and pick me up.

"We wait," she replied. "The sheriff gets to throw him out on his own sweet time. I guarantee you this won't be at the top of their list of emergencies. Could be tomorrow, could be next week. Don't call me every day," she announced.

Addison McClanahan was a glamorous Mississippi mash-up between Nancy Grace and Reese Witherspoon. I wasn't sure if she was smarty-pants zany or flat-out brilliant or a little bit of both, but she was all I had, and so far she'd done right by me. I thanked her, slipped into Lana's minivan idling in the Waffle House parking lot, and went back to meet the sweet three back at the trailer.

After four more nights of deer steak cookouts and mud puddle pancake factories, I got the call.

The Jackson County Sheriff had removed Liam without incident. Addison reported that the sheriff found him "pleasant, cordial, and entirely compliant."

What a relief.

The house was now empty, waiting for our return. We stayed one last night in the trailer. A part of me was terrified to go back to that house.

"Oh, and Alice?" Addison continued on the line. "It's legal in Mississippi to carry a firearm when you have a temporary restraining order in effect to protect yourself. Just sayin'."

I smiled, pulled my handbag with the pistol inside closer in my lap.

PART TWO

OBLIVION

LET THE POT BOIL

Jack Calhoun's office was a little row house on Convent Avenue in downtown Pascagoula, with overgrown saw grass sticking up in tufts out of the broken concrete steps out front. Mama looked skeptical. By that time, she'd been in California thirty years, and Mississippi seemed like a very foreign land, even before the storm. I reminded the kids of their manners, explained that a nice man wanted to talk to them a little bit, and we all went in.

We stepped into a little waiting room with a few mismatched folding chairs, a couple of pitiful-looking artificial houseplants in faded baskets, and hundreds of dog-eared hunting magazines. The secretary came out to meet us and told us Mr. Calhoun would be right out.

As we sat down, I took in the office. The floors were stripped down to the sub, with bits of the former hardwood broken off here and there at the corners of the room. The walls were literally still wet, with a watermark about three feet below the raised ceilings. The whole place reeked of mold.

"How y'all doing out here? You boys like them gun magazines?" boomed a voice from the hall suddenly.

I was afraid to look. Head down, I noticed first his polished dress shoes, then a very long expanse of dark dress slacks, then a well-worn brown belt, then a crisp white shirt with sharp Republican tie. And then finally, raising my head to meet his eye, I saw the most handsome black Irish Southern gentleman I'd had the good fortune to lay eyes on in some time. He had wild, curly black hair, the palest shade of oceanic-green eyes, deeply tanned skin, and a perfect white smile.

I felt myself blush a bit at my ridiculous response.

"Y'all wanna come back here in my office for a while?" he asked the kids, who sat in a silent row of chairs, magazines falling from their laps.

"Y'all go ahead now with Mr. Jack. He's going to chat with you. And be sweet," I reminded.

I watched them follow behind him down the narrow hall. Mama took my hand and gave me one of her "It's gonna be okay" squeezes.

"Mama?" I said, starting to cry.

"It's going to be fine. They're going to tell him, don't worry."

And Mama and I sat there and listened.

The place was so small, the walls so destroyed, that we could hear every word. He asked them how much their daddy drank.

"Ten beers!"

And if Daddy was nice to their mama.

"Only sometimes."

And if Daddy liked to drive his car after he drank.

"All the time, yes, sir!"

Eventually, we heard Jack Calhoun say to the children, "Now, y'all like candy, don't y'all? 'Cause I got this big ol' hunk of chocolate to share. But I have to divide it up for you, right? Now, let me see. Y'all ever seen one of these?"

"Daddy has one of those!" said Grayson.

Mama and I exchanged confused glances.

"It's a butcher knife," said Grayson in his wisest three-year-old voice.

"It is, in'nit? Your daddy got one of these?" Jack asked.

"Yes, he does," Grayson said in a serious little voice. Almost a hush. I knew what he was thinking—I was thinking of it, too.

I wished they'd remember to say, "Yes, sir." But by that time, I was crying too hard to care.

"Daddy cut Mama with a knife like that," Grayson said.

"Really?" Jack Calhoun asked.

"Really," the kids all said in unison. A hush fell then, and I wondered what was happening, until I realized they were all just sitting in there eating hunks of chocolate. Mama and I didn't say a word.

Eventually, he brought the kids out to the waiting room to stay with their grandma, saying, "I need to talk to your mama a little bit alone. Y'all mind your granny now, ya hear?"

I went back to his office and listened as he told me he'd be recommending regular visitation for Liam with the kids. He'd have them every other weekend and one day during the week.

I nearly fell off my chair.

"*What?* But you heard the kids—he tried to kill me! He came after me with a knife—he *cut* me!" I shrieked, trying in desperation to keep my voice down.

"He didn't do nothin' to them, though."

"Exactly."

"Come again?"

"Double negative. You're right, what he did to them wasn't nothing. They saw it all; they spent that night locked in the room with him."

"Aw, they fine."

"They're not fine."

"Between you and me, Mrs. Rivers, you might want to recon-
sider how you speak of kids you want to keep custody of."

"Okay, well, they're technically fine. But they've been through
their drunk daddy attacking their mama for hours on end, and
they're scared of him."

"But he didn't lay a hand on them."

"He tried to grab Aidan Lake and take him in the car and drive
drunk with him! That's what started the whole thing! He had
marks on his legs from Liam grabbing him."

"The baby ain't got no marks on his legs now, does he?"

"No, but—"

"Listen, you got three fine, healthy, well-dressed kids. You
know what keeps a father from having visitation with his own flesh
and blood? I can tell you, a nasty fight with his wife ain't it."

"It wasn't a fight, it was an attack."

"That might be, but you don't get it."

"Don't get what? If he hurt me, he'll hurt them."

It was a sentence I would repeat for years to come.

"But he didn't hurt them."

"Yet."

"Exactly, and you can't punish a man for something you think
he may or may not do at some time in the near or distant future."

"So I'm just supposed to take my chances with my children's
safety?"

"Your children are safe. They're out there with their grandma."

"They won't be safe if they have to see their dad."

"You don't know that, Mrs. Rivers."

"I do. I know it with everything I have." My voice broke, the
tears falling again.

"Look, you gotta give him the pot of water and set it to boil."

"Excuse me?"

"Enough rope to hang himself, enough heat to let the pot boil
over—that's what you gotta give him. Because I'm telling you now

the judge ain't gonna keep a man from his own children according to the fact that he beat the shit out of his wife."

"But won't the judge want to err on the side of caution?" I asked.

"Maybe later, after the pot boils over, he will," Jack countered.

"You're kidding me, right?"

"No, ma'am."

"So I'm just supposed to gamble with my children's safety until then? What if he drives drunk with them?"

"He hasn't been arrested for that, right? And he hasn't touched them. He's going to see them; you might as well just let it happen and watch the pot."

"My mama says a watched pot never boils," I whispered, starting to feel defeated.

"Oh, it boils, all right. I see it boil all the time. You wanna know what it looks like when the pot boils?"

"Yeah, I do."

"Your kids ain't got belt scabs on their asses or cigarette burns in the heels of their feet. That's the kids whose daddies can't see them. You're not there yet."

"So I'm supposed to wait to get there?"

"You don't give up, do you?" Jack asked, smiling.

"Not usually, sir."

"Best I can give you is a little extra step to buy time. But it's going to happen. You got to set his pot on the fire."

"You're basically asking me to hope that I set the pot to boil so that, what, something terrible will happen?"

"Well, that's the only way he's not getting visitation, hon."

We argued for half an hour more, and finally, Jack Calhoun, the gaurdian ad litem appointed by Judge Taylor to represent the children, agreed to not recommend any visitation, but writing in his letter to the judge instead asked that we would be interviewed by a social worker, who would then give her informed opinion.

Two days later we were in the cramped office of one Ethel Kahn, social worker, balancing on the edge of dusty couches surrounded by shelves chock-full of Russian nesting dolls. She was a sickly-looking woman, the kind of person that, though young, had a deathly pall to her, skin devoid of any life. Her eyes were dark as the Russian dolls that lined the shelves of her office— black and round. Her hair, oily stripes scraped by a comb parted right down the middle, was somewhere between mouse gray and dish brown, and her ill-fitted sweater matched it exactly. I noticed that her shoes were caked with dirt. She'd met with Liam the day before and started by telling me—in a kind of heightened, too-excited whisper that suggested we were in this together—that he admitted to drinking to excess and admitted to the violence between us, but that he'd sworn it was "mutual."

She asked the kids a few questions about their daddy, but nothing about the night of the attack. Mostly, she let them play with her endless sets of dusty nesting dolls and questioned me quite extensively about my book. I asked her how she knew about my book. "Your husband told me. He's very proud of your literary accomplishments," she said, a small smile passing her damp face.

My literary accomplishments?

This is a man who'd for the last two years had forbidden me from writing poems.

"I like poetry myself," Ethel said.

She didn't ask me a single thing about Liam.

After the forty-minute session, I left with a sick feeling in my stomach. I called Addison.

"Something's off," I said. "Is she working for their side?"

"Don't be paranoid!" Addison laughed and told me not to worry.

The next day, Ethel Kahn sent letters to Jack Calhoun, the Honorable Judge Hank "Bubba" Taylor, Liam's new attorney Buford Cooter Garland, and—of course—Addison, recommending extremely limited visitation for Liam: eight daylight hours every Saturday, with a strict provision for no drinking. Relieved, I steeled myself for those Saturday exchanges, and Mama went back home to California.

TIMBER

We exchanged the kids every Saturday in front of the Ocean Springs Police Department downtown. At Addison's urging, I carried a small tape recorder with me at our exchanges, and I had half a tape filled already with bizarre rants from Liam. Two weeks before, he accused me of giving out plentiful blow jobs to various acquaintances the last time I'd gone to California (almost two years before). This last week, I hadn't given him much chance to talk. My only goal was to inform him of a little injury Avery had suffered a few days before, seeing ahead of time that it could easily become just the fuel Liam longed for in his attempt to smear me in court.

Liam had broken the protective order half a dozen times already, following me around town, driving by the house and using his fingers to motion shooting a gun at me. In Mississippi, when someone breaks a protective order, they take a report.

They don't arrest.

There is no consequence.

That is to say, a protective order in Mississippi is goddamned meaningless: nothing but a piece of paper. I was so on edge, I needed Mama's gentle presence and her sweetness by my side. Without her, I felt lost, vulnerable. Mama had just come back, thank heavens. When we picked her up from the airport in Gulfport the Thursday before, I could see the horror in her eyes at the state of things.

Six months after the storm, and nothing was better. By now, I was used to the post-Katrina landscape—it seemed almost right to me, equal in devastation to my personal life, my family blown to bits. But as we stood in the baggage area, I could see the sadness on Mama's face. Besides, the news was covering New Orleans for the most part, forgetting almost entirely that the Mississippi Gulf Coast had been ground zero of the storm.

The terminal floor was stripped to concrete and had slick black mold growing everywhere in patches, with pure white concrete paths worn clean where the steady stream of relatives and government contractors passed each day. Great swaths of dirty plastic hung where automatic doors once slid open between the heat outside and the piped cold air of the terminal. Now everything was (by default) outside. There was a ceiling, but not much of one. The heat was stultifying.

On the car ride home, Mama sat in silence. Grayson barely spoke still. From his ocean-blue eyes stared a soul that was more thirty than three—cautious, sad, knowing too much. He didn't let me out of his sight these days, and when he did speak asked me if Daddy was going to come back and "try to kill you some more."

Aidan, still a baby, had bad dreams, wailing in his sleep, "No, Dada! No, Dada! No, Dada!" I was trying to get the kids to sleep in their own beds, but every time I'd hear that cry from Aidan, I'd rush down the hall to get him, often finding Mama standing outside his door already, tears streaming down her lined, pretty face.

My heart broke over and over, but I did what I could to make them feel safe, to let them know that we were out of harm's way now and nothing bad was going to happen. At night, after they'd fall asleep, I'd cry myself to sleep, rocking like a child. I needed Mama, and she came.

Her first night back, they all clamored for Mama's attention, climbing onto her lap and dragging her up and down the halls to each of their rooms. At bedtime, Avery and Grayson decided to take a shower together, as they often did.

After the storm, not only was the ground outside our home contaminated, the Gulf Coast Research Laboratory had discovered that, post-Katrina, there were more biting insects on the coast than in any one designated place on the entire planet. We had run out of ways to entertain ourselves months before. That big shower in the master was like a playground for them, alternative sprinklers to play in.

They had a new game they liked to play: Ice Cream Shop. In Ice Cream Shop, they filled the baby's plastic stacking cups with water and suds and soap bar "scoops" and sold them back and forth to one another. The shower was spacious, the inside tiled entirely—including the floor—with cobalt ceramic I'd chosen those many months before.

That night, I was changing Aidan on the Jenny Lind changing table in his room, looking out the window onto the quiet street, the exact same place I'd been a few months before, the night of the attack. Every time I changed Aidan, I thought not of that night but of another morning, of seeing the garbageman hop off a truck and grab our can, my entire collection of journals—probably fifty in all, kept since I was eight years old—dropping in.

The pages lifted in the damp salt air like egret wings, lifting at once in a panic in the marshes. The truck pulled away.

Liam had hassled me about the contents of those journals for years—every girl I'd kissed, every person I'd fucked, every place I'd been without him or crush I held in my secret heart, every poem I wrote that wasn't about him (all of them) was held against me.

He'd read them all: twice.

At least once a month, drunk, Liam would start in about something from the journals, his rage growing sharper with each beer, ranting sometimes for hours on end, sometimes until morning light. He was meticulous in his outrage—every book I owned written by a former lover had to be destroyed, every piece of jewelry accepted as a gift thrown out, every article of clothing mentioned in a reminiscence burned. The crudely produced student literary journal from grad school, where my poem sat side by side with one by Christina—a butch Latina from San Antonio, my girlfriend while I was at Sarah Lawrence—was torn to shreds and thrown into the fire. In Liam's mind, swirling with obsession, I had no right to a past.

"You're a whore," he insisted, "and no one thinks you can write."

I would lower my head and stay quiet, still.

"You don't *exist* without me."

His goal was to erase me.

Every time I changed Aidan's diaper on that table, I thought of my journals falling into the acrid back of the truck like so much trash, my loopy handwriting across the pages smudged with filth.

A high-pitched wail snapped me out of it. I shut the diaper quick and ran toward the master bath, meeting Mama at the top of the stairs. We got to the bathroom at the same time. Avery had fallen, slipped on the slick soapy floor, and hit her back on a plastic Tupperware pitcher I kept in the shower, which I used to help rinse her long, thick, often tangled hair.

A scrape about three inches wide by five inches long appeared on the right side of her back, breaking the skin where the rim of the pitcher had scraped her ribs from behind, bruises rising like rust on a tiny cage.

She cried and cried.

"It's okay, shuggie. It'll feel better in the morning," I reassured her. I'd been calling her *shuggie* since she was born. Liam and I had agreed to name her Hazel, but—as was his way—he revoked his "permission" when she was born. He rejected all my other suggestions, too. When he had gone home to take a shower, I filled out the birth certificate without him, naming her after Shug Avery in *The Color Purple*.

Fierce, loyal, a songbird, a girl who would know how to sing.

"It hurts, Mama!" she wailed.

"I know, baby."

I cleaned her up, put her in the new nightie Mama'd brought, and we all went to bed. In the bayou dark, all the streetlights having been washed away with the storm, her big blue eyes, set deep in her little Kewpie doll face, gazed at me, solemn.

"Do I have to go with Daddy?" she asked.

"Yes, shuggie, you do," I said, wishing already it wasn't so, a fierce dread rising.

In the morning, the bruise was purple edging into green, scabbed over in spots where the skin had broken. It was a bad scrape, and I spent the day worrying not about how my baby felt but about what her father might do if he saw it. His Saturday visitation started the next morning at nine.

"There ain't no chance in helicopter that bruise'll heal before then!" I cried to Mama. Mama didn't truck with swear words.

"It'll be okay, Alice. Don't worry, it was just an accident. Kids have accidents, for goodness' sake," Mama tried to reassure me. "He has to have some kind of reason left, right? He's not going to use the kids like that," she insisted.

Like I said, Mama had a kind streak in her longer than the thirty-two miles of Mississippi white sand beaches between the Louisiana and Alabama borders.

I had no choice but to send Avery.

In front of the police department, I hopped out of the white Land Rover. The boys were crying in their car seats, as they always did during handovers. I got them out, then wrangled with their car seats while they clung to my legs and Liam stood back and watched me. I kissed them all, hugging them, whispering reassurance in their ears, and turned to get back in the car.

"Oh, I wanted to tell you," I called, my voice shaking, loud enough to pick up on the tape. "Avery has a bruise on her back—she fell in the shower."

"Poor little shuggie," Liam replied, and he turned away.

They pulled out, and I waited until he turned the corner on Jackson Avenue to place a call on my cell to Tim Burr.

I'd hired Tim Burr to follow Liam on his visitations. It was one part legal savvy (another recommendation from Addison) and one part mama's worry—I honestly didn't trust Liam with the children. He'd threatened several times to just disappear with them. I was afraid he would hurt them. I had a tape sitting in my bedside table drawer that sent a cold dread through my heart.

"Are you going to give me visitation for the summer, or do I need to take you back to court?" Liam asks, recorded on the tape.

"The judge has already ruled on visitation for now," I replied. Of course, I was aware of being recorded, but when I play the tapes back, I sound shaky and unsure, scared, a stricken girl's excuse for the calm and pleasant voice I told myself to use.

"Well, I guess we'll have to ask the judge. Maybe I should ask for full custody, too, since you're not able to raise the children," Liam taunts from the audio.

"Of course I'm able to raise the children, Liam."

"You're a danger. You're crazy. You need psychological help."

"No, Liam, I'm not crazy," I say for likely the thousandth time in my married years.

This had become Liam's new legal tactic—gas-lighting. He'd told me, in one of the police department parking lot exchanges, "If you're not crazy now, you will be by the time me and Buford are finished with you."

This is my new reality.

"So are you going to let them come with me for the summer?" he asks on the tape.

"The judge has already agreed and ordered that one day a week is best," I state as calmly as I can. My voice sounds like I'm talking into a paper cup, shallow, hollow, flat. Ever since Ethel Kahn's letter, I've been handing the kids over every Saturday morning, retrieving them Saturday evening, and the kids were miserable about those eight hours every week. Liam wanted more.

"We can do it the easy way, or we can do it the hard way," he threatens.

"Ethel Kahn recommends you don't have the kids for overnight visitation. You admitted to drinking to excess, Liam. You're not trustworthy. You're not even conscious past 8:00 P.M.," I say.

"I want to take them to the beach house," he announces.

The beach house is our catchphrase for Gulf Shores, Alabama. When people hear *Alabama*, they don't think *beach*, but there's a long stretch of sugar-white sand stretching the length entire of South Alabama. We used to rent a beach house there for a few weeks each year.

"Actually, I think I'm going to stay in a high-rise this time."

There was a pause, a silence. The tape rolled on.

"Did you hear what I said? I really want to stay in one of the high-rises, some of the new construction buildings are forty floors at least. Did you hear about that father who took his kids on vacation?" he asks, a little fissure of sick joy spiking his voice.

"No." I hesitate, sensing something coming. I am used to his tactics.

"This dad, he was in the middle of a big, ugly divorce, and his wife was trying to keep the children from him. So the guy got summer visitation and he went to Alabama or Florida or somewhere along there and jumped from the balcony of his hotel room, thirty flights up."

"Oh, that's sad," I say, trying to keep my voice calm.

"With his kids in his arms," he adds, an unmistakable tint of threat and inexplicable glee in his voice. "What do you think of that, Alice?" he asks.

"Are you saying that's what you're going to do? Are you trying to scare me?" I ask.

On the tape, my voice is so high I sound like I'm screaming, but in a whisper.

"I don't know what you're talking about, Alice. You really need help for your mental problems. I think you need to be committed," he said.

"I'm not crazy, Liam," I reply as calmly as I can.

The truth was his tactics were starting to work—his threats, his repeated violation of the protective order, and frequent conversations like this one *had* started to make me feel like I was crazy.

Crazy. Desperate. Increasingly wild of heart.

It was after a few conversations like this, and one in which he told me he'd obtained passports for the kids and had regular dreams of disappearing with them, that I finally hired Tim Burr.

I started by looking under *Private Investigators* in the local phone book. Every person listed I either knew or knew someone related to them. (You could tell a lot in Ocean Springs just by someone's last name.) Finally, I asked around my girlfriends at the school and got the number of a detective on the Biloxi PD. I called the number my friend passed along, and a deep voice answered promptly with, "Yeah?"

He agreed to meet me at the butcher counter in Mohler's gas station on Washington Avenue, a few blocks south of the 10. They had a lunch counter there, and plastic booths. I left the kids with Mama and went to meet him. I waited half an hour, feeling like the protagonist in a bad movie of the week. Eventually, my phone rang.

"I'm having babysitting issues; can you come to my house?" he asked, and he gave me directions to a tidy ranch just a few blocks away.

He was tall, action-star handsome, with a blond buzz cut and enormous arms punctuated by tribal tattoos. When he came to the door, he held the sweetest little baby girl in those massive arms. I sat on his dark red floral couch with my manila folder full of copies of the legal documents thus far, a few photos of Liam, and a typed-up report of all of Liam's information—where he lived, worked, and an estimated timeline of his days.

He sat and listened to me, the baby bouncing on the edge of his ample, tanned knee.

"He's a little dude, right?"

"Yes, sir, my size for the most part," I replied.

"The little fuckers are always the meanest," he said. "Someone this arrogant is always easy to tail, don't worry. He's so worried about himself he won't have the good sense to notice who might be near him. No worries, I'll watch him and your kids."

I thanked him and went to leave, gathering my purse. As I grabbed the doorknob, he reached around me, pulled it open.

"One more thing—don't acknowledge me if you see me in public," he warned. "And every move you make outside of your house, assume you're being photographed. It wouldn't do any harm to be dressed up whenever you go out—like church dressed up. And carry a cake pan or a casserole a lot."

"Like, pretend I'm June Cleaver?"

He laughed. "Pretty much. Believe me, you'll thank me later."

"Okay, well, I'm thanking you now," I murmured, close to tears. Every hour or so, a great wave of sadness would wash over me, struck through with disbelief that this had so quickly become my life. But of course it wasn't quick—it's never quick.

"Don't cry, darlin'," he reassured. "You're doing the right thing. I've seen too many girls stay after being beaten up 'just once.' Lemme tell you something—it's never 'just once.' Ever."

"What if he sees you? He says he's the doctor for the Ocean Springs Police Department," I worried.

"First, for all intents and purposes, as far as he or anyone is concerned, I'm not a Biloxi detective; I'm a redneck tree trimmer. He ain't going to give me a second look."

"Thank you so much, Tim," I said.

"That's Mr. Tim Burr, tree trimmer, to you, young lady!" he teased.

I think it was the first time I smiled all week. Out front was his F-250 truck, with *Tim Burr, Tree Service* emblazoned on the door.

I knew, I just knew Liam wouldn't let that bruise remain just a bruise.

Tim Burr, tree trimmer, followed Liam and the kids the day entire. They drove straight from the Ocean Springs Police Department east to Mobile, Alabama, an hour drive down the 10. Since the storm, Liam spent a lot of time in Mobile. Tim Burr called me on the way to reassure me he was on them.

"By the way, I talked to my buddy at Ocean Springs Police."

"What did he say?" I asked.

"They never heard of him," he said.

"Never heard of whom?" I asked.

"Never heard of your husband."

"At the police department?"

"Right. Never heard of the dude."

"Ocean Springs Police? But he said he's their doctor, that he takes care of the whole department," I continued.

"Yup, like I said, they never heard of him. Trust me. I talked to my cousin, and he asked around."

"So it was all a lie to, what, scare me?"

"Yes, it was all a lie. It's not that unusual, though the doctor angle is new to me."

"What do you mean?"

"A man tells a woman he has an 'in' with the police department for one reason and one reason only—to make sure she don't call 'em when he beats the living crap outta her."

I felt as if I'd fallen from a tree and landed hard on my ass. In front of church. On Easter. Like an altogether gullible stupid fool.

Everyone kept telling me that his threats were hollow, and moments like this confirmed that he was, indeed, a liar. A bully. But he'd also been threatening to kill me, almost daily, for the last year, and he'd nearly made good on that promise. Now his biggest threat was that he'd find a way to make sure I never saw the kids again.

They stopped briefly at Magic Castle, an indoor playground. At Target, they went in and bought socks. Apparently, you weren't allowed to jump barefoot at the Magic Castle. After, they went to lunch at Liam's favorite Mexican restaurant, then headed back to Magic Castle. They stayed and played three hours while Tim Burr sat just left of a big birthday party, acting like a bored dad on his cell.

Liam talked on the phone the entire drive back from Mobile to Ocean Springs, and instead of getting off the 10 and going to his condo, he took the last exit and drove into the parking lot at Ocean Springs Hospital.

Tim Burr called and told me they were inside, but not to worry, he'd seen no one get injured. I told him about the bruise then, and he said, "Ah, got it. I'm going to stay extra close. Can you afford a few hours after he drops them off?"

"Yes, sure."

A sick feeling rose in my throat.

After about an hour inside, the kids emerged with Liam and got in his car, and they all went back to his condo.

"They're out now—looks like maybe Avery threw up on herself. They're headed back to his condo now. I'll keep you posted."

I hung up, snapped shut my phone, sat staring at it, numb.

A half hour or so passed with them in the condo, and they all came out and went to the pool. Just before the appointed time, Liam piled them into his car and brought them back to me at the police department parking lot.

They were wet-haired and long-faced when they got out of his car, falling into my arms. Liam tried to pull them back to embrace him, but they leaned away from him, staying at an arm's length. He said nothing to them, just got back in his car and drove away.

Avery burst immediately into sobs.

The story poured out of her, lurching, her little chest heaving. As she told me what happened, it was like she was coloring in the pictures of what Tim Burr had told me. The day in Mobile had gone well until, Avery said, Liam had lifted up her dress at the Magic Palace and saw her bruise. The entire drive back to Ocean Springs, he'd been on the phone.

"He says you're going to go live in a hospital for people who are sick in their brain, Mama," she sobbed. "And that we have to live with him but that's he's going to take us to visit you at the hospital but that you gotta live there for the rest of your life, Mama," she wailed.

"Yeah," added Grayson, unblinking, "why you gotta live at the hospital, Mama?" he mumbled around the thumb planted firmly in his mouth.

"He took me to the hospital, Mama, and I had to get an x-ray, and I threw up all over myself. I hate the hospital, Mama. I don't want you to live there, even a special one!" she cried.

"Me either," said Grayson. "And I don't like hospitals."

"Mama sick, Mama sick," cooed Aidan.

"And then, and then, and then, and then," Avery cried, the sobs making her inhale in sharp contractions of breath, her mouth gaping in pure sorrow.

"Slow down, shuggie. You're okay. Take a breath and tell Mama what happened at the hospital."

The tears fell in big, fat silent rows down her cheeks. Finally, she cried out, "He made me take a shower, and then he took my picture naked, Mama."

"Naked?" I yelled, alarmed.

"Yeah, but after that, we got to go swimming," she said, still crying but settling down, her sobs relaxing into quiet tears pouring down her fair little cheeks.

"You went swimming?"

"Yeah, but then Dada said that there was too many brown people at the pool."

"Avery, we don't care what color people are, right?"

"Mama, he says you hurt me," she whispered.

"I'm sorry, shuggie. I would never hurt you," I said, trying not to cry.

"I know, Mama, I know."

WELCOME TO
THE CIRCUS

Addison called first thing Monday morning with the news that Liam, via Buford, had filed an emergency motion to appear. Liam was requesting the court issue an emergency change in physical custody. As expected, he was accusing me of physical child abuse on Avery.

"There's more, Alice," Addison said, her voice quieter than usual. "Have you ever been committed to a psych ward or tried to kill yourself?" she asked.

I sat on the other end of the line, silent.

"Alice?"

"Um, yeah. I mean, no. Why are you asking me this?"

"Well, they're accusing you of much more than abusing Avery."

"Like what?" I asked in what may have been my final moment of glorious ignorance of what was to come.

Addison continued, "They're saying you're suicidal, homicidal, and an immediate danger to both yourself and the children. They say you're a habitual liar, with a genius IQ, who has had multiple abortions."

"What? He can just say anything he wants?" I asked, stunned.

"Well, he has something to back it up."

"Like what?" What could he possibly have to back it up?

"Ethel Kahn has written a letter that she believes you have dissociative identity disorder, are an immediate danger to the children, and that the children should be removed from you immediately."

"She met with me for forty minutes and never said a word!" I yelled into the phone. "And I haven't seen her since."

"Well, Liam's been seeing her, and they've apparently been going through your book. They're introducing it as evidence."

"My book? My award-winning book that was an inspiration and hope for survivors of sexual abuse? From NYU Press? My book of literary poetry? That book? How could that possibly be used against me?"

"I don't know what's in there, Alice, but they've submitted it as evidence of pornography, perversion, and parental unfitness," Addison said.

Pornography.

Perversion.

Parental unfitness.

"They submitted my book as evidence against me? To take my children away?"

"Yes, they did. Well, actually, they submitted a photocopy of the book. They left off the cover material, coincidentally."

"So it looks like I'm some coffeehouse poet with a bunch of random ramblings?"

"Pretty much."

"Did I fall asleep and wake up in 1952?"

"You're too intelligent for the likes of them."

"But seriously, that book isn't autobiography. It's literary poetry, not nonfiction. If it was, I'd have killed my father, been a prostitute in Japan, a stripper, with a sexual attraction to Jesus."

"Of sweet baby Jesus." Addison sighed. "I'm going to need a copy of that book. And can you get some, I don't know, famous writers to write you letters that it's not all a true story? I think we're going to need to educate the court."

A small sob escaped my mouth.

Years earlier, Liam had forced me to promise to never write another poem. I had never stopped, but I'd stopped writing them down. Now I silently promised to never write another poem if I could just keep my children.

If poetry makes me lose my children, I hate poetry.

"Alice, I'm sorry, but I have to ask you this." She paused. "What is your relationship with your daddy now?" she asked.

"My *daddy*?" I screeched out.

This was getting more sickening by the minute.

"Addison, he passed away two years ago. I was going to go see him one last time, but I was five months pregnant, and I had three babies. And Liam would not go visit my family with me, and he wouldn't help me with the children. And my daddy was dying and he called me and asked me if I was coming, and I said I couldn't. And my daddy died that very day. On the same day. And a few weeks later is when I lost my baby, and when the doctor dated it back to the last day of thriving, it was the same day my daddy passed. No matter what Liam says, or what they're highlighting from my book, my daddy and I had a great relationship when he finally passed. Liam was the one to encourage me to make peace with him before he died," I stuttered out.

"Well, according to this motion, now Liam states—honey, are you sitting down?"

"No, I am not sitting down. Addison. What are they saying?"

"They are saying that you had a"—and here her voice changed because the horror of it was so bad she had to speak as if quoting them because I could tell she could barely bring herself to say it

aloud to me—"that you had a lifelong, consensual sexual relationship with your father."

I dropped the phone and threw up all over the floor.

The next morning, Avery and I traipsed back over to Jack Calhoun's office to have another "talk." He had Avery come in first
and was done in just a few minutes.

When I sat down across from him at his desk, he immediately
reassured me in his deep drawl, "Alice, this whole thing is goddamned bull crap. I know you didn't do that to Avery."

"Thank God. So it's not going to go anywhere?" I asked.

"Now, I didn't say that. I wish that was how things worked, but
it's not," he said, sliding two photographs across his desk in front
of me. In both, Avery was naked, wet, hunched over sitting on her
haunches with her little behind showing, in what looked to be a
darkened room on dirty carpet. Her bruise was in full display.

"Now, this don't look good," Jack said.

"It looks horrible!" I blurted out, not sure if I was more mad or
devastated. "Jack, he's a doctor; he knows the protocol. If he
wanted to document abuse, he could have done it at the hospital
when he was having her ribs x-rayed!"

"I know, I know," Jack said, smiling, trying to reassure me. "But
the judge is going to have to give him his due process."

My fingers still rested on the two photographs of Avery. In one,
the top of her bottom, that sweet little split, showed clearly.

"These photos are the only child abuse that's happened,"
I said.

"I've seen worse."

"Jack, this is crazy. I'm not the one that did anything wrong.
Ethel Kahn is meeting with Liam, and they're deciding that I
have multiple personalities and am going to murder my children?
Does that make any sense?"

"It doesn't have to make sense, Alice, but you're going to have to fight it. I hope you took Addison's advice. Court's Friday—bring as many people as you can."

For a moment, I thought he was going to hug me. I was furious with him, wanting him to somehow call bull on the whole thing, like he said, and put a stop to it. But he couldn't. And he didn't hug me.

It felt like the whole world was imploding on me.

"Jack?" I said, a panicked sob escaping my throat. "This is bad."

"Darlin', just hang in there. What I'm fixin' to do is to set that goddamned pot to boil."

"But what if—" I started.

He held up his hand. "No what-ifs, Alice. I'm gonna tell you something: I'm goddamned fucking furious now. But the next couple of weeks are going to be hell. Pull up your bootstraps, you hear?"

"Thanks, Jack," I managed to whisper as I left. He placed his hand in the small of my back as I left his office, and I wished I could just fall into his arms and let him make it all go away. I was like the dying girl with the crush on her doctor—hope'll do that to a girl, make you all weak at the knees when your heart is breaking.

"Okay, go. Call your friends. *All* of them, hear? Every last goddamn one of them. And then call a few more," he said, laughing.

And that's how my house ended up full to the gills.

Friday morning, I would come to court with my whole family, eighteen friends, my priest, the kids' piano teacher, two Walmart greeters, Mac and Daddy, two of Liam's old nurses, three of his colleagues from the hospital, a friend's nanny, the cleaning ladies that serviced his office and sometimes our house, a doctor who used to work for him, seven teachers from the Catholic school, five neighbors, and Tim Burr.

FEMA Trailer Courtroom A would be standing room only.

Liam's only witnesses would be Ethel Kahn and his parents.

A court-appointed psychologist named Dr. Colette Colette would sit front and center. When I took my place in the courtroom, Jack Calhoun would lean in to me and whisper in my ear, "Welcome to the circus."

Their emergency hearing was granted on the grounds of erring on the side of caution for the safety of the children.

And that's when all hell broke loose.

PRETTY PICTURES

My flip phone was on double duty. In the two days since we'd received the emergency motion to appear, I'd been calling everyone and Jesus to beg them to come testify on my good behalf. Up until now, I'd tried to keep most of what happened quiet in town, but now that I was in danger of losing custody of the sweet three, all bets were off. I'd lined up half of town to come to court already, but Addison said to get "anyone and everyone and people who matter."

And they came—all my immediate family (my mama, brother, niece, nephew) from California, Auntie Rie from Fargo, and not only my brother's girlfriend but his ex-wife and her husband, too. Mama opened a new credit card to purchase most of the tickets. And now the day before the hearing had arrived, and my normally cavernous house was chock-full of everyone who loves me in this world.

The children slept with me in my room, and the rest of the

place was filled with people sleeping on kids' beds, on blow-up mattresses, on couches, and on porch lounges. Even the rocking chair in the great room was utilized—my brother's tattooed ex-wife sprawled there, while my brother and his girlfriend of ten years bunked in the baby's room upstairs. *Emergency* was an understatement.

After we had moved out of the FEMA trailer on Mac and Daddy's land and into the house, I'd tried to resume life as usual, minus the controlling, abusive tyrant. The first thing we'd done when we got back home was go room to room, taking down all the oversized paintings Liam had gifted me over the years.

Liam thought of himself as a tortured artist, but the only one who was tortured by his art was me. And anyone who came to our house. And our children. We had half a dozen paintings hanging prominently throughout the house, and they were all of "me."

Usually, I was naked. Emaciated, to be exact. Above me: doves carrying pistols that pointed at my head. My eyes bulged obscenely from my haggard face: the eyes of a wild animal. About a month after I'd lost our baby five months in (after the new nursery was all set up, after the children had long been campaigning for names), he painted and then gave me a piece commemorating the experience. Maybe it would feature an angel, symbolic rays of light breaking through the darkness? Maybe a dove suspended in a forever-blue sky.

In the painting, I'm standing, naked, on enormous flat, webbed feet with an flat aura like a deactivated halo surrounding my distorted, distended body. I seem to be holding something in my arms. On closer inspection, my arms are simply empty, but there is a dead baby, gray and lifeless, nestled under my sunken rib cage. Below me on the grass is the shadow of death, with images of my three living children, dressed as winged angels, at my feet. I'll never forget the sensation I felt when he carried it in at breakfast, the sweet three tucked into their places at the table, polished up to a fare-thee-well, on Mother's Day Sunday.

The children were silent. I was silent.

Liam, said, "Ta-da! Don't you *love* it?"

"It's, well, kind of sad, don't you think?" I ventured cautiously.

He didn't wait for my response. "Isn't it *amazing*? Don't you *love* it? Isn't it like Frida Kahlo?"

Frida Kahlo was my favorite painter. I liked the deep sense of self-knowledge, of brutal beauty in her work, the way that pain and tragedy were transformed into a kind of archetypal, redemptive truth. Liam's painting was nothing like Frida Kahlo. Despite my cool response, Liam got out a hammer and nail and went to work hanging it right above the fireplace.

From that Mother's Day on we moved around that death painting as if a cartoon of grief was acceptable mantelpiece décor. In every room in that house there was something from which I needed, for sanity's sake, to avert my eyes.

When the kids and I moved back into the house after Liam had been removed, I decided to take all the paintings down. One by one. I didn't say why I wanted them down; I just told the kids that maybe Daddy was going to want them back. The kids followed me around as I climbed onto counters and chairs, feet bare, hammer in my back pocket, balancing the oversized canvases in my arms, stacking them face toward the walls.

"Yay! Scary paintings gone!" they cheered, nearly dancing with delight. "Go away, skeletons! Go away, naked Mama!" they yelled, marching behind me.

I think seeing me remove these warped, hideous images of myself from our walls was the first time, maybe ever, that the kids saw me stand up for who I really was.

Not fat.

Not ugly.

Not stupid.

It was nice to be back in the house, but it hadn't been easy. I was forever seeing him, here or there, his stupid fake-gun finger pointing at me from his car. But would he really shoot me?

I had no doubt he'd like to. After his ejection from the house, Liam swiftly hired the meanest attorney on the coast, one Buford Cooter Garland, Esquire (a man stuffed so completely into his too-small, baby-blue polyester suit he could barely contain the good ol' belly spilling over his cracked alligator belt). But Addison had, thank heavens, worked for Buford straight out of law school before starting her own practice, so she knew his tricks and warned me to gear up for a fight.

"It's going to be ugly," she warned in her thick drawl. "Buford's mean."

"Mean how?" I asked in a tiny voice.

"He'll do everything he can to destroy you. It's not enough for him to sling half a bayou worth of salt mud at you; he's going to make your life a living hell," she warned.

"As if it could get worse?"

"Oh, it can get a lot worse." She laughed. "For one thing, Buford could spot a dumb-ass, deep-pocketed, jilted doctor in the pitch black of midnight on the last day of earth."

Addison ticked off three or four doctors in town who'd hired Buford, endured two- to three-year court battles, and spent nearly $90,000 a one. I didn't care about money, though; I only cared about keeping the kids safe.

"Also, go home and look up 'fathers' rights movement' on the Internet," she advised. "It's his mission in life to try to win custody for fathers, and Dr. Rivers's case ain't gonna be any different," she said.

"Oh no," I whispered. "But there's no way Liam could get custody—he tried to kill me!" I choked out in a panic.

"You have *got* to get something straight, right now, you hear me? Whatever Dr. Rivers did to you has nothing—absolutely nothing—to do with his role as a father," she said, a phrase she'd clearly uttered time and time again. It was a notion I couldn't quite swallow. How could a man's violent attack of his children's mother have nothing to do with his role as a father? I hadn't learned, and wouldn't for a very long time, that the world of family court has little to do with common sense, not to mention verified science.

It's true Addison tried, on several occasions, to talk me out of fighting that battle.

She told me, unequivocally, that it would be more reasonable to accept joint custody, set up a visitation schedule, decide on a reasonable child support amount, and be done with it. She explained time after time how, no matter how long and how bitter and how ugly the battle, it would likely turn out very close to what she was advising me to do right then, right there, against all my instincts. But I was still reeling, still healing from my wounds, the memories of that brutal night.

I still had a puncture wound in my chest.

I still had a bruise-colored necklace in the shape of his reach.

I still had a thousand nights of fear in my soul.

"You can stop it all now, give him visitation, and make it easy on yourself," she said.

But if he was willing to attack me, what might he do to the children?

"No, I can't," I told her. "I can't let him hurt the kids. He's dangerous. I have to fight. I can't let him do to them what he did to me, or worse."

And so she put her head down and went to work, asking for sole custody, supervised visitation, and support. Simultaneously, Buford asked for joint custody, regular visitation, and for the order of protection to be lifted. Despite my having been a stay-at-home mama since Avery was born, Buford denied that any support was necessary, as I had a master's degree and had "formerly earned $70,000 a year first as an acquisitions editor and then as a regional community relations vice president for a major book retailer."

I could hear Liam's voice echo through Buford's every filed motion.

According to Buford's motion, I was a regular career girl refusing to work out of a lazy sort of greed fueled by my desire to live off Liam's meager physician's salary. In reality, I'd recently negotiated a new physician's contract for Liam with a hospital up in Jackson, where we had planned to relocate after the storm. Liam was anxious to get away from any signs of a hurricane. We'd interviewed everywhere from El Paso, Texas, to Aiken, South Carolina, since the storm. In the end, Liam couldn't leave behind the money to be made in Mississippi.

Low population translates to the lowest per capita HMO coverage in the country; hence, Mississippi was the last bastion of fee-for-service medicine and had the doctor salaries to prove it. With student loan reimbursement, an income guarantee, and funds to open a brand-new independent practice, we'd negotiated a deal that equaled more than $250,000 per year for the next four years. Problem was, I didn't have a copy of the contract. I hadn't thought to bring it when I left the house the morning after the attack.

But I was on friendly terms with the recruiter up at the hospital in Jackson. In Mississippi, a doctor's wife is part of the package, and I played the part well. In the recruitment process, I'd come along to a slew of dinners out and real estate tours and hospital picnics, the children dressed in matching, monogrammed outfits. One afternoon in Addison's office, she wished aloud I had proof of Liam's new contract. As she went over our answer to Buford's latest motion, which argued that Liam made less than $5,000 a month, I asked, "You mind if I use your phone?"

I still had the hospital recruiter's number in my address book. She answered on the first ring. "Hey, Cindy. It's Alice, Dr. Rivers's wife?"

"Well, hey, Mrs. Alice! How are you? Did y'all find a house yet?"

"Not yet—there's so many pretty new houses, it's hard to find one I like best!" I blathered. "It's so lovely up there." I added, "I just can't wait to get up there and start fresh! We even looked in my old neighborhood I lived in when I was a little girl," I gushed.

"Well, when y'all get up here, I want to invite you to my Bunco," Cindy offered sweetly.

"That would be so nice. I just love Bunco!" I lied. I'd never played.

"I know, right? It's so much fun, and you'll get to meet all the other wives!" she continued.

"Well, gosh, thanks. You are so sweet. Anyway, I wondered if you could do me a favor? I'm down to our lawyer's office here in Ocean Springs getting our taxes and whatnot dealt with, and I plum forgot to bring that contract. Is there any way at all you could fax it to me here?" I asked, sounding as stupid as I possibly could. "Dr. Rivers is counting on me to get this paperwork finished, and he'd just kill me if he knew I was as absentminded as a hound behind a butcher shop."

Cindy laughed knowingly. "Oh my gosh, no problem at all, hon. My husband's like that, too. What's the fax?"

And in less than ten minutes, scrolling out of Addison's fax machine was Liam's new contract, every financial benefit in stark detail.

"Holy smokes." Addison smiled, looking over the contract. "Buford's not going to like you. He's not going to like you at all."

Together we went over her reply to Buford's motion, and I signed it. I asked her about Jack Calhoun and if I could trust him.

"Here's one thing you should know about Mr. Jack Calhoun— he's my neighbor and he's a single dad."

"That's two things."

"And he and Judge Taylor are in the same hunting club."

"That's three."

"Third time's the charm."

"I'll take what I can get."

"And Judge Taylor is going to be our judge still, right?" I asked.

"I heard he used to be a Baptist minister."

"He did, and he left because he thought they were too liberal," Addison started.

"And now he's going to be deciding on my fitness based on my scandalous, queer, sex-with-the–Virgin Mary book of poetry?"

"Let me ask you this. Was the book published when Liam met you?"

"No," I said.

"But was it published when he married you?"

"Yes."

"Was it published when you had your children?"

"Yes."

"Then it's a nonissue."

"You're sure?" I asked, feeling a rising dread.

"I'm sure."

Addison knew me as another mama at St. Alphonsus Catholic School. She knew me as the girl who sat in front of her in church at St. Paul's Episcopal, keeping three small children quiet and well-behaved. She knew me as the girl at the park every day after school, surrounded by kids. As the mama organizing the country store at the St. Al's annual fall festival fund-raiser. As the wife of the Ocean Springs Hospital's chief of staff. She knew me as everyone else in town knew me—as a wife, a mama, a nice gal, and nothing more.

"Look, I'm going to need a copy of that book," she said. "Make it several. Hardcovers, if you can get your hands on them. And you haven't worked at all during your marriage, is that right?" she asked.

"Well, I do review literary fiction and poetry for *The Times-Picayune* Sunday book review," I offered.

"You do? How much do they pay you?"

"One hundred dollars per review, and books," I said.

"That's not work, darlin', that's a hobby."

I felt like I often did at dinner parties and social outings—like the slightly ridiculous, foolish wife of an accomplished man, with delusions of becoming a "writer."

It was a long way from Sarah Lawrence and winning the Bobst Prize.

"Let me give you a bit of advice, okay?" Addison asked.

"Sure," I said, holding back inexplicable, furious tears.

"Don't ever marry a man on whose head you could set a plate and eat your supper," she ventured, smiling.

"It's a little late now," I managed, through tears.

"Second piece of advice?"

"What's that?"

"Court's going to be brutal. Wear armor."

BE SWEET

Every last person in my house, save my niece, Katie, and the boys, came to court that day. My nephew, Josh, drove me over in the rental car with Mama and Auntie Rie and a few other people in the back seat. I was moving through a fog akin to shifted night sugar—everything was thick with an otherworldly fear I'd never felt before in my life, not in the dark nights of my childhood, not when Liam had held the tip of that eight-inch butcher knife to my heart.

We crossed over the Pascagoula Bridge, and I watched the flattened marshes, devoid still of cranes. Mama kept saying every now and then, "It's going to be okay." And then, when no one answered, "Well, surely it will."

I was silent. Avery sat between me and Josh in a gathered pink peplum dress with her pink cowboy boots, her hair tied up in a matching bow. I didn't want to talk about it in the car. She and I held hands the whole way there. We'd talked about it into the night, and she'd fallen asleep in my arms. The last thing she said was, "You'd never hurt me, Mama—never, ever, never."

"Never, baby. Never. Now sleep."

I stayed up half the night, watching her eyes flutter behind the milk-blue tender skin of her lids, wondering if tomorrow would be the day they'd take her.

Never. No way. Liam had told so many lies so far, and none of them stuck. This one wouldn't either.

We drove through town. Even after the storm, the fast-food signs still stood tall, but with their plastic interiors missing. Did anyone else notice they looked like framed art of sky and clouds and, at night, stars? Did anyone else wait for birds to appear in those stark black frames again?

Finally, we drove up on the fairgrounds. In my mind, I heard carnival music of years past, pumping away in unbridled cheer. Instead of endless rows of FEMA trailers, I saw Ferris wheels and frozen horses, turning round and round on fading merry-go-rounds. I saw carnival barkers with alphabet candy necklaces tattooed around their necks and fathers with enormous stuffed mice perched on their sturdy shoulders. I smelled the sweet scent of cotton candy and saw a little girl in a maraschino cherry–print dress, standing in the middle of it all, dirty faced and lost. I heard a gun go off, and saw thin dogs the color of a hurricane race around a track in tufts of dust.

"Alice? We're here," said Josh, his hand on my shoulder.

I stepped out of the sedan, my low pumps crunching on the sandy gravel of the fairground. Cars were lining up, parking the way they pull in to a revival come a Friday afternoon when they mean to stay, folks pouring out in their finery, greeting one another, friendly but solemn, ready for the task at hand.

In one glance, I saw my friends Miss Wanda and Miss Lou, the greeters down to the Walmart; Miss Charlie Jones and Miss Sweet, Grayson's preschool teachers; Avery's first-grade teacher, Mrs. Trigiani; my girlfriends Charlotte and Deidre and Lana and

Susan and Stephanie and Alma and Jane; my priest, Ellen Gautier; Liam's former partner Dr. Stephanie Jensen; Liam's former nurses Becky and Louise; our across-the-street neighbors Huck and Misty; Tim Burr; Mac and Daddy; and my dear friend Miss Oenida, who sold beer by the can and homemade tamales out of the front window of her house on the wrong side of the tracks in downtown Ocean Springs, one of my "secret" friends whom I could never reveal to Liam.

I didn't have the heart to talk to anyone as I crossed the scabbed earth of the fairgrounds. So there I stood, in my Sunday best—a blush linen suit to the knee and white cotton blouse—in the strangling summer air rising off the rough-hewed slats of the walkway outside Jackson County Chancery Courtroom A set up in one of dozens of FEMA trailers strewn like Chicklets thrown into the dust of the Pascagoula County Fairgrounds in Gautier, Mississippi. I entered the trailer and stood on one side of the folding table, an old, rail-thin, bent-to-the-waist bailiff with silver pompadour stood on the other.

"ID, ma'am?"

"Yes, sir." I smiled, handing it to him.

"Your bag?" he asked, one brow raised.

"My bag?"

"Yes'm, I need to check it."

"Oh, yes, sir," I said, handing it over.

The bailiff unzipped the squat bag, holding his elbows high as he pulled out items, inspecting them like they were treasures from another time. He pulled out my lipstick, my reading glasses, a copy of Emily Dickinson's collected, some folded legal papers. He was taking his time.

He looked me in the eye, smiled. Paused. He remembered me from the first hearing. I had seen him catch a tear before it fell, and it gave me such an overwhelming feeling of safety and tenderness I thought I might die of gratitude.

"Ma'am?"

"Yes, sir?"

"I believe," he said, drawing it out with a wink, "ya left something in your car."

"Come again, sir?"

He leaned over the table then, his eyes the color of a South Mississippi sky right before a storm, deep blue bleeding into sulky gray. I was still in that fog of fear.

"Ma'am, you may want to head back to your vehicle before you enter the courtroom." The way he said vehicle, it rhymed with pumpernickel. He looked down at my purse, made his eyes real wide, nodded pointedly toward it.

It was then I remembered: the gun.

But my heart didn't race even then.

My heart was steeled: not stolen.

"I'll be right back; give me the keys," I told Josh, who looked at me quizzically.

When I got to the car, Addison was just stepping out of her Mini Cooper.

I slipped the gun into the glove compartment.

"Okay," she said. "So today is going to be brutal, but same deal as always. Stay completely calm, no matter what happens. They're going to say crazy things about you; they're going to portray you as depraved and insane. So even though the reaction of any normal person would be to be hysterical and wild and angry, you have to be incredibly calm. Stepford wife calm. Bizarrely calm. Patron Saint of Calm. Anything else and you'll be playing into their hands."

"No problem. Seriously, I can handle it."

I thought I saw red birds cross the sky, but I knew there weren't any. Avery waited outside the courtroom, and her pink boots had little tooled red hearts that flashed in the sunlight.

"Okay, let's go."

We walked into the courtroom, and I couldn't believe it: the tiny trailer was stuffed like a tin of sardines—standing room only.

I knew people were coming, but this was beyond the pale. Three rows of metal folding chairs lined the courtroom, and every seat was taken. Another row of people stood behind those seated, and another row still of people sat on the floor in front, and then people crammed in along both walls of the courtroom. Someone had saved a seat for me in the front row.

Liam was there. His parents stood next to him. I saw him wave at his nurses and our neighbors, wrongly assuming they were there for him.

I felt like I might throw up. I felt like I might start laughing and never stop. Tears stood at the edge of my eyes, about to fall. I tried my best to turn them into the shining confidence of a smile: happy gratitude of a mother whose community had come out in support.

Skittering at the edge of desperate: passing it off as calm.

Jack Calhoun walked by me, whispered in my ear, "Welcome to the circus, act two."

I looked to Addison, asked, "Is there a bathroom?"

She pointed with her hot-pink fountain pen to a nondescript door behind Judge Taylor's desk. I walked across the room, my shoes thumping on the hollow floor, just a few feet above the scraped earth of fairground, conspicuous.

Once inside, I looked at myself in the fake, wavy mirror above the sink. I looked stricken, hollowed out. In the last month or so, I'd lost forty pounds. First the storm hit and we'd had the oppressive heat, then Liam's increasing abuse, the weekends in New Orleans and Oshner and the threats of killing me, the lack of food with the Walmart still missing a refrigerator, now the weeks since the attack: I was whittled down to an inch of my being. I stared back at my wobbly fun house reflection in that cheetah-print scarf around my neck, and suddenly I looked like someone in a carnival attraction: THE LADY WHO COULDN'T BE KILLED.

I stood a moment, lost.

Above the toilet, there was a handwritten sign taped up: IF
YOU SPRINKLE WHEN YOU TINKLE PLEASE BE SWEET AND WIPE
THE SEAT! SIGNED, THE HONORABLE HANK "BUBBA" TAYLOR

It was written in lime-green crayon.

This is who was to decide my fate? How did I end up here? I'm
supposed to walk out of this bathroom and, in front of this room
full of people, hear myself called mentally unfit and a pornographer and an abuser and suicidal and homicidal? After I *tinkle*? If
there were a window, I might have climbed out of it, hitched back
to Ocean Springs, and left forever. But Avery was in that courtroom, and so was my fate.

And so I opened the door, took my seat, and court began.

Well, it didn't begin right away. Judge Taylor announced that
we were missing an "expert."

As if on cue, a woman appeared in the doorway at the back of
the courtroom. The alabaster morning light behind her allowed
us to see only the outline of her form: imposing. She walked with
a cane, deliberately, but with a certain joy. Liam immediately went
to her, assisting her over to her place at the table next to Buford
Cooter Garland, Esquire, and Ethel Kahn. I heard him mention
her "surgery," and he made a point to put her cane somewhere
where she could reach it easily. He was sickeningly accommodat-
ing to her, asking her if she was comfortable, if he could get her
anything, acting as if he himself were her personal physician.

Something about that seemed instantly familiar.

Ethel Kahn actually stood up when she saw Liam, embracing
him. I couldn't believe my eyes: Ethel Kahn, who was supposed
to be an impartial witness and a professional, had just hugged
Liam in open court.

When they pulled back, Liam kept a hand on her shoulder as
they gazed into each other's eyes.

Birds gathered into a great mass of wild panic and swirled
within my heart and burst out my chest like a galaxy of silver wings
into the paneled ceiling of the courtroom, circling three times

before flying out the door. My ears roared with their beating. Liam patted her kindly in the small of her back as he returned to his place holding up the east wall of Courtroom A.

The "expert" was one Dr. Colette V. Colette, a "court-appointed psychiatrist and child custody and high-conflict divorce specialist." She had a silver crown of hair that can only be described as a heavy metal beehive, a formidable rose floral dress, knee-high panty hose, hiking boots, and a cane decorated to the hilt and halfway back with Mardi Gras ribbons and bows.

"I do apologize for my taaaaardiness, Your Honor," she boomed with equal parts volume and sugar-sweet cordialness. "I've just had surgery, and I find it ever so hard to get around, you know."

"Yes, ma'am. Not a problem; we were just about to get started."

"I also apologize for my appearance. My patients love me so dearly I must wear something quite extreme to remind them that they cannot embrace me, and *this*," she said, with a grand gesture with her good arm toward her bandaged shoulder, "is the only solution that seems to work."

"Yes, ma'am, well, it's certainly original," remarked Judge Taylor, a slight blush rising in his cheeks.

The courtroom broke out in hesitant laughter.

Only then did I notice the maxi pads affixed to Dr. Colette V. Colette's bandaged shoulder. Attached to said maxi pads were just under a dozen Christmas bows and what appeared to be decoratively trimmed Post-it notes that read, I LOVE YOU, BUT DON'T HUG ME, tacked on, too.

Again, I thought, *This is the person who'll decide my fate?*

Just then, my brother's ex-wife, always a bit of a rebel, had a sneezing fit next to me. I noticed she had a large, rainbow pagan pentagram tattooed on her chest in full display. I wished I could shove her out of the courtroom. Did she think we were in America? *This is Mississippi . . .* I wanted to scream at her, *Cover yourself, girl!*

I looked over and saw Liam pointing to my brother, Gene.

Josh, who was standing closer to Liam, came over to me, whispered, "He just told Buford that Gene is your boyfriend."

Liam had cut all ties to my family many years before, and he didn't even recognize my brother.

Buford watched the exchange between me and Josh, then made an obscene gesture at me. Ashley had warned me ahead of time of his tricks. He would stop at nothing to get a reaction out of me, and I wasn't giving him the satisfaction. I looked over at Buford in his baby-blue, ill-fitting suit, his shirt straining at the buttons over his bulging belly, his black alligator boots, and flashed him my prettiest beauty queen smile.

Two can play at that game, motherfucker, even if I was disguised as a Mississippi Sunday school teacher.

But then suddenly Judge Taylor swore everyone in—the lawyers, Ethel Kahn, Dr. Colette V. Colette, Liam, me, and Avery—and we began.

All the air in the courtroom left when the single door slammed shut. A single bead of sweat, and then another, and another, and another ran from my neck, where the cheetah scarf hid the deepest scrape from my own nail where I'd pried Liam's hands off me just before losing consciousness, all the way down my spine to the waistband of my skirt, where it blossomed into a growing waistband of cold, damp fear.

"Good morning, everyone," said Judge Taylor, smiling. "Obviously, we have a very full court. We have a minor with us this morning, I believe, Miss Avery?" he said in a kind voice, the way one speaks to children. "Hello, Miss Avery."

"Hey," Avery said in a very small voice, sitting right behind me next to Mama.

"Come sit by me, Avery," Liam said, out of turn.

"No," Avery replied.

"Can we have someone take Avery out for now?" Judge Taylor asked.

Miss Charlie took Avery outside by the hand.

"What I want to do first is ascertain who is here on behalf of what party. Those who are here for Mrs. Rivers will be going in Courtroom B across the way to talk with Mr. Calhoun first, then those who are here on behalf for Dr. Rivers will follow. Can I see a show of hands from those who are here for Mrs. Rivers?"

Every hand in Courtroom A except Liam's and his parents' went up.

I didn't bother to raise mine.

"I see," said Judge Taylor.

Jack Calhoun cleared his voice loudly, coughed. I might have seen him stifle a laugh, but it could have been wishful thinking.

"And can I see a show of hands for those who are here on behalf of Dr. Rivers?"

Liam and his parents raised their hands, high.

"Okay, then, y'all wait outside. Everyone who is here to speak on Mrs. Rivers's behalf, please follow Mr. Calhoun into Courtroom B."

Like a swarm of bees abandoning a hive, all the people willing to come to court to say that what Liam and his lawyer were saying about me was a lie exited the tin can of justice and followed Jack out.

I stayed.

I testified.

My life entire depended on it.

I told them, in front of my attorney and Ethel Kahn and Dr. Colette V. Colette and Liam, about how Avery fell in the shower. I told them about how I told Liam about it. There wasn't much to tell but what I knew.

No, I didn't throw Avery out of my moving car.

No, I didn't stomp on Avery with my boots.

No, I don't want to kill Avery.

And no, I did not have consensual sex with my father willingly my entire life.

And no, my poetry collection was not autobiography; it was poetry, which is to say, fiction.

No, I did not consider it pornography.

No, I was not suicidal.

No, I was not homicidal.

No, I did not want to kill my children.

Yes, I was a Christian.

No, I did not go to my father's funeral.

The questions were so outrageous and yet I answered them calmly, with as much grace and kindness as any good Southern mother should. That's the thing about family court: there is truth to the term "courtroom drama."

I did not get emotional.

I did not cry.

I did not get mad.

I was pleasant.

I was kind.

I was loving in demeanor.

I behaved as if these were silly questions, you silly men.

I behaved as if I were happy to answer their silly questions.

I did not get mad, because anger is unbecoming of a mother.

Mothers don't get mad.

Mothers aren't negative.

Mothers don't say bad words.

My poetry? Oh, that old thing? That was in my twenties. Didn't you do silly things in your twenties? My goodness.

Yes, I was molested.

A little.

Daddy drank.

Whose daddy doesn't?

Gosh, I forgave him.

I'm a Christian.

Aren't you?

Bless his heart, poor Daddy.

I'm happy to do whatever's best for my babies.

Oh yes, I sure do want them to have a daddy.

All kids deserve a daddy.

Sure they do.

Yes, this is sad, I agree.

Yes, sir.

No, sir.

Oh, dear.

Gosh.

Me, worried?

I just want whatever's best for everyone, including Dr. Rivers.

Yes, sir.

No, sir.

Happy to.

Thank you, sir.

This is how one acts when one is filled to the brim of the brim of the deepest back corner of one's heart with fear and dread. This is how one acts when one is being questioned in a metal folding chair in a trailer courtroom when one's published poetry book is being used against you as evidence of "pornography and perversion and unfitness to raise children." This is how you act when everything you hold dear—when the babies who are made of your flesh, whose bones are your bones, whose hearts are your heart, whose sweet bodies lie next to you at night because they are still afraid their daddy will come back and finish killing you, who smell like starlight and sugar cookies and sing like birds filling blue skies in a thousand tomorrows—is being held just out of your reach, might just very well be snatched away from you, forever.

This is how you act when you'll do anything, anything at all, to hold on to the only thing in the world you want.

I stand outside while Avery testifies for almost an hour without me present, without an attorney of her own. I'll read the court transcripts later about how Judge Taylor asks her if she knows the difference between right and wrong and asks her if she's a Christian and then asks her if she goes to church and then asks her which one and then tells her about his daughter and then tells her he told his daughter how she, Avery, was coming to his court today and how his daughter asked him to give her this Jesus bear. I'll read about how she explains to the court over and over again about how she slipped in the shower and scraped her back against the Tupperware pitcher Mama uses to rinse the shampoo out of her long hair. I'll read about how she goes off in a tangent about her favorite cartoon, *Charlie and Lola*, and speaks in a British accent and no one can understand her when she's referring to a character called "Marv" and they think she's saying the color "mauve."

"So then Mauve," Avery says in her British accent.

"I'm sorry, the color mauve?" Judge Taylor will ask.

"No, Marv," Avery will correct.

"The color mauve?"

"No, Marv."

"Mauve?"

"Marv."

"Let's move on."

I'll read how Daddy took her to the emergency room and made her get x-rays but still took her swimming after at his pool. I'll read how he didn't have photos taken of her back at the ER but he made her strip naked on the dirty carpet of his condo and took photos of her with his phone. I'll read how, when asked how I punish her, she says, "Sometimes I even have to clean my room." I'll read all this and be thankful that I wasn't in the courtroom with her, as all of it would have made me think I'd be going home with her, to put this horrible day behind us once and for all and for good.

Judge Taylor calls us all back in.

"Thank you all for coming today. These situations are never easy. When serious allegations such as these are made, I am bound by law to see them through. Therefore, I'm ordering that the children be placed in the custody of Dr. Liam Rivers as of 4:00 P.M. today. I'm also ordering that Dr. Liam Rivers, Avery Macen Anderson Rivers, and Alice Mary Anderson Rivers undergo a complete psychological evaluation over the next ten days in the office of Dr. Colette V. Colette. While this evaluation is under way, Mrs. Rivers shall have no contact whatsoever with the three minor children."

I have a photo from that day: it's of the sweet three and me sitting on the stair landing just before they left. We're all trying to smile. There is an Adidas bag packed with their things. Grayson looks stricken. Avery looks exhausted, afraid. Aidan's diaper shows above his shorts. It's the first time any of them will spend the night without me.

At the bottom of the stairs, discarded, is a purple teddy bear with a white cross emblazoned on the belly.

EMPTY

The next morning, there was no reason to get out of bed. For once, I wished I had the addiction. I wished I could drink myself into oblivion, swallow a handful of pills, plunge a needle in my arm, anything that would dislodge the horrible glass shard of pain that was angled between heart and lung. I wanted to go into Avery's room and crawl under her covers, but someone was in there—someone who'd flown to fucking backassward Mississippi to my rescue, to no avail, was in there.

I'd failed.

The kids were gone.

I wanted everyone out.

I should have gone out and told everyone thank you. I was too destroyed to be polite. I'd used up a lifetime of polite in that metal folding chair the day before. At least I thought I had; I had no idea how many years of polite the battle still ahead would require.

I was about to get a Ph. fucking D. in polite.

But one by one, in the days that followed, everyone flew back to their normal lives, in normal states, where they had no-fault divorce. Where they had courtrooms. Where judges don't hand out Jesus bears. Where poetry isn't pornography. I could tell they couldn't wait to get out of Mississippi, and I couldn't blame them. I stopped pointing out, on the drive to the airport, the way the moss hanging in the oaks looked like torn lace. The way the moon hung over the low gulf, the exact same white as the sugar-spun beach. I stopped trying to convince anyone there was beauty in the place I loved so much. Because I could see the disdain in their eyes as they passed the bombed-out, post-Katrina state of the place. I knew they didn't see the empty Waffle House signs in the sky as frames of something beautiful, as possibility. One by one, they each said the same sentence to me before they left: "You have got to get out of here."

My life had become something I needed to escape.

"The court will never let me leave," I answered.

I wondered, when I'd cried myself to sleep at night, why no one ever warned me how much I'd lose by trying to leave? That's the part no one ever tells you.

People ask all the time: Why did she stay? What they don't understand is that leaving is often—maybe always—much, much worse.

There are women who don't survive the leaving.

There are tiny tombstones of tiny humans who don't survive the leaving.

Why hadn't I just taken the three crisp hundred-dollar bills Liam left on the counter the day after he attacked me, bought some bikes, and gone on with life as usual? At the very least, why hadn't I secretly saved money instead of running away? Made some kind of plan? Tricked him? Built up evidence against him? Anything but this? It seems so obvious in hindsight. But the wounded bird doesn't know to build the secret nest.

A wounded deer leaps highest? Fuck you, Emily Dickinson.

He'd told me exactly this would happen for years.

If you try to leave me, I'll destroy you.

If you try to leave me, I'll good ol' boy you into the ground.

If you try to leave me, I'll have you put away in an institution, declared insane.

If you try to leave me, you'll never see the kids again.

All of it was coming true. The children were gone. And I was about to start an intense psychological evaluation with a doctor who wore maxi pads affixed to her dress. I'd been called a pornographer, a pervert, a child abuser, suicidal, and homicidal, a murderous danger to my own children.

I stayed in bed most of the day, watching the flat, lifeless sky.

How was it that my husband had beat me nearly to death and now I was alone, in bed, while he had custody of my children and I was accused of abuse?

Maybe I am crazy.

Is this justice?

How do you leave a husband, covered from foot to crown with knife wounds and hand-shaped bruises, file for divorce, and end up the accused?

This is why people stay. This.

There was no choice but to keep fighting.

All day, I obsessively Googled *custody evaluation* and *parental alienation* and *fathers' rights* and realized that I wasn't in for a fair fight. I would have to not only defend myself and tell the truth, I'd also have to be smarter than Buford.

I hated him at least as much now as Liam.

If there was one thing I knew how to do, it was research. I read snippets of books online and tracked down e-mail addresses and phone numbers of experts. Something inside me told me this wasn't going to be an ordinary fight.

A single day without them made clear I'd never survive a life without my babies. No way, no how was I letting that happen.

PINK FLAMINGOS

AND QUANTUM

PHYSICS

I woke up and chose a nondescript outfit from my closet. Long, sand-colored linen skirt, peachy-pink T-shirt from Walmart, pair of Clarks Mary Janes. Typical mom-wear. I was going to be there for eight hours straight for psychological testing, I wanted to be comfortable. I also wanted to look as non-murderous as possible.

I drove over to Gulfport. On the road leading to Dr. Colette's office, a man stood on the outcrop with a big handmade sign that read, THE WAGES OF SIN IS A HURRICANE! REPENT, SINNERS! NO GAMBLING ON LAND! There was a great debate going on if the casinos should be rebuilt as barges, as they were before the storm, or if they should be finally allowed on land. I guess the good Christians of the Gulf Coast felt gambling wasn't so bad if they weren't doing it on God's green earth. But when multimillion-dollar casino barges were torn asunder in the storm, the fate of the city's coffers were in jeopardy if they didn't agree to change the ordinance and allow casinos landside.

I felt like I was gambling with my children. Say one wrong word, answer one question wrong, and that's it—they're gone. Addison had already warned me to "be honest, no matter what."

She'd also told me that if I lost custody, even if in error, there was little to no chance they'd reverse it back to me in the future, as the courts believed that was too much wear and tear on the children.

The stakes were high.

I pulled into a long strip mall of one-story offices in a horseshoe formation surrounding a gravelly parking lot with an Arby's in the middle. Sitting there in the car, I felt such a sense of panic and dread. How could strangers, people I don't know, who don't know me, have the entire fate of my children in their hands? What if she believed everything Liam has said about me? I'd already been to one social worker who met with me once and then decided, with Liam's help, that I was a murderous multiple personality that beat my children. That might murder my children.

It felt like the world had gone mad.

I dialed Mama.

"Mama. Am I crazy? Is it possible I'm crazy and I don't know it?"

"Hush up! Of course not. Go in there and let her see who you really are and what hogwash this is."

I stepped out of the car, walked to the office, opened the door, and went in.

In the small waiting room, the floors were linoleum, and the receptionist, Mr. Matthew P. Colette, was partitioned behind a bulletproof glass wall. Taped up next to him as he greeted me was a very large, smiling picture of President George W. Bush, signed to Dr. Colette V. Colette. He had me sign some documents and asked me to take a seat. The walls were hung with posters about drug abuse and domestic violence, and there were AA pamphlets on the end tables.

"Alice?" Dr. Colette announced my name, loud and clear and friendly from an entrance to a hall to my left. "Come on back!"

She was wearing a long skirt, a T-shirt with a flamingo appliqué, sturdy walking shoes, and was still walking with a cane. Her well-coiffed beehive was again impeccable. Stepping into her office was a sight for a panicked mama's sore eyes: every inch of shelf space and desktop and floor space was covered with pink flamingos of every kind. Carved ceramic flamingos. Cartoon plush flamingos. Blow-up plastic flamingos. Rubber dog toy flamingos. Wooden carved flamingos. Flocked holiday ornament flamingos. Big lawn flamingos. Candle flamingos. Fluffy pillow flamingos.

"Avery sure got a kick out of those."

"Oh, was Avery here?"

"She hasn't had her eval yet, but she came in with Liam's folks when they were dropping him off and picking him up."

"How did his evaluation go?"

Oh, my Lord, did I just ask that? That is the worst, most horrible way to start my day, I thought.

Dr. Colette didn't seem to mind, saying, "Well, let's just say it was interesting. Does he always dress like that?"

"Dress like . . . ?"

"He's an interesting little fellow, that's for sure. I can't even imagine the two of you married."

This is sure getting off to an interesting start. Is she trying to trick me into being inappropriate?

I felt so nervous I could hardly speak. Dr. Colette explained what we'd be doing all day and that she'd be recording everything and that there were no right or wrong answers on any of the tests and to just be honest and do the best I could.

No right or wrong, except if my answer costs me my children.

The first test was to be an IQ test.

"You ready?" Dr. Colette asked, a wry smile spreading on her wide face.

"I guess so. It's not quantum physics, right?"

"We'll see," Dr. Colette said, winked, and laughed uproariously. She pressed Record on the cassette deck on her crowded desk.

And so it began. I can't really remember most of the questions; it all passed like a blur—math questions, logic questions, reasoning questions, philosophical questions. How my IQ had anything to do with my fitness was beyond me, but at that moment it felt like I was in a race to save my children and every question was do or die. But as we got into it, I started to relax, mostly because, much to my surprise, Dr. Colette Colette was approaching it like it was Friday night game night down to the First Baptist. My answers to the language questions plum cracked up Dr. Colette Colette, and I started to feel like maybe she was going to be okay. Maybe I could trust her. When we got to the final question and I answered it, she paused, said, "Come again?"

I answered it again.

"Tell me how you got that."

I explained.

"Well, *hot damn*. That does make sense!"

It was my turn now. "Come again?"

"Alice, you just explained why Buford called you an 'evil genius'! I don't know about evil," she said, and lowering her voice to almost a whisper as if Liam and Judge Taylor were eavesdropping on the other side of the door, she continued, "but I already suspect that's a big load of bullshit. But I'm not going to be surprised at all if you're a genius. I ain't never in twenty years of practice had anyone get that question right."

"Well, uh, thank you, ma'am."

"Call me Dr. Colette; we're going to be here awhile."

She took me through a battery of tests: word matching, strange strings of questions, long lists of questions about my parenting style and skills, what I knew about Avery (apparently, she asked Liam and me the same list of questions and then planned to ask Avery and see which one of us got more of them right).

After a short bathroom break—where there was flamingo-shaped soap and flamingo-printed hand towels, my face peering back at me with a desperate pink sheen to it I barely recognized like some mama beast who'd been searching three days for her babies in the wild, half-starved and furious, whittled down to ache and deprivation—I headed back into Dr. Colette V. Colette's office.

"I forgot to take your picture!" Dr. Colette boomed.

It amazed me she still had this much energy. She held up a Polaroid camera and told me to smile. I tried to look as pleasant and motherly as I could. The camera flashed, and the photo spit out, and Dr. Colette set about waving it in the air like a fan at a Sunday late service.

"Oh, that's a nice one," she said, turning the photo toward me. I looked like I was stricken with sorrow, as if someone had just died. "Did you bring the binder?"

"Yes, ma'am."

I handed her the carefully constructed binder I'd put together in the last few days. Inside were letters from dozens of friends attesting to my fitness as a parent. There were letters from the kids' teachers, the priest at church, Sunday school teachers, relatives, the ladies from Walmart even. And at the back was a long letter from Thomas Lux, an esteemed American poet who also happened to be my mentor and teacher when I was in grad school at Sarah Lawrence College studying poetry. Tom had taken time to write about my book of poetry, my work, who I was as a person and a mother, and what poetry on the page meant. And he was very clear about why it should have no effect in the determination of my fitness as a mother. He was willing to drop everything to come and testify on my behalf as well.

When I'd called Tom and told him what was happening, he

cut me off midsentence, "Are you fucking kidding me?" he'd boomed.

"I'm not kidding."

"What do I need to do? Where do I need to be?"

"For now, just write a letter, if you can," I asked.

"I can't believe this shit! It's not the nineteen fucking fifties," Tom said. "Tell me where to send it and I'm happy to be there once you get to court."

Dr. Colette took her time reading Tom's letter, then asked if I didn't mind if she shared it with her husband.

"Well sure, of course not. But why?"

"Well, Miss Alice, we happen to be big fans of poetry."

Now, that was the last thing I expected to come out of Dr. Colette V. Colette's mouth.

"And we like to dabble in the poetry a little bit ourselves."

Well, hot damn.

"We have taken the time to read your book."

Where is this going? Please let this be good. Please let this be good.

"And frankly, we find Dr. Rivers's assessment, as well as Miss Kahn's assessment, to be complete and utter horseshit!"

There was total silence in the room.

Every pink flamingo looked at me with its one black beady eye to see what I might do.

And then, Dr. Colette V. Colette and I broke out laughing.

"Dissociative identity disorder!"

"I know!"

"She diagnosed you from a poem!"

"A single poem!"

"She got dissociating confused with a whole diagnosis!"

"Amateur hour!"

"Hack!"

"Loser!"

"Buford's babe!"

We were laughing so hard that Dr. Colette had to ask me to pass her one of the client tissues from my side of the desk. I had never been so relieved in my life. I took a deep breath and a swig of water from my water bottle, and Dr. Colette said, "But anyway, I do have to ask you about the thing."

"The thing?"

"The father thing."

"Oh."

"That's the other part of what brought us here, and honey, I'm almost embarrassed to bring it up. I read your book. I've been evaluating you all day long. I've already evaluated your husband. So, not to divulge anything, but I have learned a thing or two. However, I am obliged to address all the issues. And this is the remaining issue, so I am required to go there."

"I understand. Please. What would you like to know?"

"Your father molested you."

"Yes, yes, he did."

"Did you, as your husband alleges, have a 'lifelong consensual sexual relationship with your father'?"

"Of course not. No."

"How long did your father abuse you?"

"From when I was about three or four to about ten."

"How severe was it?"

"I would say it was mildly severe. But how do you define these things? Any sexual abuse is extreme. Was I brutally raped? No. Was it subtle inappropriateness? No."

"But it seems that you, through writing this book, have dealt with it rather well."

"Yes, I think so. It has been a shock to have it dragged up this way, considering."

"Considering?"

And that's when I started to cry.

"Because I didn't speak to my papa for nine years. Nine entire years. After my book came out, I stopped speaking to him.

Completely. No contact. I had my babies, I got married, I moved away. I moved on. I tried to heal. And then one night, one ordinary night, the phone rings in my kitchen in Mississippi, and it's Mama, and she says, 'Your daddy is dying.' So I tell Liam. And Liam, who is really better about death than any doctor I know, says, 'Don't let him pass without trying to resolve it.'"

"Wow, he said that?" asks Dr. Colette.

"Yeah," I say, "he did."

"So he encouraged it."

"Yes. So the next day, I pick up the phone. Just like that. After nine years, I pick up the phone, and I call my papa. And he answers the phone."

"And what happens then?"

"And then he doesn't die for four more years."

Dr. Colette laughs, and I laugh, too. Everyone laughs at that line. It's a funny thing, how in a hurry I was to call before his death and how he stuck around four more years. But it's what happened in those four years that is the important part.

"So what happened in that first phone call?" Dr. Colette asks.

"Right away in that first call, he admits to everything. He says he violated me and he's sorry and he wishes he could take it all back and he knows he can't and he's read my book and he's proud of me and I've made art of the pain he caused and he knows that while he hurt me I'm helping someone else and he knows he doesn't deserve my forgiveness but he's asking for it anyway."

"Wow."

"I know."

"That's pretty—"

"I know."

"And basically we had four years. Four years of making amends. And having fun, too. And he met my children. I mean, he was never alone with them, but he met them. And we became friends again. And I was able to forgive. Like, really forgive. And by the time he died, I wasn't locked in that cage anymore, that cage of shame. It was never him keeping me in the cage anyway; it was me and my anger and my shame and my inability to trust, but who gets that? Your abuser willing to make amends? And all along, Liam encouraged it. Liam helped me. Liam was there for it. And the last time I talked to my papa, he called me and he asked me if I was coming, and I was pregnant with my fourth. Fourth baby. And I told him I didn't think I could make it. Because Liam would never come to California with me. Hated my family. Didn't care that my papa was dying enough to come and help me, really. So I told him it was okay and he could go. And he hung up the phone and he did just that. He had the hospice nurse help him with a bath, he sat in his chair, and he passed away."

I forgot for a moment that Dr. Colette was evaluating me. I was telling her my most sacred story: the story of how I freed myself. And the second part of the story is how the freedom story became a story that shattered me again. I continued.

"The thing was, at that very same moment that Papa died, I miscarried that child. She died. And Liam never forgave me that. So maybe this is all his payback. But my papa? He left his body to the medical school that saved my life when I was in a scooter accident at nineteen. He told me he was going to do it before he passed. He told me: *Babe, my body for your body. Amends.* This was one of the most sacred things in my life that Liam has now dragged through so much misery mud. And for what? To make me out to be what? A whore? A pervert? What he did with this is unforgivable. But I guess I'm not supposed to say that, right? I'm not supposed to say he's unforgivable. I'm supposed to say I'll work with him to co-parent no matter what, right? But I'd be lying if I said that this, this thing with my papa, was okay. It was the ugliest thing he could think of. And that's who he is. And that's why I worry about him with my children. So, no, I don't have proof he'd do them any harm, but I do have proof of his character, and this is that proof. And if that makes me terrible, then I'm terrible. But this broke my heart."

"Miss Alice, I'm going to go ahead and mark you down an A plus for honesty. People come into these things and they bullshit me and they tell me everything they think that I want to hear. They don't dare tell me what they really think. So thanks for just being honest. That's what I need to hear: the truth. A parent willing to tell the truth is a good parent."

Avery would be evaluated the next day, and Dr. Colette would give her formal recommendation in a week.

THREE LITTLE BIRDS

The days after the psych evaluation passed by in silence. I didn't leave the house. I didn't eat, didn't watch television, didn't read, didn't listen to music. I mostly slept. I would go from room to room, crawling into each of the children's beds: first Avery's firm twin in her sky-blue room, the hot-pink walls of her bathroom giving the bedroom a constant sunset hue. Then to Grayson's little fortlike bunk, where I'd flip through his truck and train picture books mindlessly. I even crawled into Aidan's crib once, watching out the high windows for sandhill cranes that never passed now.

Aidan's first word was uttered in that crib, upon awakening from a nap: "Bird."

I said it now, aloud: "bird."

So much house and no one but me in it; I wished I could fly away.

I heard the garbage trucks come, heard the crunch and creak of mechanism crushing what I'd thrown away. I thought of all my journals, all those plain white pages covered with my wide, looping cursive, like wings. I imagined each page rising up, taking flight, escaping into the slate-gray sky.

Liam was erasing me. My history, voice, my writing, my children. Soon I'd no longer exist.

They called me crazy, and I felt that I was losing my grasp on reality. I shut the slatted wood blinds against the misty bayou sunlight. Everything fell to shade.

I must have fallen asleep. The next thing I knew, there was a horn honking insistently in the drive. I crawled from Aidan's crib, peeked out of the blinds, and saw Addison standing next to her Mini Cooper, honking the horn and looking up at the house, her hand in a salute above her eyes to shield the sun. Addison had never stopped by before. Heart racing, I ran down the stairs, out the front door, and to the drive.

"Dr. Colette made her recommendation," she announced, a stack of papers in hand.

"And?" I thought a whole flock of cranes had crowded in to my lungs at once.

" 'Dr. Rivers shows a tendency toward violence toward the vulnerable . . . ,' " she read off one of the papers.

"Oh, my God . . ."

" 'Dr. Rivers speaks of minor child Avery with profound disrespect . . .' "

"Oh, my God . . ."

" 'Dr. Rivers admits to a profound substance addiction . . .' "

"Oh, my God . . ."

" 'Dr. Rivers admits to bringing the knife from the kitchen on the night in question . . .' "

"Holy fuck . . ."

" 'It is my recommendation that Mrs. Rivers be given full physical custody of the minor children, commencing immediately . . .' "

"Addison!"

"I know! I couldn't wait to call you."

"When?"

"He'll be delivering them here in the next hour."

"Oh, my God, I can't believe it!"

"You did good, Alice. She saw through everything. She saw the truth."

"Thank God. Thank God someone saw the truth. Finally."

"Oh, and by the way? I'm sure Liam isn't thrilled your IQ came out *much* higher than his!" Addison added, throwing her head back and laughing.

"So much for 'stupid'!"

It was the first time I'd laughed in weeks.

And, as promised, Liam's parents drove up in their rental car not long after with him smashed in front between them and the three kids in back. The kids poured out of the back seat, crying, "Mama, Mama, Mama!" and ran into my arms.

Liam got out and tried to hug them goodbye, but they ignored him. He looked at me and said, "Try not to kill them."

I hoisted Grayson up on one hip, Aidan on the other, took Avery by the hand, turned our backs on him and locked the door. That night, we all piled up together in my bed and slept in a tangle like bears—content in the warmth of each other.

PAJAMARAMA

We fell back into a routine. Avery went back to first grade, Grayson to kindergarten at Magnolia Park Elementary, and Aidan to preschool at St. Alphonsus with Miss Charlie. We had simple dinners, and the kids did things they'd never been allowed before.

We had mashed potatoes and hamburgers with no buns (their choice, something they'd never had power over before) for dinner one night, and I casually passed Avery the salt shaker.

"I get to put it on myself?" she asked, eyes huge with wonder.

"Yes, ma'am."

Sometimes I let them eat on the couch and watch TV when they ate, and they thought they'd been given the keys to some wild castle of abandon. Gone were the days of the formal dinners skating around Liam's perfectionism and unpredictable rages. It was a little bit like the summer before our house was finished being built. We sold the old house before this one was finished, so Liam sent us over to a rented beach house in Gulf Shores. He'd stay in the clinic during the week and come join us every weekend. You'd think the best part of that arrangement would be the wide sugar-sand beaches of Alabama; the warm, shallow waters of the Gulf of Mexico; the way you could stand in the Gulf at sunset and a school of stingrays would slip right around you, their sleek edges skimming your skin as they passed. Instead, we lived for the quiet easiness of days without Liam. The minute he walked through that beach house door on Fridays, everything changed. Towels could not be left hung cockeyed on a ledge, a glass could not be stray in the sink, a single grain of sand on the landing could set off a rage so intense the baby would run away and hide under the coffee table.

So those days after the custody evaluation were like the beach house summer, and everything relaxed. I had to stop myself from turning boxes and cans to perfectly line up in the pantry. I took the hundreds of perfect white hand towels I usually kept folded perfectly in baskets in each of the six bathrooms, stuffed them in a black trash bag, and shoved them to the back of a hall closet. I wore my nightgown all day long.

On Friday nights, after the kids bathed and put on their pajamas, we started what we liked to call the *Pajamarama*—which was just the four of us piling up in the car in our pajamas, going down to the Sonic, and ordering ice cream sundaes and fries and people-watching and picking shapes out of stars and clouds and listening to kids' music CDs too loud in the car.

Appearing in public in our pajamas? Scandalous.

Out past bedtime on a Friday night? Unheard of.

Laughing and carrying on without a care in the world and a drunk man to manage? Heaven.

Those were the easy days, when everything seemed like it might be almost over.

The only difficult part was every other weekend, when I had to exchange the kids with Liam. He'd meet us in a Denny's parking lot, just as nasty as ever, cussing me out under his breath. I tried to ignore him completely—as if he were a ghost. The only thing strange about it was every time we exchanged the kids, he was driving a minivan.

Liam in a minivan.

Liam always had the nicest car. He never even went to a car lot to pick them out. When you're a small-town doctor in the South, you have certain perks. Liam would call up dealers in Mobile, tell them what car he was interested in, and they would deliver the latest Mercedes, BMW, Range Rover, or Porsche to our house. Just like that. He'd drive it for a weekend and decide. He'd lease them for a year at a time, then get a new one (after a year, a car had too much wear and tear for Liam's OCD standards). So to see Liam pull up in a rented minivan week after week was just odd. I figured he was trying to be a Disneyland dad.

On one of those weekends, at 2:00 A.M., I woke up with a strange feeling about the minivan. My hair stood on end, and my skin was afire. The van: something wasn't right. I just knew it. He wasn't trying to be a Disneyland dad and drive a van for the kids' sake; that wasn't in his nature. If he wanted the kids to watch movies, he'd have screens installed in his Mercedes. As my feet hit the floor, the vision of him crammed between his parents in that front seat when he'd had to bring back the kids flashed in my mind. I ran down the stairs to my study, turned on my computer, watched the screen flash on in the pale Mississippi night. The shadow of the big magnolia still standing after the storm swayed slowly across the pale-green wall behind me. The search screen connected and filled the study with a filmy light. I typed in five words:

Liam Rivers Arrest DUI Mississippi.

And there it was: He'd been arrested almost two months before for DUI with not one but six—count 'em, *six*—counts. He'd barreled through a sheriff's checkpoint, took them on a high-speed chase, ran several red lights and stop signs, and finally ran into a ditch before being arrested on scene.

I called Addison's office machine in the middle of the night, voice shaking, and read off the report from the newspaper clipping on the screen.

Hey, Addison, it's Alice. I know it's the middle of the night but well, this is going to sound crazy but I had this weird feeling because it bothered me that Liam always exchanges the kids on the weekends in this minivan because you know, he'd never be seen in one, anyway. Um, well, like I said I had a weird feeling so I Googled it and guess what? Liam Rivers, arrested, DUI, six counts, reckless driving, driving through checkpoint, driving through red light, excessive speed, resisting arrest, refusing alcohol testing. Anyway, you can read it all online, it was almost two months ago. He can't possibly have a license. He's driving the kids without a license. He knew all this during the psych evaluation and everything. I can't believe it. Call me in the morning. Can you get the arrest report? I can't believe it. Okay, call me in the morning. We need to file our own emergency motion.

Here I had been telling everyone from day one that it was dangerous for him to drive my children, and everyone—Addison, the judge, Dr. Colette, Jack Calhoun—had told me that you can't keep him from driving the children based on what he *might* do. What he *could* do. Well, now he had done and he did do, and it turned out I was right all along.

I went back to bed, heart pounding. I don't know what woke me up in the middle of the night: Mother's intuition? Grace? Whatever it was, I felt like it was about to change the entire course of my life.

Addison called me right away the next morning to tell me she was putting a motion together and requesting the arrest report. She said that since Liam didn't have any visitation scheduled until the next weekend, we should wait to get the arrest report to file the emergency motion.

I agreed.

I can't tell you how much I wanted to call Liam and tell him what a lying, reckless, minivan-renting, slimy piece of shit he was, driving the children around on a suspended license. (Clearly, the van had been so his plates wouldn't get pulled, a kind of "just in case" stopgap.) He'd been sitting in Dr. Colette's office calling me a homicidal maniac and pervert all the while failing to disclose he had lost his license. But I held my tongue. I had learned well how to hold my tongue in my marriage, and I could hold it just a little more.

Besides, I was busy with everyday life. It's funny how in the midst of total chaos, normal life just keeps rolling along. The kids had school and homework. I was chairing the "Country Store" at the St. Alphonsus fall festival. The town of Ocean Springs has a huge art festival, The Peter Anderson Festival, every year that about a hundred thousand people come to from all over the world, and St. Alphonsus has a school festival the same weekend to raise money for the school. It's a win-win, because people at the art festival have some fun things to do for their kids. There are rides and games and food and the Country Store, where we sell various homemade items—mostly holiday items but other stuff as well. If you've ever been to a Southern craft fair, you probably know exactly what I mean. For my part, I made onesies with little iron-on sayings like *got milk?* and *thunderpants* and *eat, sleep, cry, repeat.*

The morning before the fall festival, the arrest report came in. Addison called me on my cell.

"You're not going to believe this. He *was* arrested with six counts. He did, indeed, crash through the sobriety checkpoint. He actually drove through the barriers and took them on a high-speed chase."

"No! You're kidding!"

"Yes, ma'am, he did. Ran several red lights, charged with reckless endangerment, too. The best part is he ran off the road, and they had to basically pull him out of his car and drag him into the back of their squad car—he was so drunk. He *refused* all testing, *and* he was falling off the seat of the squad car asking to talk to his lawyer, *and* he was blaming it all on you!"

"On me?" I laughed.

"It actually says in the report that he says, 'This is all my ex-wife's fault.'"

"Oh, now that is rich."

"You can't make this shit up!"

"So you're going to file a motion?"

"Yes, today. I've already called Jack. You might imagine he was pretty entertained. I have my legal assistant working on the motion today. We're asking for a halt of all visitation until we can have a hearing. We will be asking that he no longer be able to transport the minor children, which will essentially put him back to a Saturday visitation in a prearranged spot. You will drop them off someplace, and he will visit with them there, and you will pick them up later. He may not take them anywhere."

"How long will it take to get a hearing?"

"Probably a few weeks—but the emergency motion will be sure to be granted. I'm also forwarding it to Dr. Colette. Both Dr. Colette and Jack will be writing recommendations to the court in the next day or two. So just go about your life and don't worry."

"Thank you, Addison."

"That's what I'm here for. See you at the festival."

"See you there."

The next morning, we woke up early and drove the five minutes downtown to get the Country Store set up before the festival started. Parking on the street was filling up fast, and the only place I could find was in front of Ethel Kahn's office. A fissure of rage snaked up my spine as I got the kids out of the car, seeing the high window of her office in the morning light, lined with her dusty collection of Russian nesting dolls.

I wondered how she lived with herself, being Buford's paid gun. Of all psychiatric disorders, dissociative identity disorder (DID) is one of the rarest and most complex to diagnose. The idea that Ethel Kahn met me once for forty minutes with all my children in the room and then she met with Liam for a month, twice a week, and they went over my book of poems and diagnosed me with DID was perhaps the most ridiculous thing I'd ever heard. Even Dr. Colette had suggested I file a complaint. A court in any other state would never have even entertained Kahn's letter of diagnosis. At least that's what I thought at the time, having still not learned the ways of family court.

I felt a strange pang in leaving my car sitting there in front of Kahn's office, but I stuffed it away, plastered on a smile, and went to start the day. It was not lost on me that the whole town knew of my personal business. Liam was, after all, chief of medicine at the hospital, as well as on the board of directors at the bank. There were plenty of people who thought I should mind my business, shut up, and be grateful for my fancy house and my three children and ask God's forgiveness for dragging my poor husband, who, yes, likes to drink a little, through the mud. I'd undoubtedly run into more than a handful of those folks today. But I'd also stocked the Country Store with my girlfriends, and I could hide out among the hair bows and chokecherry jam and baby quilts and drink lemonade and feed the kids dollar bills and know that soon, I wouldn't have to send off my three little birds to terrifying weekends any longer.

I sold through my onesies by two o'clock, and the hair bows were half out. My friend Tammy offered to go get more hair bows from her car. She'd been holding back some for her tennis team fundraiser but capitulated to the festival's market demand. Aidan, who was always starry eyed at Tammy's New Zealand accent and her wild blond golden ringlets to the waist, said, "I go? I go, Miss Tam Tam?"

She looked over at me with a cocked brow, and I said, "Sure, take him!" and watched them disappear into the crowds.

And less than thirty seconds later, I heard Tammy's voice raised, shouting, "Let him go!"

The crowd moved back immediately. You'd think someone would have rushed in to help, but people backed away like a bomb had gone off, the rings getting wider and wider as Tammy's voice rose. I couldn't see whom she was talking to from my high stool at the back of the Country Store.

"Back off, you drunk bastard! I'll call the police!"

The crowd gasped. I got off my stool and started running.

"He's a baby, and you're not allowed to take him. Fuck off, you!"

By now I could see Liam, his hand squeezing Aidan's arm, grabbing him from Tammy. Aidan was crying, being pulled the same way he was the night Liam attacked me.

"Noooooo!" My voice sounded like a bird's cry, from high, high in the sky, a screech, desperate and desolate.

When he heard my voice, Liam let go, turned, and disappeared into the crowd.

Tammy was on her phone and calling the police in an instant.

Another mom from St. Al's got in her face. "Put that away! The man just wants to see his son!"

"Oh, shut up, Christy! You don't know what you're talking about."

Both Tammy's and Christy's husbands were also doctors at Ocean Springs Hospital.

Just then, two Ocean Springs policemen walked up and asked what happened. Tammy told them, "This bastard tried to steal her baby!"

By now, the crowd had gone back to their own day. The police officers came into the Country Store and took a report.

"We'll never find him in these crowds, ma'am. We probably wouldn't arrest him anyway, as he didn't actually take the child."

"It's attempted kidnapping! Are you fucking mad?" Tammy protested. She was clearly not from these parts.

They looked at her like she was a frothing dog.

"I understand, sir," I said calmly, resigned.

"I would recommend you leave for the day, ma'am. You don't want him coming back. Go home, keep your doors locked, and call us if he comes around."

This was the level of help I was used to in this town.

I started gathering up our stuff to go.

"Mama, Daddy tried to steal Aidan!" Avery said.

"I know, baby," I said, weary. "Let's talk about it later."

People were staring.

Tammy offered to walk us to our car.

"It's okay; there's so many people out. I'm sure it will be fine."

I felt a kind of numbness sink in. I just wanted to be with my babies and go home. It felt like it would never end. No matter what I did, no matter what I discovered or what the court ordered, we would never be safe, and he would never leave us alone. We walked through the grounds of St. Alphonsus in silence. Past the upper grade classrooms, through the garden. When we came through to the front of the school, I looked across the street to see our car parked there in front of Ethel Kahn's office. At first it didn't register: Had someone left flyers on my car? Why so many?

"Mama?" Avery asked as we crossed the street, getting closer.

There was white paper all over the car. Across the windshield, on the back windshield, under the wipers, tucked into the side windows, folded into the door handles. It was like the car was covered in white feathers, a winged creature, ready to take off and fly. Some paper was flat, some folded, some had fallen in the gutters, while others skated quietly down the street toward the beach a few blocks south. I pulled the papers from the door handles and told the babies, "Get in."

Quickly gathering all the pages up from off the car, then from the gutters, then running and capturing the loose ones on the road, I ran back to the car, got in, and locked the doors.

"What are they, Mama?" asked Avery.

"Just some papers, sweetie."

They were all the same: a printed page from the journal I kept on my computer. I'd started it after Liam threw away all my handwritten journals. On each and every one, Liam had burned out or knifed out the places where his name appeared:

```
I am starting this journal on the computer today,
after weeks, months, really, of thinking about it.
I will protect it with a password and hope that
███ does not break in somehow. It is ridiculous
that I have a marriage that does not allow me the
simple act of keeping a private journal, something
that I have done my entire life, since I could
write well enough to do so - third grade, I
believe. Of course all of those journals are gone
now, decaying in some landfill. ███ read them all
and held every detail and uttering against me,
whether they were from before I met him or not. Of
course I have tremendous bitterness and resentment
that I seem not to be able to overcome. Sometimes I
am nearly able to forgive this breach, attributing
the act to his lack of impulse control, yet another
symptom of OCD. Other times, I know that I deserve
respect and privacy, and his disease does not
supercede my value as a human, as a woman, as a
soul. But I woke up this morning, about four-
thirty, with one thought being spoken inside - what
if you just went back to the person you were, the
person you are? I heard my own voice say those
words and I knew that finally my inner spirit had
given me the answer to my unhappiness, uneasyness,
in my marriage.
```

The date of the entry was the day Liam attacked me.

I drove straight to the police station.

The whole way there, I imagined that at any moment Liam would step out behind a magnolia or a cottage and shoot me in the head.

It was all I could think of—how the bullet would pierce the windshield, would go into my forehead so cleanly, how the back of my head would come off like a broken shell, the blood exploding like a wave crashing, how it would splatter the children, how the car would keep going, roll up into the lawn of First Baptist, come to a thud against the old stone façade. I thought of the way my torso would sound the horn, a long wail that would go on and on, and how many people would turn to watch in slow motion before they ran to help.

That is what fear does to you. That is what living every moment wondering if he's going to kill you does to you. That's what going from watching him try to take your baby and no one thinks it's an emergency to going to your car plastered with a page from the day he tried to kill you does to you.

It makes your death real, and you know one thing: it's coming.

But this day, you make it. To the police station. With your children. Who get cans of pop and packs of crackers and sit on a bench in the hall and you hope they'll still be there when you come out, and you go in.

And so I sat opposite the detective in a tiny square office in the police station, explaining the chain of events. The divorce, the attack, why I hadn't pressed charges because I didn't want the kids to end up in foster care.

"That was very smart; you put them first."

The officer looked up and saw how many reports I'd made when Liam had broken the restraining order.

"Pardon my French, but he don't give a fuck. You said he's a doctor?"

"Yes, he's the chief of medicine down to the hospital. He actually had me convinced that he was y'all's personal doctor, sir."

"Our doctor?"

"Yes, sir, he told me he was the doctor for Ocean Springs Police, so I could forget about calling y'all if I ever need help."

"Oh, fuck that. So the bully uses *us* to scare a woman? And you say your lawyer just filed a new motion today?"

And that's when I put it together. Ever since Liam filed that emergency motion to take the kids from me, I'd been reading up on fathers' rights tactics and I'd read enough to know that the higher the stakes, the more dangerous it is. When we filed the emergency motion, Liam knew that we knew about his DUI and had filed the motion to stop visitation.

He had nothing left to lose.

"Look, I can't tell you what to do, but—"

"Can't you? Really? Because I don't have anyone to tell me. My papa passed away. My mama's no help at all, really. I don't have any family here. I need someone to tell me what to do. I wish my papa was alive. I tell you what he'd do—he'd be buying us plane tickets and getting us on the first plane out of here. But I don't want to be charged with kidnapping. I really don't know what to do!"

"If you were my daughter, that's what I'd do. You got family out of state?"

"My mama's in California."

"Honey, get on a plane. Tonight."

"Really? What if I get in trouble? I have to ask the court."

"Call your lawyer. Tell her what happened. Call her right now."

I did. I called Addison, told her I was calling from the Ocean Springs PD and that Liam had not only just tried to kidnap Aidan at the fall festival but that he'd scared me half to death papering my car with burned-out, knifed-out pages from my journal from the day he attacked me, which seemed like he was coming back to make good on the promise he made to kill me on that day. And that I wanted to leave.

And then Addison said this: "Leave. Go. Get out. Now."

I called up Tammy and said, "We need help."

We drove to Tammy's house from the police station, spent the night, and got on a plane in the morning. We never went back to our house again. We left everything behind. As the plane took off at sunrise the next morning, rain began to fall right, slicing sideways through the sunlight.

Avery held my hand and said, "Look, Mama, it's sparkling."

PART THREE

BADLANDS

CALIFORNIA
DREAMING

It was like stepping back into my own soul.

We found a sweet house in a leafy old neighborhood. You know those helicopter scenes at the opening of *American Beauty*? All the tree-lined streets and rose gardens and walkways that inexplicably wind their way up to strange little doors in white cottages and brick or stone houses? The way old pines dipped so low against lazy old power lines hung like holiday lights with burlesque seams instead of gaudy garlands? How cats lolled on streets, not even bothering to get up and half the windows have rainbow flags and the community center has socialist community organizing meetings on Friday nights? We moved into that kind of neighborhood, and no one delivered us a layer cake and no one invited us for drinks, and, frankly, that was just fine.

I started right off teaching community college at the same South Sacramento community college where I'd started out, and I enrolled Avery and Grayson in the local public school while

Aidan lolled away his mornings at a co-op church preschool not far from our house. I remember the night before Avery and Grayson started at their new school, the secretary in the office invited us to their annual multicultural night dinner and festivities. There was a potluck with fare from all over the world and dancers and performers from indigenous California tribes, Southeast Asian lands, and African nations. Grayson smiled wryly at me, his sideways grin, and said, "We're not in Mississippi anymore."

Thank fucking God.

I saw a few old friends here and there, but I was still on high alert, watching out for Liam to show up on every corner. Mostly, I just worked and tried to get the kids settled in and acclimated to California living. The kids' teachers requested I get them to stop calling them "ma'am" and "sir" at school.

Fat chance.

Addison, of course, was successful in getting all visitation stopped. Both Jack Calhoun and Dr. Colette Colette had written stinging letters to the court not only reprimanding Liam for lying to the court about his DUI and alcoholism but for driving the kids without a license for months on end. Then Addison had filed a second motion to get official approval for me to stay in California as my permanent residence. Given what had happened— that little something about attempted kidnapping and stalking with a little hint of *maybe I'll murder you*—she seemed confident it would happen.

But I couldn't sleep at night, terrified the court would order me back to Mississippi. They could order me back. But I did have full physical custody. I was now employed; even if I was only an adjunct professor, it was a start. Just as Addison had warned me that if the kids were given to Liam after the custody evaluation they'd be unlikely to be given back, she assured me it was unlikely they'd be forced back to Mississippi after they were already settled in California.

She was right.

So I settled in. It was like I went from being a placeholder self—Mrs. Dr. Liam Rivers—to the real me—Professor Alice Anderson or, fuck it, just Alice—all at once. People could see me. Hell, I could see me. I was no longer a ghost self in a wavy trailer park funhouse mirror.

One Saturday morning, as I was dropping the sweet three off at Mama's house on my way to a comp class to teach *To Kill a Mockingbird*, I got voice mail from my friend Frank, another poet, telling me that Norman Mailer was in town and giving a talk the next day. Frank was from New York, had known the Mailer family for years, and said Norman wanted to have dinner with some "real" writers that night. Norman told Frank to invite only the best people, and Frank thought of me. I listened to the message standing in Mama's driveway.

"Should I go? I shouldn't go, right?"

Norman Mailer had been one of Papa's favorite writers, but I hadn't gone out once since I'd moved back to California. Hell, I'd not gone out since I'd filed for divorce.

"Why not?" Mama said, adding, "I can come over and watch the kids."

"You think? Why would Norman Mailer want to have dinner with me? What would I even have to say to him?"

My self-esteem was at an all-time low. I was just getting the feel of my own skin again, but I had vowed off writing for good after Liam used my poems against me in trying to take the kids away.

"Because you're the best," Mama said sweetly. Mama always said that; she'd been saying that since the first day of kindergarten.

"You're okay with watching them?"

She nodded. I told her I'd call him and tell him I'd go.

That day in class, I remember two things: one, I was lecturing on *To Kill a Mockingbird* and was on a particular high until one of my students kept motioning to me strangely—finally, I realized she was trying to tell me the side zipper on my dress was open—and two, in my excitement, I casually name-dropped to the class the fact that I just happened to be having dinner with Norman Mailer that evening, and not one of them had any idea who Norman Mailer was.

I put on a little black dress and met Frank at the steak house at the Hyatt Regency downtown. I was a little late. The hostess pointed me toward their table. I remember walking toward the table and seeing Norman first—he looked exactly like his author photo, the same silvery sleek mane of hair, the same blue smiling eyes. Frank rose with arms wide to hug me and introduce me. As I pulled back from Frank's embrace, I saw the third man at the table.

John Buffalo Mailer: the man I was about to fall in love with.

Damn it. Liam had been a fluke with me. I'd dated girls my whole life, and I wasn't about to make that mistake again. But in the back of my mind, I also knew this: *You've got an ongoing custody battle in Mississippi. No girls allowed. Not yet.*

It was fucked-up logic. But I was living under the fear of the great state of Mississippi.

Buffalo took my hand in his, kissed it, and said, "Lovely to meet you."

"Charmed, I'm sure."

"Dad, did you hear that? I think I just died."

"You're in trouble, son."

I laughed, added, "I think you're both in trouble if I'm the only 'real' writer Frank could come up with for dinner companionship."

"What's worse," Norman added, "he's counting himself as the other real writer!"

Everyone laughed, even Frank, while Norman assured him he was kidding. Then Norman looked me in the eye and said, "I hear you're a fine, fine poet, Alice."

"Yes, I did read your hearing was failing."

Buffalo and Norman laughed and told Frank, "You picked a good one."

This was the most fun I'd had in approximately ten years—other than the Pajamaramas at Sonic.

The conversation flowed easily all night. Frank pressed me to tell the story about how I'd used Norman to get out of trouble as a girl, and I did.

Once, as a sassy sixth grader, my papa was being a drunk ass when my friend was over, and I called him a motherfucker. Well, that snapped him out of his drunkenness pretty quick, and he chased us down the hall where we quickly locked ourselves in his office while he banged on the door, threatening to beat our smart-ass asses. After about twenty minutes of this banging, it came to me.

I yelled out, "Papa, I was being funny! I didn't say you were a *motherfucker*; I said you were a *muggafugga* like in Norman Mailer's book!" Well, Papa thought that was the funniest thing he ever heard, and we came out of the office and he made us Coke and rums (Cokes with a splash of rum).

The second half of dinner was mostly Frank and Norman reminiscing about New York days and Norman's run for mayor, while Buffalo and I fell into an easy, intimate conversation. It was obvious neither of us wanted it to end. But when Norman tired out and wanted to go back to his room (he had a big talk at the Crest Theatre as part of Sacramento Lectures the next day), Buffalo got up to take him. Norman's age and fragile state meant he needed someone on the road with him. With his wife of many years, Norris, sick with cancer, Buffalo, his youngest child, was in Sacramento to help. In the hall, when Buffalo embraced me to say goodbye, he whispered, "Wait out front for me; I'll come back down."

I got my car from the valet and sat with the door open, watching the stars pass slowly over the state capitol dome while cars left ribbons of light down L Street on a busy Saturday night.

Eventually, Buffalo appeared.

He was tall, rugged, handsome, with bright blue eyes, chiseled jaw, strong shoulders, wearing Levi's and boots and a T-shirt and leather jacket. He had soft lips and a heavy brow. I had no idea how old he was, but I was sure he was too young for me. His voice was low and had that East Coast prep school clip to it. He was a Mailer. I was some girl from Mississippi with three kids and a disastrous life and a book of poems from a zillion years ago. He leaned on the open door to my car and said, "Well, hey there, stranger."

From him, it didn't sound like a line.

"What are you doing?"

"What do you mean?"

"You can't be interested in me."

"Oh, I can't? And why not?"

"Well, I'm pretty sure I'm way too old for you. I'm into girls. You live in New York, and I have a terribly messy life the likes of which you don't even want to begin to know about."

"I don't care about age. I don't care about distance. And I like messy. I can fix things."

I laughed. He had to be kidding, right?

"Just give me your number, okay?"

I sighed. "Okay, but this is not happening. I mean, you're incredibly handsome and seemingly brilliant, and you smell like a forest and, well, you're tall. But yeah, not happening."

I wrote my number on a scrap of paper from my car and handed it to him.

He laughed.

"What?"

"You could have texted it to me."

"I don't text."

"Oh, my God, I think I'm falling in love."

"Shut up," I said, laughing. I shut the door and drove home. When I came home, the phone was ringing. Mama was walking out the door and the babies were sound asleep. I picked up, not imagining who would be calling so late.

"You gave me your *land*line?" said a familiar low voice.

"Why are you calling me already?"

"I've been calling you; I thought you weren't picking up your cell."

"You are insane."

"I'm persistent."

"Aren't you waking up your daddy?"

"I don't call him *Daddy*, and no, I'm lying on a table out in the hallway."

"Isn't that uncomfortable?"

"Why, yes, it is. Should I just come over?"

"Oh, God, no!"

"Seriously, can I?"

"No! I have children here!"

"But they're sleeping."

"They could wake up. They don't need any strange men in the house."

"Seriously, stop saying things that make me fall in love with you."

"Put your daddy on the phone, please."

"Stop. Are you coming to his talk tomorrow?"

"I don't know. I hadn't planned on it. I already got a babysitter tonight. And this morning while I was teaching."

"Teaching?"

"I teach community college."

"I wonder if they sell engagement rings in the lobby."

I had to laugh. It felt good to laugh. It felt good to talk to someone who was interested in me. Who found the things I loved to do—write, teach—admirable and not a threat. But Buffalo was so disarming and, yes, charming, that we ended up talking for four hours more, into the early morning hours. And I did go to Norman's talk the next day. And I went backstage for just a few minutes and kissed John Buffalo Mailer, and from that day on we talked every single day and e-mailed, and we started, slowly at first, then all at once, to fall in love.

When Addison called to say the court had agreed that Liam could come visit the children in California for six days as long as he brought his parents with him and did not drive them, I agreed to go to New York to see Buffalo.

He sent me sweet texts on my BlackBerry several times a day, trying to get me to text him back. The day before I left, he texted: *out getting a present for you.*

I texted back, my first text: *in this world / love has no color / yet how deeply / my body is stained / by yours.*

It was an Izumi Shikibu poem. Buffalo texted back: *perfect. you'll see. i love you. you are my angel.*

The next day, he met me at the gate at LaGuardia with a dozen roses and my "present": he'd tattooed my name on his arm. After only one kiss.

Truth be told, I was terrified to sleep with him. Terrified. Because as much as he'd said about age not mattering, I was thirteen years older than he was. I had had three children, including one C-section. I'd had major trauma surgery, and my body was crossed over by scars. Thankfully, we went straight from the airport to his parents' storied loft in Prospect Park. I'd already been befriended by Norris by e-mail, and we'd become fast friends. Southerners, models, writers: hell's belles. It was like coming home to a family that I belonged to. Not that I don't love my own family with all my heart and soul, but here was another family who first thing asked me about my poetry. Norman had already bought and read my book, even. I was starving for them.

And now I was seen.

We went back to Buffalo's place and the night was long and we made love and I could imagine a life here. A life of literature and love and no cruelty. I could write a thousand journals and line every wall with them if I wanted.

I spent six idyllic days in New York, making love and going to dinners out every night, meeting Norris and Norman's friends, shopping with Norris, visiting Buffalo's grandma, lazy mornings in bed with Buffalo. The Mailer family propped me up when I was sick with worry. Which was every day. They bought me presents for the three little birds. They talked about them like they were already part of the family. Norris bought them three white stuffed buffalos. Buffalo always had me put them on speaker when I spoke to them, so he could hear their voices. The time flew, even when we weren't doing much at all. There were hours on end of reading quietly, side by side. I wondered why I'd lived a life with anyone who didn't let me be who I'd always meant to be. Even far away, I felt like the kids and I were all being folded into this great family and that here we were safe. That we belonged. And that someday, I would bring them back with me. And then, just like that, it was time to be home at last.

I flew in to Sacramento, picked up my car, and went to pick up the kids at the Hyatt, the same hotel where I'd met Buffalo not too long before. They were happy to see me, but quiet. When we got home, Grayson wanted to take a bath.

Our house was an early-twenties two-story with a long, tiled bath that took a long time to fill. Grayson was a slight boy, with shoulder blades like sharp wings protruding from his pale back. He climbed in while the warm water still ran. He pushed a little bright green tugboat back and forth, silent.

"How was your week, sweet pea?"

"Okay."

"Did you do anything fun?"

"I don't know."

"Did you ride the train?"

"I don't know."

"Did you see any movies?"

"I don't know."

"How were Grandma and Big Poppa? Were they happy to see you?"

"I don't know."

I let him sit in silence then for a while, playing with the tugboat. He'd steer it near the running water, let go. It would float in the tide back to him. He'd steer it into the wake, let go, it'd float back again.

"Mama?"

"Yeah, sweetie?"

"Daddy hurt me."

Suddenly, Grayson threw up in the water, the whole bathtub turning a kind of muddy orange pink, the color of Thousand Island dressing

"Oh, baby, oh, baby," I said, pulling him out, wrapping him up in a big white towel. "What happened?"

His little body racked in sobs, he leaned over and threw up again into the tub.

"Daddy h-h-h-hurt me. He lock me out."

"Locked you out?"

He started crying again. I held him close to me, rocking him back and forth, trying to soothe him, saying, "It's okay, you're okay, baby, you're okay, it's okay, you're home safe now, you're safe, just take a deep breath. Everything's okay. Mama's here. It's okay."

When his breathing evened out, I wrapped him in another clean, dry towel. "You wanna get dressed?" He nodded and went off to his room. I waited near the door. He came out in little yellow SpongeBob pajamas. I picked him up, carried him downstairs and to the couch.

He sat down next to me and told me what happened.

"Me and Avery were sleeping by each other, and Aidan slept with Daddy. Avery kept touching me and bugging me, and I told her to stop and then she told me to stop and then I told her to stop and we was supposed to be sleeping, and then Daddy got mad. So he got out of the bed and he take me by the ear and he pull me out of bed and he drag me across the floor. Then he open the door and he kick me out and he lock me out."

"He locked you out of the room? Like in the hallway?"

"Yes."

"What did you do?"

"Cried and screamed and banged on the door."

"What did he do? What did the kids do?"

"He wouldn't let me in. The kids try to let me in, but he yell at them and wouldn't let them. Somebody finally let me in."

"So then it was over."

"Then we went to bed and we try to tell Daddy why we was fighting, and he got mad again so this time he throw me on the floor then he kick me right here on my ribs and he open the door and he kick me again real hard and I out in the hallway locked out again. It late at night."

"Oh, my gosh, baby. I'm so sorry. So sorry. What did you do?"

"I cried, but this time I decide not to bang on the door. I just walk down the hallway."

"Where were you going?"

"I was going to the elevator. I was going to go down to the lobby and ask for a key."

"Did you?"

"No, Daddy open the door and run down the hallway and grab me and throw me hard back in bed and tell me to shut up and go to sleep."

"I'm so sorry, baby. You know that's not right. Daddy should never do that to you. Never."

"Mama?"

"Yeah?"

"When I was in the hallway?"

"Yeah?"

"I was only wearing my red underpants."

I called CPS the next day, who did an investigation. Of course, Liam's parents were supposed to have been supervising the visit, but it turns out that not only did they have their own room, but it wasn't even on the same floor. And all the things

Grayson said turned out to be true. Liam was put on supervised visitation through the California courts immediately, and we had temporary jurisdiction for one year in California.

I felt a deep, soul-torn sadness that Grayson (and Avery and Aidan, too) had experienced such trauma. But surely now, in the California courts, things would go my way, and they'd be spared future trauma at the hands of their father. I often felt a wretched guilt that I had escaped from Liam's wrath, but now instead I simply put my children in his path alone—without my protection. I still e-mailed and called Dr. Colette sometimes, and she told me that having me in the picture would raise the stakes and the danger quotient exponentially and that what I was doing was the best option, but I still felt like I was throwing them into the fire while I ran and jumped into the cool lake of relief.

Visitation was changed to limited, supervised visits with Liam, and we would go on with our lives. And we were happy. We ate out, we laughed uproariously on our walks in the park, we got a puppy we named Coconut, we went on day trips. I was wildly in love with Buffalo. On some days, it seemed we might even live happily ever after.

Buffalo came to see us in Sacramento and met the kids. He brought them the stuffed buffalos Norris had bought and told them we were the Buffalo family and that someday very, very soon, everything would be very different. We walked to McKinley Park and walked around the path around the lake full of ducks and geese and two slightly evil swans, and he hoisted Aidan on his shoulders and Avery and Grayson held each of his hands and Aidan raised his fat little hands into the cherry blossoms and petals rained down on us all like a blessing.

Then I swore them to secrecy.

All we need do was keep fighting, all we need do was make it through the still-looming final trial, all we need do was make sure none of us was hurt in the meantime.

All we need do was stay alive.

"FAMILY" COURT

The thing about family court in the United States that anyone who has been through it knows is that it makes no sense. For example, if a father beats his first-grade son, locks him in his underwear in a hotel room hallway in the middle of the night, all while enraged and intoxicated, and is given supervised visitation, one would assume he would have to jump through some pretty high hoops to get unsupervised visitation back, right? Especially if he has a history of severe domestic violence (documented in the courts) against the child's mother as well as repeated DUIs and driving the minor children without a license, making false allegations, and losing custody of the minor children. That would seem a pretty steep hill to climb, wouldn't it?

The truth is, the minute that father has a CPS case opened and is ordered by the court to be supervised during his visitation, the entire goal of the court becomes not to protect the minor children but to "reunite and reunify" the minor children and the father. The goal is to "remedy" the "breach" as swiftly as possibly. The children are immediately put into counseling with the parent who has just abused them, whether they want to or not. Pity the mother who resists or protests. The abuser is also put into counseling, often with the same person who is supervising the visitations. And the supervised visitations? They are not conducted in a staid counseling office somewhere. No, the supervisor comes out on Saturday outings to the fair or the park or the zoo, all while the abuser buys the supervisor lunch or dinner or admission to the attractions. And after several weeks or months of this, the supervisor writes a recommendation to the courts. The children are observed and the supervisor comments on their "fear level." Well, what would your children's "fear level" look like at a public fair when they have a supervisor with them at all times? When they know that at 4:00 P.M. they get to go home with their mother? When they know they get to go home long before their abusive father starts in on his nightly drinking binge and the rage that soon follows? This is how abusers can go from an abusive incident to supervised visitation to unsupervised visitation in a matter of months.

I fought Liam hard in the California courts. I presented all of it. The original court documents from Liam choking me, stabbing me. Avery's testimony. Dr. Colette V. Colette's report on Liam's likelihood to abuse the children. Liam's false allegations that I abused Avery. Liam's driving the children unlicensed. The kidnapping attempt. The stalking and papering of my car. The police reports. His multiple DUIs. His mental health records in which he professed the uncontrollable urge to kill me. The CPS records from the most recent case.

The court ordered that supervised visitation be lifted, commenting that all my evidence was neither "recent nor relevant" to be a concern. The court actually admonished me for interfering between the relationship between the minor children and their father.

He was ordered, as a result of how hard I fought to protect my children, more visitation than he'd ever had before: ten consecutive days a month, every month.

Forget the history: *not recent.*

Forget the violence: *not relevant.*

Ten days a month: uninterrupted, unsupervised.

TINSELTOWN

Liam didn't give up on me, even if he was still living in Mississippi. He hired PIs to follow me and go through my trash. He contacted my landlord, an old Portuguese man who lived across the street from me, and convinced him I was a "lesbian whore" who had left my husband for another woman and stole the children and run off to California. (Eventually, the landlord evicted us, and I was too depleted and too broke to bother fighting it in court.) Now you see my reasons for avoiding dating girls. For these reasons, I kept my relationship with Buffalo secret. There were other reasons, too.

In my mind, I heard Liam's oft-repeated words: *No one but me will ever want you or put up with you.*

Buffalo was young and terribly, heartbreakingly handsome.

He had written a book, *The Big Empty*, with his father.

Buffalo was one of *People*'s Sexiest Men Alive.

Buffalo was literary, worldly, an actor, everything Liam wasn't. Those were the "good reasons" to keep him a secret.

There were "bad reasons," too: Buffalo had an open history of girls, drugs, sex, and running with criminals. One of his best friends was an international opium dealer who'd spent time in federal prison. He was the former senior editor of *High Times* magazine. Any one of those things could put my custody in danger. Sometimes I wondered what I was doing. Sometimes he did. But he'd pursued me, and it'd worked; I was in love.

Probably would have been easier to just date a nice girl.

It's what a part of me really wanted, but the great fear inside me couldn't allow. The fear of that Mississippi courtroom had a lock on my heart.

But most of our time together was spent somewhere other than my place. One Thursday, I left the kids with Mama and flew down for a long weekend to meet Buffalo, Norris, and Norman in LA, where Norman and Buffalo were giving a talk at the Disney Center. The Mailers had swiftly become my family.

A car picked me up at the airport and delivered me to a chic downtown hotel. I left my bags at the front desk, and Buffalo came down to meet me.

"Hello, my love," he said, leaning in for a kiss. Every time he kissed me, I broke open into galaxies, places I had closed down exploded into shining darkmatter of planets and stars. I never remembered being this in love with Liam. The thing about divorcing Liam was that, by the time it happened, I had been so beaten down for so many years that I no longer loved him. There was only escape, only relief, only fear and fury and the need to never be at the other end of a knife again. Heartache was never part of the equation.

With Buffalo, it was all heart. A kind of wildness.

We rode the elevator up to a penthouse room, and Norman and Norris were there at a long table with another friend, Lawrence

Schiller. Norris stood and embraced me, her thin limbs fragile as a gilded cage, her auburn hair aflame. I kissed Norman on the cheek and top of his head. Lawrence stood and shook my hand, and that's when the photographs caught my eye.

"Oh, good Lord."

Spread out across the long glass table were at least thirty glossy photos of Marilyn Monroe I'd never seen before. Most next to a pool, looking natural and luminous, happy. The world was about to see them, too.

"Who took these?" I asked, astonished.

Everyone laughed. I got the feeling they got a kick out of my cluelessness from time to time. I'd been in Mississippi a long time.

"I did, my dear," Lawrence said, "and I must say you strike a little resemblance."

"Oh, good Lord, you are too kind. These are astonishing."

"Alice, you must be wanting to freshen up before dinner," Norris said. "We're going to meet downstairs in about an hour."

"Oh, an hour? I'd better get changed!" Norris always looked exquisite, even now, when she's melted away to nearly nothing. Just last week, she'd e-mailed me photos from *British Vogue*, who'd come to take photos of her for a piece they'd done about her new book.

"It was very nice meeting you, Mr. Schiller."

"Call me Lawrence."

With that, Buffalo and I went down to our room to get ready for dinner. The room was small but luxurious, with patterned walls and heavy drapes overlooking the Pacific. The bed was high and piled with down and luxe pillows. The floor was covered in carpet so thick the only sound was the beating of the sea. There was champagne waiting on the little mirrored desk next to the bed, and two highball glasses. Buffalo poured us two glasses and pushed me down onto the bed, in my bra and panties.

I didn't bother to protest.

He bit my lip, hard, and gathered my hair at the back of my neck in his hand, looking me in the eye. "I got an e-mail today."

"You did, did you?"

"I did."

"What did it say?"

"We got the house in Carroll Gardens."

We'd put a deposit down on a big, rambling four-bedroom house the last time I was in Brooklyn.

"We did? Well, hallelujah."

"That's not the right answer."

"It's not?" I said, and I kissed him again.

"I thought you were a nice, Southern girl."

"You know I am."

"You want to live with a half-Southern, half-Jewish New Yorker in sin?" His eyes smiled at me.

All at once, things became real to me, and everything crashed in on me in pounding waves. Of course I couldn't live with him.

I couldn't live with anyone.

I couldn't be with someone like Buffalo.

I couldn't date someone with his history.

I couldn't move my children in with someone who edited *High Times*.

It was like that luxury hotel room morphed into FEMA Courtroom A in my mind in an instant.

Buffalo could see it happen.

"You're thinking about him, aren't you?"

"Yes."

"What are you scared of?"

"Everything."

"What do you want to do?"

"I don't know. I want to be with you, but I'm afraid of losing my children."

"What can we do to make sure that doesn't happen?"

"We could kill him."

Buffalo kissed me hard then, harder and harder. I thought my lip would bleed.

Finally, he stopped, leaned back, pulled something from behind the pillow under my head, a tiny black box. "Or, we could get married."

STORMÉ WEATHER

Liam's visitation progressed from ten days to ten weeks in a row that summer. I didn't think I'd survive it. Worse yet, the ten weeks were prior to the final trial date. I was sure he'd pull some kind of trick. He was to have the kids with him all summer, and I was to pick them up when I came to Mississippi for the trial.

It felt like death.

A trick.

I was in a panic.

Norris and I had a daily e-mail exchange by that time that rivaled any letter-writing exchange I'd had in days gone by; we were up to five or six e-mails back and forth a day.

Norman and Norris paid what I would have made in salary teaching adjunct classes that summer and bought me a ticket to New York. It was in many ways the best and worst summer of my life.

Buffalo had started a new gig with *BlackBook* and was busy.

We went out to Provincetown on the weekends. I spent my weekdays writing at Poets House or seeing friends.

Even after I arrived, Norris and I still e-mailed every day.

Once I discovered it, we ate nearly every night at a Cuban joint with ocean-green tiled walls and music spilling into the street. Every night, they played my favorite song, "Perhaps, Perhaps, Perhaps," and the owner would come and dance me up and down the sidewalk while I sang and Buffalo clapped and laughed. Usually, at some point, my cell would ring with my court-ordered "phone visitation" with the kids. I'd run, sprinting down the street as far as I could get, as fast as I could get there.

Liam made the kids call me on speakerphone, because he wanted to hear our conversations. My biggest fear—that he would discover not only that I was in New York and not Sacramento, and that I was with Buffalo Mailer—I couldn't let come to pass. Buffalo and I talked about it almost daily, made sure not be photographed together or mentioned online. I was, for the moment, his secret fiancée. I knew if Liam discovered I was engaged to be married to one of the Mailer clan, he'd drag it all into court.

Buffalo had written several pieces about his "experiments" with drugs. It didn't matter that I'd never smoked a joint or for that matter partook of any drugs at all: it was a storm I couldn't afford to bring to my impending final trial date back on the Mississippi coast.

So I would run to the corner, flip open the phone, and speak to the kids, upholding the farce that I was home alone in Sacramento, waiting in terror, alone, for the coming trial.

Sometimes, I admit, it gave me an inexplicable secret thrill that Liam didn't know what I was up to. And after living under his sanitary and overwhelming thumb for the last nine years, my afternoons with Norman Mailer were a balm to my very soul. It was like the old me, the real me, had reappeared. For all the years it took for Liam to erase my true identity, being embraced by the Mailers was an instant reboot. I was back: literary, fearless, funny, wild. One afternoon, Norman pulled *The Outlaw Bible of American Poetry* off the bookshelves of the Mailer apartment at the top of a Brooklyn Heights brownstone and handed it to me.

"I have this at home."

"So you're familiar with my poetry?" Norman asked, that legendary twinkle in his sharp blue eyes.

"Ummmmmm . . ." I smiled.

"Ha! It's just one poem. Read it, tell me what you think. Page 183."

I opened the book and read Norman's poem. Then I read it again, not looking up from the book. I felt like I was staring at that book for an hour.

"Well? Let's hear it! What do you think of Norman Mailer, poet?"

There was a long silence.

"You want to know what I think of Norman Mailer, poet?"

"That's what I said, isn't it?"

I took a deep breath.

"Norman Mailer. Poet. Fucking sucks."

That uproarious Norman Mailer laugh then, booming through the room.

"Thank you!" He laughed, his hand on my head now, in that tender Norman way that only his close friends and family knew.

"For telling you your poetry sucks?"

"For having the balls to be honest."

"You're welcome?" I asked, smiling.

"Well, aren't you going to ask me?"

"Ask you what?" I asked, genuinely confused.

"What I thought of your poems." He smiled.

"Oh, God," I moaned, feeling set up. "Okay, let me have it."

"Alice Anderson, poet. Fucking brilliant!"

We laughed then, and he gave me a hug and I reached up and hugged him back, my hands on his thick fleece jacket resting on the increasing frailty of his shoulders.

"You make a fine future daughter-in-law, Alice Anderson."
"Why, thank you, Mugga Fugga."

Sometimes Buffalo'd have to socialize for work and I'd tag along. One night there was a big party happening out in the Hamptons. Somehow, instead of feeling hopeful and celebratory, I felt panicked and blue. Apart from the trial, Norris was fast disappearing from cancer every day. I just didn't have it in me to celebrate. I wanted to be with friends, not in a crowd.

Although his pitch was quite enticing, I decided not to go with Buffalo to the *BlackBook* magazine party in the Hamptons. Despite the temptation of a tranquil pool and requisite sunset, despite cocktails and minor celebrities and more time with my love, I said no. I had a feeling. Sometimes my intuition is pretty damn good.

Instead I met Kate West at East of Eighth, our regular Chelsea watering hole, the basement-level bar a few steps from the Chelsea Hotel. We'd been meeting about once a week that summer. I walked through the falling light of Chelsea in a sheer white T-shirt dress, my heavy black boots stomping the pavement, weaving my quick way through the throngs of New Yorkers heading into whatever their evenings held. When I arrived, I could see through the low, golden window that Kate was already there, had already ordered our regular two pizzas from big-muscled Jimmy at the bar, already had my glass of wine ready and waiting, next to hers.

Every time I saw Kate West, I thought back to our grad school days at Sarah Lawrence, and a relief—the kind of relief you find when you recognize an instant friend, a true friend, someone who'll cut through the bullshit (especially MFA program bullshit) and just be who you need them to be, and let you be who you are—came over me. I thought back to the way she and her dad were the only ones who came to my graduation, smiling from the audience like family when mine were nowhere to be found.

So when Kate West texted me, *East of 8th tonight?* first thing that morning, despite the promise of the Hamptons *BlackBook* party, a party that was important to Buffalo, I texted back, *Yes.*

I'd been to East of Eighth so many times that summer, and every time Kate West would say, "You just missed Stormé" or "Stormé was here earlier." The pull to Stormé was stronger than a swanky party in the Hamptons. Because even though I loved John, the call to the true me sang out to me. Liam was my exception, and John was, too. Being with queer folk was who I wanted to be, and feeling like I couldn't do that was one more thing that the Mississippi courts was taking from me. It was like I was shoved in the closet all over again. Every time I heard Stormé's name, I knew I needed to meet her. That's the thing about my intuition—I don't give up on it.

When that voice tells me to wait, I wait. When the voice tells me to go, I go.

That day, the voice said one thing: *Stormé.*

And so I went. And when I descended the outdoor stairs into East of Eighth, I could see two things: one, Kate West at the bar, the glasses of wine sitting in front of her; and two, the legendary Stormé DeLarverie at the corner back end of the bar, khaki-green fisherman's hat perched askew on her head, hovered into her multipocketed jacket, a face lined with a life of pain and courage, looking quietly down into her beer.

"That's her, right?" I asked, coming in for a big Kate West hug.

"That's her, all right." She laughed. "I can't believe you finally get to meet her."

I didn't go over right away. We had a glass of wine, talked about Kate's day at the Manhattan Chamber, my afternoon shopping with my mother-in-law-to-be. We'd been out all afternoon, trying to find the perfect outfit for the final trial date, set for one week from that day. I'd followed Norris through Saks, through Macy's, through Barney's, stood mostly naked in dressing rooms with Norris's ghostly hand passing in dress after dress, most too formal, too earth-toned, too unabashedly cool. I needed something just right for the final day of trial in Jackson County Chancery Court, and even the best of New York's finest department stores had to offer didn't fit the bill.

It's not as if Norris didn't try. She did. Even though she shared the same simple Southern background as I, Norris had been in New York a very long time now.

It still amazed me every day how much she gave to me—some girl from Mississippi and Sacramento who, compared to the circles she ran in, was pretty much no one. One book of poems decades before, but she introduced me as "America's Next Great Poet!" with enough fanfare to make it seem as if it were true. I laughed it off every time she said it.

And while we shopped, she saw me as I would someday be—back to being a writer, back to owning my own life, powerful, smart, deserving of something great. I don't know if what she tried to buy for me that day would have worked in court or even made a difference, but I knew I couldn't see myself in those expensive dresses and swanky sweaters. I didn't feel worthy yet.

After shopping for some hours, we hopped in a cab, and Norris turned to me, put her hand on my cheek, smiled, said, "Hey, I have a million beautiful things. Come over, I'll pour us some wine, and we'll raid my closet."

This sounded like the best plan I'd heard in a good while.

We went back to the apartment in Brooklyn and weeded through her closet for the perfect court outfit. She was tired from the day, wasted to nearly light and bones from the cancer by then. Her wild auburn hair rose from the sharp planes of her face like fire licking at the wind, her skin so pale it was nearly translucent. She disappeared into the little galley kitchen, poured us two glasses of dark wine in big glasses, then came back and lay on her bed and watched me come out, time after time, in increasingly wrong outfits.

I mean, I started looking for things that were right, but when it became clear that Norris's clothes were too Bohemian, too ritzy, too late-era Heart meets Ladies Who Lunch, I just gave up and played an hour of dress-up.

"Yes, Your Honor, I plan to raise these children in a fine Christian home," I drawled as I emerged in a pair of tight embroidered bell-bottoms and a crocheted vest over a hippie-chic, long-sleeved golden tie-dye tissue T. She laughed.

I went back in to find something new.

"Your Honor, I meant no disrespect when I wrote that poem about Jesus and masturbation—the secret to good sex is old-time religion!" I intoned, walking slack-hipped across the room in a burnt umber velvet minidress and metallic pink cowgirl boots.

Norris doubled over on her side, laughing. "Oh, God, it's not the cancer that'll kill me, it's you!"

I went back in for more.

"I do solemnly swear that I will never ever, not ever write another poem again—at least not a naughty one, Your Honor!" I mock-shrieked in a beaded russet-hued Bob Mackie that sparkled like a sunset galaxy.

Applause, more laughter from the bedhead redhead.

Norris screamed, "More! More!" like repeated encores at a theater of the ridiculous.

"Why, Your Honor, I have no idea why anyone would even imply I'd be mixed up with that horrible, sin-soaked Mailer family and their wretched, woman-hating patriarch," I whispered in mock fury, clad only in a tiny black nightie barely covering my naked ass, where I held an open copy of The Naked and the Dead I found on a shelf as camouflage to hide my nether regions.

Norris stood up on the mattress, intoned in her best Southern patriarch judge voice, "Mrs. Dr. Liam Rivers, I now pronounce you

divorced, and please may I see you in my chambers immediately."
She leered at me, taking a finger behind the left arm of her eye-
glasses and making them bounce up and down on her face like
a couple of "hubba hubba" eyebrows coming on to a talentless
tart. She then put her hands on her heart and fell back onto the
bed in a featherlight heap. I ran back into the closet, covering my
behind, laughing hysterically, almost in tears.

Finally, in a last-ditch effort to coax more of the music of her
pure laughter, I put on one of Norman's old suits and his spare pair
of black Uggs up to my knees and tied one of his old wide ties
around my neck in a big bow, and came into the room arms out-
stretched and bellowed, in reference to Norman's daily Dove bar,
"Somebody get me a Dove bar!"

And there I found her—sound asleep, the sound of her wet
breath like the gentle Provincetown tide coming in and out, her
arms still resting on her heart. I sank down on the floor, the back
of the bed at my back, in Norman's pants both too short and too
wide, with my face in my hands.

The fear that drove me came over me then. What if I lose?
What if the kids are ordered to live with Liam in Mississippi forever? What if I'm ordered to move back to Mississippi? What if I
never get to live the life this summer had reminded me I wanted?
What if I get nothing at all? What if the judge says I can never
write about any of it? What if I lose custody altogether? What if I
lose everything?

As I sobbed silently, eyes behind my palms, I saw then in my
mind's eye the lines of Norris's many e-mails. She wrote still me
daily, even though I was in town. Besides stories of her life back in
Atkins, Arkansas, and her early days with NM (as she always
called him in correspondence), she talked to me of what-ifs I'd
never allow anyone else to utter.

How *if* I lost my children, I'd start a new life in New York.

And *if* I lost my children, I'd write a bestseller, make loads of
money, and hire the biggest shark attorney in the country.

And *if* I lost my children, she would get me a job at *The Paris Review*.

And *if* I lost my children, life would go on—tragic, lonely, glorious.

It might be all lies, but it was something.

Norris gave me the one thing I almost lost daily: hope.

From Norris, I'd entertain the terrifying idea that whatever happened was meant to be. *Besides, she'd always say, if I can hold on to Norman Mailer for thirty-odd years, surely you can hang on to your own damn children.* And anyway, she reminded me, she was in need of extra grandchildren, and she was counting on my three. She already had a closet corner full of things for the sweet three, like our future set and ready at the waiting.

I hung up all the dresses and frocks one by one, put Norman's stuff back where I found it, and quietly slipped out of the room, climbing the strange ladders of the apartment to the upper perches, where I sat looking at the river, the passing barges slow as gators in the bayou back home, cutting swaths of wake into the silent, black water.

Even though Norris made me feel safe and calm, like no matter what everything was going to be all right, that summer I existed in a near-constant state of terror. I knew anything could go wrong in Pascagoula, and when "go wrong" meant losing my children, that was a "go wrong" that inspired a torrent of frustrated tears. It's difficult to live in fear among the Mailer clan, with their wide bravado and literary inclinations, where any confession turns into a story recollected, a literary reference called up, as if life itself were a chapter of a novel, unfurling in reason and interconnection.

So I pulled up my unofficial Mailer bootstraps, climbed down the ladders, put on that white T-shirt dress and black motorcycle boots, smoothed on a gash of deep red lipstick, left Norris a note, texted Buffalo my apologies for not going with him to the Hamptons, and set out into the night.

In the dark of East of Eighth, our pizzas arrived.

Each time the door swung open, a wall of sound—taxi horns, footsteps in the metal stairs—filled the small room. The sound reminded me of the slow roar of a symphony warming up, then falling silent. Kate and I were sitting at the little ledge seating in the bar area, with our backs to the actual bar. In one of those silent moments, a voice bellowed, "West! Who's your friend?"

It was Stormé.

We walked toward her, and I extended my hand and said, "Stormé, it's such an honor to meet you."

"You brought Mississippi Coast trash to East of Eighth?" Like anyone who grew up on the Gulf Coast, Stormé could parse from my thick accent exactly where I was from. She leaned in and embraced me with strong arms, kissing me hard on the cheek. It was the first time she called me "Mississippi," the first of thousands of times I'd hear her gravelly voice intone that word with love from that night to the end of her life.

It was a slow-motion moment—an instant where fate arrives like a silent movie, showing you your shaky-framed future.

I asked Jimmy for a new beer for Stormé, on me.

"Nope, drinks for Stormé are on the house, indefinitely."

I tipped him twice the cost of a beer, and he set her a new full glass and a pizza down on the dark mahogany bar.

She was wearing the fisherman's hat, and the big army-green jacket with pockets everywhere, a ratty sweater over a worn denim snap-up shirt, baggy cargo trousers, and big black combat-style boots. Her face was lined the way my grandmother's was—the wrinkles not revealing a lifetime of smiles or furrowed brow, but crossed over like scorched earth, lined with life entire. If she were sitting at a bar in Ocean Springs dressed as she was, not a soul would guess that under that garb was a woman.

Kate had to work early, and so we all said our goodbyes and I sat back down next to Stormé.

"What's your trouble, missy?" she asked, looking me in the eye.

"How can you tell I have trouble?" I asked.

"Hey, I lived in pain most of my life; I know it when I see it. You got on that pristine white dress, but it might as well be smattered in blood, you're bleeding so much pain, Mississippi."

I was taken aback. Tears sprang to my eyes.

"Let me tell you something," she added, tapping the edge of my wineglass and nodding at Jimmy, who topped me off. "I grew up in New Orleans, that whole Southern thing," she said.

"I know."

"Oh, you know?" she teased. "You know this how?" She laughed her classic cackle, shaking her head back and forth like I'd said something she couldn't believe.

"Um, I Googled you?"

"Oh, you did, did you? What did you find?"

"I know you grew up in New Orleans. That you're mixed. That you were the only drag king touring with the Jewel Box Revue. I know you were a bouncer at several gay bars in the Village over the years, *and* I know you threw the first punch at Stonewall. And that you've lived at the Chelsea Hotel nearly forever."

"So, in other words, you don't know jack shit."

"Come again?"

"Let me tell you a few things, and you tell me if any of it sounds familiar, or if it—as they say—applies to whatever pain you're carrying around now, yeah?"

"Yeah," I said, grateful already. Comfortable. I laid my head on Stormé's shoulder for a moment there, and we just stayed like that, in a bar in Chelsea, while the world kept swirling and I found peace with a stranger at the end of a bar.

THE MARK

"Listen up, Mississippi."

Stormé wasted no time.

"When I was a little squirt in New Orleans, I had a daddy who wanted me with each damn ounce of his gin-soaked mean-as-a-snake being to be every perfect thing he thought a daughter of his shoulda been. He wanted me to be the upright Southern girl—pretty, polite, obedient, fuckin' *girlie!*"

She laughed and shook her head at the same time.

"You ever have someone in your life who don't see you? Don't recognize you for who you really are?"

"Oh yeah, sure 'nuff do." I nodded.

"And my daddy, the fact that he didn't want me to be the tomboy scrapper that I was? The dapper dan? The lezzzzzbian? The *sinner?*" she intoned in the deep New Orleans drawl of an uptown preacher. "Well, you know he saw that as a damn solid reason to whoop my ass on the regular. Anyone ever beat you senseless, Mississippi? Beat you halfway to your funeral and back?"

"Yeah." I nodded, my eyes filling.

"I mean, damn," she continued, "I wasn't ever going to be a sweet, Southern, pretty girl. I mean, I coulda. I could play any part anyone wants me to. But I couldn't be that on the one hand and be true to myself on the other, and I ain't got a third hand. And I sure as shit wasn't going to grow up and get me a husband. If he wasn't so good at connecting his fist to my face, I'd say my daddy saw me as a ghost. Invisible. Y'ever feel like that?"

"Erased, that's how I feel," I confessed. "Like the real me is wiped away and some unreasonable facsimile is standing in my place. I'm not a poet, I'm not a writer, not a person who loves people, knows how to sing, loves to laugh. To dance. That girl got pinned up to a board in the shed a long-ass time ago. In her place? A maid, a wife, a mama, a fuckin' ghost without a past. And really, without a future. He told me every day, 'You're fat. You're stupid. You're ugly.'"

"It's like a waking death, ain't it?" Stormé said, placing her gnarled hand on my knee.

"It is," I squeaked out.

"How'd he hurt you?"

"It was just the one night," I whispered through tears I willed not to fall.

"One night's enough."

"That's true. I left the next day, for good."

"Good on you, Mississippi. But it's never just one night—I bet you had half an eternity of leading on to just the once. But you left? Bet that chapped his pussy hide! So why are you still so scared? I could smell your fear across the room."

"I have to go to court next week—the final date of my long-ass, dragged-out Mississippi divorce trial." I sighed, resigned.

We had fallen into conversation the way two people from the

same somewhere else plunked down in a foreign city are likely to do.

"*In Mississippi?*" she bellowed.

I nodded.

"Well, *fuck!* No wonder you scared, girl!"

"They used my book against me, my poems. They said I had a 'lifelong consensual sexual relationship' with my own now-dead Papa. They're trying to take my kids away."

"Awwww, *hell* no! We ain't gonna let that happen, Mississippi. Ain't no backwoods, backward, religious-ruled court going to steal your own damn children out from under you."

"The judge used to be a Baptist minister."

"Nope."

"My ex has a nasty attorney who calls me 'the Black Widow' and says my ex never laid a finger on me."

"Nope."

"That I left a choker of hand-shaped bruises around my own neck."

"Nope."

"That I threw myself down the stairs."

"Nope."

"That I took the butcher knife in hand and scraped and punctured my own chest."

"Holy *fucking* nope!" Stormé slammed her fist down on the bar then, hard. "We're getting you out, Mississippi. I'm going to help you, and you're going to win."

"You are?" I asked. "You barely know me. Why would you help me?"

"Because you and I? We're the same breed, we got the mark. We recognize our own kind, and we don't let each other slip through the damn tragedy cracks of life."

I sat there nodding, big fat tears rolling down my cheeks. Jimmy topped my glass, and Stormé fished out and handed me an old-fashioned hankie from one of her pockets.

"When's court?"

"Next week."

"You ready?"

"I guess so, I mean, mostly."

"How're you not ready? You got an attorney, right?"

"It's not that. It's actually sort of stupid."

"Just tell me; I'll help you."

"I don't know what to wear."

"That's not stupid; that's wardrobe, baby."

"And I've been in New York all summer being the real me, and I'm not sure I can go back and play Sunday School teacher, perfect, June Cleaver mom again. I mean, look at me! I am the scandalous girl they said I am. I write sexy poems, I'm engaged to a man the court would not approve of. Honestly, I don't know why I'm even engaged to a man."

"Yeah, I was going to . . . but that's another story for another day, girl."

"Fucking Mississippi."

"I know. But I'm all the bad things they say I am. I'm not allowed both. I can't have my sweet three and and have this wild, literary life, too. I can't be me. Nobody gets both. Or at least not me."

That was it: that was the truth of all the self-hatred that had been stored up in me for the last nine years.

"Oh, hush that nonsense, Mississippi. You can worry about all the rest later. For now? Here's what you're going to do. You're going to get the perfect outfit."

"I already tried that."

"Not with my help you didn't."

"You're going to help me get the perfect outfit?" I asked, skeptical.

"Damn straight I am! You're going to pick me up at the hotel first thing tomorrow morning, and we going shopping, girl."

"Okay." I wiped my tears from my cheeks with her hankie.

"And you're going to wear whatever I tell you, and then you're going to behave exactly the way I tell you in court."

I laughed. "Here I thought I was done with people telling me what to do."

"Here's the thing, Mississippi. I ain't trying to boss ya. I'm tryna help ya. And I ain't going to let you lose everything you hold dear. You're going to go into that final trial date in drag."

"*Drag?*" I blurted out, too loud. Every head in the place turned to look at the loudmouthed Southern girl, assuming all the wrong things. For a moment, I thought Stormé was either drunk or out of her damn mind.

"Yes, girl, drag. Like you said, I was the only drag king with the Jewel Box, right?"

"Right?" I said, still not getting it.

"Well, you gonna go into court next week in another kind of drag. You gonna go as the most upright, pretty, perfectly Southern Republican mama they ever fuckin' seen. And you gonna play that part like you know how to play it, the best you've ever played it."

Suddenly, it made sense. I could do that. I could dress the part and play the part. And I could fucking win. I knew it like I knew my own heart. Stormé walked me out, and we walked arm in arm to the door of the Chelsea, and she gave me a big, dry smack right on the kisser.

I went to the curb and hailed a cab. When we were crossing the Brooklyn Bridge, I texted Buffalo.

i'm on the bridge, be home soon. met and kissed the most bad-ass girl in nyc tonight. how was your party?

Buffalo texted back.

wtf? i hope you're kidding! you know i don't share. party was boring.

When I got home to Carroll Gardens, he buzzed me in, and we stayed up half the night talking about his party and my night with Stormé.

Buffalo said, "You gotta write her story someday. How do I not even know her name?"

I loved how whenever I told a story, Buffalo told me I should write a book about it, like I had a lifetime of books to write in my future. I fell asleep in his arms, thinking about that book, about Stormé, feeling less like a wounded animal and more like the luckiest girl on the planet.

The next morning, I took the subway back into town, met Stormé in the lobby of the Chelsea, and we walked arm and arm all the way down to the Banana Republic in Soho.

"Banana Republic? You sure?" I asked.

"Girl, you gotta look right, not rich. You gotta look perfectly middle of the damn road. Like you went to the mall in Metairie."

When we got there, she bossed me to get in the dressing room and get undressed. Five minutes later, she passed a cream-colored taffeta suit with a straight, over-the-knee skirt and a three-quarter puffed-sleeve matching jacket, along with a little pure white silk shell. It fit, and made me feel like a blond Jackie O, with a Southern lady going to Easter early service twist.

I came out and stood in the three-way mirror with Stormé behind me, smiling.

"What'd I tell ya, Mississippi? The magic of drag."

We walked all the way back up to Chelsea arm and arm, reminiscing about New Orleans the way only two Southerners in New York can. Stormé told me about her days as a girl in the Quarter. She asked, "There must have been some good times over there for you, too, huh?"

"After the storm, we'd go over to the Quarter just to get away from all the destruction, you know?"

"Yeah, I do; it was pretty untouched. Still had some musicians and restaurants, too."

"Exactly. Of course, Liam would abandon us to get drunk, but me and the kids had some sweet times."

There was a ragtag Tremé pickup band that would play in Jackson Square in the Quarter every weekend, busking tips from tourists. One weekend, one of the hundreds we spent living our new good life with babies in tow, the band started to play my favorite song, and I—with big girl Avery on my hip—commenced to sing along.

"C'mon up here, darlin', and sing!" called the trumpet player.

I didn't need to be asked twice.

I stepped up to the mic and sang with every ounce of my wounded soul, "*Some bright morning when this life is over, I'll fly away. To that home on God's celestial shore, I'll fly away.*"

It was about four weeks after Katrina, and we'd escaped to the French Quarter for the relief of an air-conditioned hotel room, hot gumbo in bowls, strong drinks, and a life away from the destruction that was Ocean Springs.

"*When the shadows of this life have gone, I'll fly away. Like a bird from these prison walls I'll fly, I'll fly away.*"

After that, every time the band saw me coming with a kid on my hip, they'd just quit full stop whatever song they were on and break into "I'll Fly Away." And weekend after weekend, as the days after Katrina grew long, I'd sing that song again and again, wishing I really could fly away.

HANDGUNS, HARD-ONS, AND THE HEADLESS HORSEMEN

The day arrived for the final trial. I flew into Gulfport the night before, the spare lights of the coast a stark contrast to the bright lights of New York. I checked in to a depressing residence near the courthouse. Long gone were the FEMA trailers in rows on the fairgrounds. Now a brick courthouse with white columns stood in downtown Pascagoula. Everyone kept mentioning what a fine building it was, but to my eyes, everything looked miniature and insignificant. I could have stayed with friends, but I found myself wanting to be alone. I felt like Ocean Springs was no longer my home. I just wanted to go to court, get it over with, get my babies, and get out.

Morning came quickly. I woke, took a long shower in the dark, and put on my drag. I looked in the full-length mirror attached to the bathroom door and tried to see what the people in court would see: blond, Southern, upright, sweet, motherly. Buffalo texted me: *you got this. we don't need him or his money. after today we are free.*

Buffalo and Norris and Norman had all cautioned me against fighting too hard. They knew what fighting had cost me in court in the past. All that mattered was keeping custody, getting divorced, and being free to live outside of Mississippi, away from Liam.

I walked over the courthouse. Lana and Tammy were already there, waiting on a bench outside the courtroom.

"Addison's inside," Tammy said, adding, "Is Dr. Colette coming? Hopefully no maxi pads today!" We laughed and they both stood up and hugged me.

It wouldn't be the huge crowd of that one, terrible hearing almost a year before, but I was lucky to have a group of people who were willing to testify for me. Tim Burr would be here, and a group of my closest friends, and the kids' teachers. Jack Calhoun walked by and winked at me. "Lookin' good, California," he said quietly.

Right on his heels, Liam came in with his new attorney. Buford had fired him when his DUI came to light. Buford was a shark, but there was one thing he would not tolerate and that was a liar. And Liam made Buford look like a fool. So Liam got fired.

I'll never forget when Addison let me know. She'd called me up and as soon as I answered, she said, "Buford fired him."

"Come again?"

"He fired him."

"I didn't know you could get fired by your own lawyer."

"Well, you can. I mean, that's what Buford calls it. He's just removing himself from the case. After all his nastiness, he has this weird moral high ground and claims to refuse to work for clients who lie to him, so Liam has to get a new attorney."

"This has to be good news, right?"

"Right."

I didn't know much about Liam's new attorney, but he looked

to be at least a normal human being in comparison to Buford Cooter Garland—no baby-blue suit, no black alligator boots, no swollen red face.

Just then, Addison popped out of the courtroom wearing a black suit, strappy silver high-heeled sandals, her hair a copper blond that set off her eyes.

"Wow, you look great," she said to me. I knew I looked very different to everyone. It was like I went away and brought the real me back to town.

"Thanks, Addison; you, too. Are we starting?"

"Judge Taylor is about to announce the day's docket. Do you want to come in?"

"Sure." I picked up my handbag and walked in. The formal courtroom put me at ease and made me more nervous at once. No more FEMA trailer courtroom.

Judge Taylor called the court to order and went over some business. It was all a blur to me. The courtroom was full of people from various dockets. Addison addressed the court, pointing out that I had flown in from out of town and requesting that our case thus be given priority to be addressed today. She didn't want us pushed back to another day. Judge Taylor agreed and said he'd like to tackle one simple divorce ahead of us that involved no children or property and that we'd start our case immediately following. Addison signaled us to sit tight. She leaned and whispered, "Dr. Colette isn't here yet anyway." I nodded.

The other case got off to what seemed like an easy start but quickly devolved into a huge battle over custody of a talking parrot. The lawyers argued, the plaintiff and defendant cussed and spoke out of turn, and finally, when the defendant screamed out, "She taught him to call me 'Fucking dickhead'!" Judge Taylor had had enough.

He banged his gavel on his stand. "Order! Order! We will recess this case while the parties meet with their attorneys in conference regarding custody arrangements of the bird. I would like to advise the parties that I have a case involving actual minor children, and I will *not* waste time listening to y'all bicker and complain about a talking bird. Is that understood?"

Both parties agreed, and all involved left the courtroom. Addison and I and Liam and his attorney came forward to the plaintiff and defendant tables, and Jack Calhoun approached Judge Taylor with some documents, stopping to give the court reporter copies.

"How'd you do at camp this weekend, Bubba?" Jack asked Judge Taylor.

"Pretty good, pretty good. You?"

"Fantastic. Shot two. Set for fall. Saw you got a new firearm."

"Sure did. It's a looker, too, pretty nice piece."

There I sat, worrying about losing three vital pieces of my heart, and they were talking hunting.

They might as well have shot me on the spot.

There was a little more discussion, and it was discovered that Dr. Colette was on her way. Addison said we'd get started shortly.

I went to the restroom, fixed my lipstick.

Back out in the hall, I texted Buffalo: *about to start, terrified.*

Buffalo texted back: *we are strong, it's almost over. we will be the buffalo family and he will not be able to touch us. he has no idea what he's up against.*

Many times, the Mailers had told me that if I just got out of Mississippi with custody of the kids, got to New York, and established residency, we'd get one of their many attorney friends to decimate Liam the next time he tried to cross me. It felt good to have their collective power secretly behind me on this final day of battle.

I still believed this was the final day.

Eventually, court began. Everyone had to take the stand: me, Liam, Tammy, Lana. Everything that happened in the last year was rehashed. The original attack, the abuse allegation against Avery, the DUI, the kidnap attempt at the fall festival, my departure to California, the abuse of Grayson in the hotel. I kept expecting them to spring Buffalo on me, but they never did.

When they put Tammy on the stand, they asked her what Liam's demeanor was that day at the fall festival.

"Creepy!"

"Can you be more specific?" Liam's attorney asked.

"Just creepy. Look at him," Tammy said, her New Zealand accent stronger than ever, pointing at him sitting across from her. "Look at him right now. Look at his pants! I can't tell if that's a handgun or a hard-on!"

The courtroom burst out in laughter.

Judge Taylor banged his gavel and asked for order.

Jack Calhoun looked at me, and I, holding up three fingers casually next to my skirt, mouthed the words, *Circus, act three.*

He smiled.

They let Tammy step down and called Dr. Colette. Liam's attorney didn't want to talk about Dr. Colette's report or the letter she'd written after his DUI and deceit had been discovered, of course. He wanted to talk about my poetry. About "the masturbation Christianity" in my poetry. About the prostitutes in my poetry. About sexual abuse in my poetry. Dr. Colette V. Colette had already made clear to me how she felt about this line of thought, how small-minded and backward she thought it was. Soon enough, she lost her patience.

"Look, the headless horseman!" she bellowed, her Southern accent drawling the words as she pointed a finger to the back door of the courtroom. So convincing was she that the courtroom entire turned and looked toward the back door.

"Excuse me, Dr. Colette?" Liam's attorney inquired.

"You're talking to me about a book of literature as if it's a personal diary, as if it's the truth. Do you not know the difference between imagination and truth, sir?"

Liam's attorney stood silent in his tracks for a moment.

Dr. Colette continued, "Mrs. Rivers is a writer. We tend to

grow them here in the great state of Mississippi. You may have heard of one or two. If Mrs. Rivers is not fit to be a mother because she wrote some poetry, then there are a great many people in this great state whose children y'all better be ready to go round up and collect. Furthermore, Dr. Rivers married her when she'd already published this book, which, I might add, the very reputable publishing house of New York University Press saw fit to print. Now, if you'd like to ask me about how Dr. Rivers is addicted to alcohol or how he falsely accused Mrs. Rivers of child abuse or he lied during his psychological evaluation or he failed his evaluation miserably or how I recommended Mrs. Rivers receive sole physical custody of the minor children, I'd be happy to answer those questions. I am not, however, prepared to entertain questions regarding how a work of literature affects one's fitness to be a parent, because the two have no correlation whatsoever except that perhaps being a writer makes Mrs. Rivers a more sensitive and insightful parent."

Liam's attorney had no further questions.

After that, there were very few remaining issues. Liam wanted his paintings back, and Judge Taylor allowed him, because they were a gift, to purchase them from me at some cost. Judge Taylor divided the marital assets (what was in the bank) evenly. The trickier part was investments, commercial properties, and the like. It became clear that these negotiations would require several more days of trial. I texted Buffalo.

Buffalo texted back: *give him what he wants. give him everything. he can keep his dirty money. we don't need it. we'll create our own life. bring the kids and come home.*

And at the end of the day, that's exactly what I did. I gave him all the things that were important to him: money, his paintings of me, the house, the commercial properties, the cars, investments, the clinic I'd built him.

And I walked away with only this: sole physical custody of the sweet three, and my freedom.

In a terribly inconvenient twist, Liam negotiated, in a last show of power since the children would continue to live on the other side of the country from him, for the last two weeks of summer until school started. I signed the final divorce papers, booked a new flight back to New York, and went back to my Buffalo and my beloved Mailers.

THINGS LOST

I stood at the luggage round for a good twenty minutes at LaGuardia, wondering where Buffalo was before I started to entertain the notion: maybe he wasn't coming. Just then, my matching black suitcases with the pink leather trim came out, landing with a thud in front of me. Suddenly, I wished I could chuck my stupid suitcases in the dumpster. I fished my phone out of my handbag and dialed Buffalo. No answer.

Dragging my bags behind me, I made my way out to the taxi line. Maybe something went wrong. I texted Norris: *hey, beautiful. i'm back. no buffalo at the airport. is everything okay? love you.*

Norris replied: *love you sweet girl. i think buffalo will text you soon.*

The taxi line was long, and the night was hot and sticky. Finally, I got a cab and got inside.

"Where to, honey?"

"Um, Carroll Gardens, I guess."

"Address?"

"Can you just go in that direction for a bit first, please?"

I was getting worried. Buffalo always met me at the airport. Where was he?

Oh. Maybe they were planning a surprise.

A party.

A celebration!

That must be it.

I texted Norris again: *no word from the buffalo, can i swing by there and see you on my way home? tales to tell.*

There was a long pause before she replied.

I imagined a great panic in the Mailer apartment, great arguments and discussion about game plans, and shifting of champagne bottles popping ahead of time. I leaned my head back on the taxi seat, letting the lights of Brooklyn wash over me, finally relaxing into the realization that I'd finally endured the final trial day and won. Even though they weren't with me now and it didn't quite yet seem real, I had won full custody and nothing could stop me now. Sure, I'd given up security and the future was unknown, but I would build a new life. Anything was possible. I had a whole new family and a man who loved me at my side. And in two weeks I would pick up the sweet three, and happily ever after would begin at last.

Just then my text chimed.

Norris: *i don't think so, love.*

My heart dropped.

The text chimed again.

Buffalo: *meet me the cuban place.*

Okay, settle down now, crazy girl. You've been in Mississippi two days entire and you've lost your mind. Poor Norris is probably not feeling well, Buffalo worked late, and you're expecting their whole lives to revolve around your silly little Mississippi trial. The disaster's over. Relax.

I gave the cab driver the address of the Cuban place on Court Street and closed my eyes until we arrived.

Buffalo came out to meet my cab, paid the fare, took my bags out of the trunk, and took and stored them behind the bar. He had a table on the street already, and two beers and something for us to munch on while we waited for our meal. We'd been here so many times he already knew what I loved.

The walls were lined with cool green tile the color of old 7UP bottles, and almost every table was filled with people enjoying the summer evening. The sound of "Perhaps, Perhaps, Perhaps" wafted out over the tables and into the street once again, as if on cue.

Buffalo took my hand in his, absently turning my engagement ring the way he always did, and said, "Here's to you, angel, you did it."

We clinked bottles of Red Stripe and pulled long drinks of the cold, cold beer.

"Now are you going to devote your life to making sure this doesn't happen to other women?"

"I'm not sure about that."

"Are you fucking kidding me?"

The tone of his question took me aback.

"Well, you know me; I'm an activist at heart. Of course I want to make a difference. The family courts are broken at best, abusive by nature. But before that, I need to build a career and raise my children and write again and, hell, make some wedding plans!"

It was then I saw the clouds pass over his eyes.

"That's why I wanted to meet you here."

From the moment I'd left the court the day before to this moment, I'd been filled with a victory song. Suddenly, it all went silent.

"I didn't think you'd be strong enough. I mean, it wouldn't have been fair to tell you before the trial. I wanted to tell you after the trial—I knew you'd win. I have already taken my stuff and gone to Provincetown for the rest of the summer. You can stay in the apartment until it's time to get the kids."

"You're saying we're over?"

"Yes."

"Why today? Just yesterday you told me to give him everything. I gave up alimony, all the property, all the investments, you *let* me give it all away. You *told* me to give it all away. And you *knew* you were going to dump me?"

"You don't need it. You will create a new life without his blood money."

"Why? Why did you do this to me?"

"It's not *to* you, it's *for* you."

"*For* me? For me how?"

"I'm a danger to you. My history, my past, and the future I want puts you and the custody of your children in jeopardy. What if I want to do drugs? What if I want to write about it?"

"How about you decide not to for the sake of me and my children?"

"I can't live a life with boundaries set by Liam."

"Not for me?"

"Not for anyone."

With that, he walked out of the restaurant, never looking back.

I went back to Buffalo's place, stunned. I sobbed, cried, screamed. I was outraged. I lost my mind. I went through his apartment, searching for some other reason. Maybe he'd found someone else? I could accept any other reason except that Liam had stolen one more thing from me. I looked through Buffalo's papers. I searched through his bathroom for a stray hair or scrap of tissue with lipstick in the waste bin. Sobbing, drinking wine we'd bought before I left for the "celebration" upon my return, I tore the place apart. Eventually, I found his journals. I sat on the floor and read them all. I learned almost nothing new. I read how much he adored his parents mostly, which I already knew. I learned that he'd proposed and dumped several people before me. When I got to the end of his journals, I sat on the floor, sobbing, realizing that I had become the thing I hated.

I was the person who read the journals.

I was Liam.

Was I?

Where was my victory song?

Had I learned nothing?

Sitting there on the floor, I felt like I'd lost the dignity I'd come in on. Not only had I lowered myself to Liam's level, but I'd become the stupid girl once again, putting my needs aside in order to depend on a man.

I was so desperate to find an answer—any answer. Between moments of utter despair, I had moments of fury at how Buffalo had done it. Part of me knew he was right, that it would have been dangerous to dump me before the trial, but it certainly was reckless to encourage me to give away everything when he knew he had no intention of staying with me.

Then again, I was the idiot who didn't care for myself.

The self-hate was torrential.

I called Norris, sobbing, asking her why and how long she'd known. She was very kind, bewildered. She wished he'd made another decision. She, too, was losing a dream. She was sure we would marry and become a family. She knew she was dying. She wanted to know her Buffalo was married and had a wife and children before she departed. Instead, he seemed to be self-destructing. But she knew she couldn't change his mind. Although he asked her not to talk to me, we stayed on the phone for hours in those two weeks.

It was torture to be stuck there in his place, but what could I do? I had to pick up the kids in Mississippi in two weeks. No use flying home only to fly all the way back to Mississippi. When I could bring myself to get out, I'd go drink with Stormé at East of Eighth. One morning, Norris showed up and told me to pack an overnight bag. She took me by the hand, and we went out to see Norman, who'd retreated to Ptown for the summer to write.

When we came in, Norman was sitting at the bar overlooking

the beach. I didn't ask where Buffalo was. Norman looked at me and said, "My dear, you were too damn smart for him anyway." The kindness of that statement made me well up, and he laughed and said, "Knock off the tears." We had drinks, then went out to dinner. The next day, Norris took me shopping, loading me up on handbags and dresses and jewelry and all kinds of things I'd never buy for myself.

Before we headed back, I went up to the top floor to say good-bye to Norman. He had put on a clean white shirt. He sat at the end of his bed. I sat down next to him. We both knew it would be the last time I'd see him.

"You have safe travels, Alice."

"You, too, Norman." He knew I didn't mean on the ferry. "Thank you for letting me be a part of your family. It has meant everything to me."

"You're going to make it, you know that? You're the real thing."

"I don't know about that, but I sure am going to miss you."

"You're beautiful."

"No, *you're* beautiful."

"Well, I guess you're right," he said with a smile.

I gave him a kiss on the head as I stood to leave. It was the last time I saw him, sitting on the edge of his bed, in pale-blue cotton boxer shorts and a crisp white dress shirt, gazing out to sea.

EVERY SECOND

SATURDAY

I stopped off in Mississippi just long enough to pick up the kids (I never even left the airport) and hop the next plane to California. I walked from my gate to the walkway to meet them, and the floodgates of the rest of my life opened up. The whole world felt right again with my sweet three at my side.

Even so, my heart was shattered. I never shed a single tear at losing Liam; I had long since fallen out of love. But I was broken, ripped wide-open raw with pain at Buffalo's brutal betrayal. I, of course, saw fucking Buffalos at every turn, every song reminded me of him. I cried myself to sleep at night after the kids were fast asleep. I sent him a string of humiliatingly desperate e-mails. Begging, then cussing him out. Norris told me to bill him for everything I'd given away in the divorce, and I did.

Cruelly, he'd write me back that maybe it wasn't forever, this split.

As if I'd ever take him back.

The only way I knew to ease my wounded heart was to soothe it with the passion of new lovers. The truth was, until Liam, I was never much interested in men. Just like Stormé, I grew up in a household with a father figure who left no room but his way, and his way did not include the homosexual way. So although my first love was the redheaded girl who sat in front of me in math, and my first girlfriend was the trumpet player in the high school band, when it came time to have children and marry, I talked myself into Liam. Liam was nonbinary before we called it that, as close to "girl" as a boy could get. After Liam, Buffalo sort of steamrolled me into a romance with him, and I was so aching for love and so afraid of the Mississippi courts that by then I went willingly. And I did love Buffalo—I loved him with a wild, passionate abandon. But now that I had no court battle, no Southern Baptist Mississippi judge looking over my shoulder, I could finally just be whom I wanted to be with, and who I wanted to be with was women.

Every second Saturday in Sacramento, there are open art studios in the city's midtown art district. My friends, who witnessed my total devastation, took it upon themselves to help me secure a date for each Second Saturday.

I wasn't looking for love; I was looking for distraction.

I was reckless. I both wanted to get involved quickly and not get attached. I tended to come up with nicknames for each date. "The Badass Banker" was an Indian teller I met at my local branch who drove a Prius and had a lot of piercings.

"Crème Brûlée" was a chef I met at an event who liked to feed me during sex.

"Violence, Esquire" was a defense attorney with a masochistic exhibitionist side who liked to text me very bad things from court.

"Professor Fuck" was an English professor who gave all her students As on their papers and liked to drink whiskey and write poetry all over my body in Sharpie.

I would do almost anything to keep me from thinking about Buffalo, so raw was my heart.

I don't remember who it was who introduced me to "Quantum Starlight." All I know is that when someone introduces you to a trans Italian quantum physicist who was the only girl in a family of brothers named after *The Brothers Karamazov* (her name was Alyosha), you pay attention. She was doing her postdoc at UCLA, and we talked online late into the night and on the phone for months before I finally agreed to go down to meet her.

My friend Dana agreed I could stay with her in her loft downtown. I drove down and bunked out with Dana, catching up with each other on everything in our lives. I told her about the wild route to Alyosha and how it'd all come about by my heartache about Buffalo.

When I told her he was Norman Mailer's son, she said the truest thing that would ever be said about the situation: "Well, honey, of course Norman Mailer's son broke your heart!"

Later that night, I left to go meet Quantum Starlight at her flat. She waited for me on the street. I was surprised by her physical presence. She was smaller, more catlike than I'd expected. She had wild, curly dark hair, freckles, and a guttural tick in her throat.

"Do you mind it?" she asked, a childlike look in her eyes.

I peeled off my shirt, exposing all my surgery scars and knife wounds. "Do you mind it?"

We made love into the morning hours, until we fell asleep, spent in each other's arms.

The next morning, my phone chimed with a text.

It was Dana: *turn on CNN, it's Norman.*

I scrolled the news on my phone and saw the headline: LEGENDARY AMERICAN WRITER NORMAN MAILER DIES IN NEW YORK.

I must have howled because Alyosha shot out of the bed in fear, then seeing my tears, came back and wrapped me up in her arms. I wanted to get out of there. I wanted to be in Buffalo's arms.

I texted Buffalo: *i'm so sorry. i love you.*

Something happened to me then; I just went numb. It was if all the pain I'd endured the last few years overwhelmed me. I couldn't feel it. My lips went numb. They tensed up and took on an ugly, taut slash. I started to shiver, though I wasn't cold.

Alyosha looked at me, pushed my hair from my eyes.

"You're in shock, love."

I gazed up at her deep green eyes. Maybe it was her accent, but I couldn't understand a word she said.

"I'm going to help you now."

Alyosha began to pinch me, all over. Her fingers were fine and pale and slender. She pinched me along my thighs, on the underside of my breasts. She took tiny bites of my skin here and there between her teeth. These weren't love bites or playful pinches; they hurt. They hurt a lot. Between these wounds, she kissed me. Bite, kiss. Pinch, kiss. Bite, kiss. Pinch, kiss. Eventually, my whole body felt on fire.

I started to cry. I couldn't stop crying.

"That's the quantum science of sorrow, my love."

AND JUST WHEN

Life went back to normal after that. No more Second Saturdays, no more pining for Buffalo. I went back to simple days with the sweet three. Teaching. Cooking dinners. Enduring the visitation schedule of dropping the kids off with Liam one week every month to his house in Sacramento. Keeping to myself. Writing poems.

In some ways I gave up on life. I certainly gave up on the idea of love. I felt like I'd come so close to the edge so many times I couldn't take that risk again. Every time I tried to have a little something extra, things went terribly wrong. So I finally accepted that custody of my children was perhaps the only thing I got.

And that was enough. The years stretched out, and Liam bounced back and forth between supervised and unsupervised visitation. I knew now that when he was put on supervised visitation, it was only a matter of time before he'd win back unsupervised again. The only thing that still hung over my head unresolved was the house in Ocean Springs. Houses in that part of the world didn't sell for four, sometimes five years after the storm.

On the day the house papers came in the mail, offering me a paltry sum for my part of it (roughly 4 percent) and making the ten-day monthly unsupervised visitation permanent forever, I called both Addison and Dr. Colette. Both of them were in agreement: if I'd learned one thing over all these years, it was that the path of least resistance was always the safest for my children.

I signed the papers.

A strange feeling came over me.

Grayson, ironically, was home from school that day. When I asked him what was wrong, he said, "I just can't go." He'd wandered out from his room that morning and announced, "I'm not going to school today." I don't know why, but I let him stay home. Avery's friend Leilani's mom came to pick up Avery and Aidan, pulling into our drive in her minivan, stepping out to wave through the window at me. As soon as I saw her wave, I saw the van begin to move, with Leilani and her two little brothers inside.

Backward.

Rolling.

Down our drive.

Across the street.

Headed into the yard of our across-the-street neighbors.

I screamed, pointed. Mrs. Yokomoto ran desperately, catching up to the van, tucking in by grabbing the wheel, and slamming her flip-flopped foot into the brake right before it hit the neighbor's house.

My heart was pounding double.

Part of me thought, *I can't let this woman drive my children to school.* But it was already time to go, and the kids were outside and everyone was laughing like it was all a great escapade, and in my brain I could only hear my own heartbeat, with a rhythmic song.

My cell phone rang, and I answered it. I told my friend Patrick about the wild van chase and the court papers.

Then I heard my voice say, "I don't feel right; I gotta go."

That's the last thing I remember. The next thing I knew, I was lying on the kitchen floor, with Mama yelling at me, "Alice Mary, get up! Did you take something?"

Grayson sat at my head, with his small hand on my shoulder, his wide blue eyes staring down at me, quiet as a midnight hotel hall.

"I'm fine, I'm fine," I mumbled.

"You most certainly are not fine!" Mama shrieked, grabbing a mirror I'd brought out to my desk to pluck my brows in better light, "Look at yourself!" She thrust the mirror in my face, and then I saw myself—black eyes, what looked like a broken nose, a horrible scrape between my nose and upper lip, busted bottom lip, chin broke open like a too-ripe plum.

"I'm bloody."

"You called 9-1-1, right, Grayson?" Mama asked over my head.

"Yes, ma'am, I called them first. Then you. Then I put the dog in the crate, then I opened the front door. Then I came back and sat down here with Mama," Grayson reported.

His voice sounded so far away.

"What happened to her?" Mama asked.

"I was in the other room. I heard her tell someone on the phone she didn't feel right, then I heard a big bang, then I ran in here and she was jerking around on the floor and her chair she was sitting in was way over there, and there was blood, so that's when I called 9-1-1."

"You did good, honey," Mama cooed. "Let's get her up."

I could hear the ambulance in the distance, and I remember Mama and Grayson leading me over to the couch, where I was lying when the local firehouse paramedics came in. I knew them from the field trip in Aidan's class the week before.

"Alice, can you hear me?" one asked, shining a light back and forth in my eyes.

"Yes, I have ears."

"Do you know what happened to you?"

"Mama says I'm not okay. I think I broke my face," I said quietly.

"Did you take anything, Alice?"

"No, sir."

"I need you to tell me if you did. It's important."

"I didn't."

"Even if it's something the doctor gave you."

"I didn't take anything."

But I'd been having seizures for years, hiding them from almost everyone. They started shortly after Liam choked me. I went to a lady doctor in Mobile after the first one and convinced her to not keep a record of it. If Liam found out I had a seizure disorder, the motion to reverse custody would have come at the speed of light.

"Sometimes I fall down," I told the medic.

"Is that what happened?"

"I don't know." I really had no idea what happened.

"Young man," the medic asked Grayson, "are you the one who called?"

"Yes, sir," he answered.

"Did you see her fall?"

"No, sir. I heard a big crash, but by the time I came in, she was just shaking on the floor."

"Shaking, like convulsing?" the medic asked.

"Yes, sir, I guess so," Grayson answered.

"Alice. Alice—look at me! I need you to stay awake."

"Yes, sir," I mumbled. I felt as if I was looking up at them all from the bottom of a steamy terrarium.

"Do you know what year it is?"

Silence.

"Alice, can you tell me what year it is?"

"Nineteen sixty-six."

I heard Mama gasp then, a little cry escape, before she said, "That's when she was born."

"Do you know what street you live on?"

"I live on this lane."

"Which lane is that, Alice? Can you tell me the name of it?"

"This one."

"Alice, let me ask you another question. I need you to think about it and answer for me if you can, okay?"

"Okay," I said from my resting place on the dirt at the bottom of the misty glass terrarium of my mind.

"Who is the president?"

"Of what?" I asked.

"Who is the president of the United States?"

"The flycatcher in chief." I heard Grayson laugh, and then there was movement, and I felt myself strapped to a board and then slid into an ambulance. And sliding backward down the highway like someone going down a very clear drain.

It was only later that we all pieced together what happened.

First I opened the court papers: *Recent, Relevant.*

Then Mrs. Yokomoto lost control of her van.

The kids that were going to school went.

I answered a call, hung up.

Then I had a massive grand mal seizure, the worst I'd had since sustaining an acquired seizure disorder due to lack of oxygen to the brain.

Due to lack of oxygen to the brain, while being strangled. By Liam, all those years before.

I seized, while sitting in my zebra-striped office chair at my desk in the kitchen, under the window.

Hit my head on the desk, smashing my keyboard with my face.

Two black eyes and ruptured eye sockets that would take three years to heal.

Broken nose.

Split lip.

Still seizing, I bucked in the chair, and it tipped and slipped out under me, shooting across the kitchen floor.

Slammed my head on the floor.

On the floor. I still seized. Grayson came in. The ambulance came.

A few days later, I learned my fate: not just a fall, a traumatic brain injury. I'd hit my head so hard I'd injured my brain, permanently.

The skull is like a bowl, with sharp-edged ridges lining the inside. When shook, the brain hits on these ridges and gets ripped and torn.

A coup contrecoup with diffuse axonal shearing of the brain.

In layman's terms? Shaken baby syndrome.

Only I'd survived.

Thanks to Grayson, yet again.

I could no longer read books. About an hour after the fall, I could not speak in sentences. The neurologist finally stopped me as I said, "But I say, I say, I say, ambulance, I say, words, row words." I was trying to explain I spoke in sentences at first.

"When the edges of the brain are torn like that, the damage keeps settling in for hours."

The damage keeps settling in.

Just like abuse: the damage keeps settling in.

I went home a few days later, dragging my left leg, unable to move my left arm, unable to speak in sentences, no longer able to read a book. My short-term memory had about a ten-minute span. While the kids were at school, I'd lie in bed for hours, then get up finally and drag my leg across the room to my bathroom. Once there, I'd stand perplexed, not sure what the toilet was.

Then the pee would run down my leg and it'd come to me: toilet.

I slept about eighteen hours a day the first few months. When I rested my head on the pillow, lying on my side, I could hear my heartbeat in my ear like a conch shell, roaring.

Recent. Relevant. Recent. Relevant. Recent. Relevant. Recent. Relevant.

I could no longer drive. A few weeks after the injury, the permanent visitation schedule kicked in. Mama drove me and the kids downtown to Liam's second residence (by now, he had a place in Midtown not far from where we met originally, as well as in New Orleans). The kids got out of the car, crying silently. They each came to the passenger side of Mama's Oldsmobile.

I embraced the kids one after the other with my right arm around their necks and said the same thing to each: *Don't tell him.*

With no other choice, I complied with this visitation schedule for several years, despite his cruelty, despite his drunken nights. Despite the frantic, sad texts the children sent. None of it was enough to stop visitation.

I kept working and working at it, learning how to walk and talk, how to read and especially write. For years. I kept taking the kids downtown to Liam's, reluctantly, but knowing that failure to do so would mean losing custody altogether.

For years.

I took them, time after time and month after month.

For years.

Despite the times he was drunk.

For years.

Despite him taunting Avery with a saw, telling her he'd slice her pneumonia cough out of her.

For shame.

Despite his collection of real human skulls, scattered around his house.

For fear.

Despite the verbal abuse.

His habit.

You're fat. You're stupid. You're ugly.

Without me to aim his insults at, he now divided them evenly among the kids: Aidan was fat, Grayson was stupid, Avery was ugly. She looked the most like me.

A neurologist had told me about six months after my injury,

after I'd undergone some extensive testing: 1. You'll never speak in sentences again 2. You'll never teach again 3. You'll never write again.

But year after year, despite being uninsured, I made up my own rehab. I'd watch Gabby Giffords on YouTube, and re-create my own rehab in my bedroom. Grayson would get up early before school and run through the paces with me, doing exercises we created with broom handles, pool balls from the dollar store, jumbo rubber bands, Silly Putty.

To speak again, I "echoed" stories on NPR for hours a day and memorized poems until my brain was rewired. To write again, I placed an "X" in every third or fourth place where a word, because of aphasia, should be. Then I'd go back later and Google "thing that goes over body of water that joins two pieces of land" and finally arrive at "bridge."

Eventually, after years, I started to return to myself.

It seemed I was always fighting to return to myself. And I was always relinquishing my children. And over the years, Liam would have long stretches of unsupervised, and then supervised visitation. He had several CPS cases, followed by the immediate "reunification" process.

This went on and on, endlessly. Almost unbearably. Until one night in July, about four long years after my injury.

I was back teaching a composition class at a wretched as-seen-on-TV tech college, lecturing on the Socratic method of argumentation. The criminal justice room where the class was held had walls decorated with crude student-made collages of crime scenes. Above the instructor's desk, a poster board monstrosity with red paint splatters splashed across candid photos of students awash in fake blood and fake gunshot wounds; and another where one student (perp) choked another student (victim), which kept coming loose, hanging slantwise before I pushed the corner of tape in once again.

My students had moved onto group labs, working quietly

together at long, white, plastic tables. The room was freezing, and I took my blazer off the back of my chair and put it back on. Almost instantly, I felt my phone start to buzz in my pocket. I didn't check it the first time—a student came up to my desk to ask a question, and I spent a few minutes showing him how to turn his sentences inside out so they would have varying music and form. After he returned to his group, my phone buzzed again.

I pulled out the phone: there was near a dozen texts from all three of the children.

Aidan: *call the police daddy drunk*

Grayson: *daddy just beat me up. now i'm crying.*

Grayson: *call the police please*

Grayson: *please*

Avery: *daddy just basically beat up Grayson and we both started crying. Grayson said he was going 2 call the police but daddy was saying NO. help us!!!*

Grayson: *please answer*

Grayson: *please*

Me: *oh my god*

Grayson: *please call please*

Me: *okay I'm calling.*

Grayson: *are they coming?*

By this time, I'd left my class, announcing an emergency. I was flying down the 50 in the moonlight with the Sacramento PD on speakerphone.

"Ma'am? What time did the first text message come in?"

I was driving ninety miles an hour and checking and sending text messages and trying to direct the police to Liam's big craftsman house.

"Ma'am? You don't remember the address, but it's the second house in, right?"

Avery: *are they coming?*

Me: *yes, i'm here too. i'm waiting. they told me not to come in.*

Avery: *i see you outside*

Me: *they're coming*

Avery: *thank you for coming*

Avery: *we have everything packed*

I stood partially hidden behind a palm in front of Liam's house. My heart was pounding double.

I could see the kids in the upstairs windows, their arms waving frantically at me like they were stuck in a burning house and couldn't get out. I saw Liam cross the living room. I could hear his fancy boots stomp across the hardwood floor.

Me: *i am here, waiting for police. we are on the phone. what did he do?*

Grayson: *we were hiding from him then he found us and just started screaming at us*

Grayson: *then he started getting mad and started to kick and choke me*

Grayson: *i started to hit him back*

Grayson: *i didn't know what to do*

I stood behind the fat palm, shaking. The night sky was full of stars, a galaxy of lost hope.

Avery: *MAKE THEM SEE HOW DRUNK HE IS TOO*

Avery: *with the test thing*

Finally, a Sac PD patrol car pulled up quietly behind me. I walked to the window.

"Are you the one who called, ma'am?"

"Yes, sir. Here are the texts."

I handed my phone and watched, and he scrolled through the texts from all the kids, flipping between the three. He called for backup, got out of his car, and started toward the house, with me behind.

"Ma'am, I need you to stay out here. No matter what happens. I need you to stay out here. Do you understand?"

"Yes, sir."

I saw him mount the steps, knock quietly on the door. Liam answered, and the officer went in.

Me: *they're in there with him now*
Grayson: *ok*

I heard Liam raise his voice, saw the officer take him down. I heard voices—his, the officer, his girlfriend. I moved from behind the palm and to the bottom of his gracious stoop. A second later, he was back up and cuffed, being led down the front steps by the officer to a second Sac PD car I hadn't even noticed pull up.

I heard Avery scream, *"Finally!"*

As I rushed up the stairs, I could hear the kids running down Liam's dark wooden stairway. The minute they saw me, all three started wailing. A kind of keening I'd never heard from them before—panicked, animal, full of all the sorrow they'd been holding these long years.

In a matter of minutes, the house was filled with a dozen officers, interviewing everyone, a CSI photographer put Grayson up against a wall and had him remove his shirt, taking photos of his torso. Of his neck.

Flash.

Recent.

Flash.

Relevant.

Flash.

Recent.

Flash.

Relevant.

Liam sat glaring out the window from the back of the car in the street. He watched me pass from room to room helping the children. It was the first time I'd been in his house.

After a while, they drove off with Grayson in an ambulance, me and Avery and Aidan following behind in our car. It was almost midnight as we pulled away from Liam's house. Avery sat in the passenger seat next to me. As we passed by Liam, he turned his head and looked right at us.

"Finally, you got what you deserved, fucker! Everyone knows

now, finally!" Avery screamed. She was fifteen, and it was ten years to the date from when he strangled me. It was the first time I'd ever heard her cuss.

From the back seat, Aidan said, "Well, Mama, now you only owe Grayson once."

"What do you mean, sweetie?"

"He saved your life twice now, and you just paid him back."

"This is the last time any of us are going to need to save each other, baby, I promise."

There was a silence in the car. The stars passed overhead, closer than they'd seemed in years, like a blanket of truth, finally thrown down upon us.

Liam was booked, charged with felony child endangerment. We wouldn't be seeing him again anytime soon.

And back into the carnival of court we went. This time, I knew how to perform more tricks.

FINALLY

We got out of the hospital around four in the morning, driving through the night with the sunroof open, stars passing silently above. I tried to convince myself what I'd always believed: that every pine tree pointed to a corresponding star. I needed to believe in some magic, some order in the world. I parked out front, and we all went in and piled on my bed, together, and fell fast asleep in dreams. Every hour or so, I'd wake up and look at Grayson's neck, see the raised red marks there. The night was quiet and I could hear them all breathing and it sounded like stars scraping the sky.

In the morning, a woman from CPS came to visit.

It always felt like we were in trouble, even this time.

The DA called on day one.

The Victim's Advocate Office called.

Liam's parole officer called.

Liam spent less than twenty-four hours in jail.

We were notified by text when he was released.

I filed for a protective order with the family court on the second day.

At his first hearing in the Sacramento County Superior Court, the DA asked for a criminal protective order.

We had consecutive cases in the family court and the criminal court.

It took over my life entire.

Liam hired not one but two high-powered attorneys: one family attorney and one criminal attorney. Both were big, nasty sharks who were used to swimming in rough waters.

His family attorney had one goal: go after me, hard.

His criminal attorney sang one song: Grayson had no injuries.

If a stranger tackled a thirteen-year-old child and strangled him, he'd be in prison; if a father tackles a thirteen-year-old child and strangles him, he hires a high-powered attorney and starts negotiating.

Liam's first motion in the family court was to ask for reunification therapy and supervised visitation. Without an attorney, it was me who had to go and fight his attorney.

Luckily, I won.

With all I'd learned, I knew how to fight. Several attorneys who were in court that day came up to me after and congratulated me for taking down Liam's attorney. I had pointed out that there was a criminal court pending, and therefore Liam could not be honest in therapy if he could go. That my children had no interest in seeing him, that seeing them, even in a therapeutic setting, would be breaking the criminal protective order. I also pointed out the obvious: we'd done supervised visitation, reunification therapy, and court-ordered counseling before. It hadn't worked.

I took a deep breath before I said the next thing. "Although I argued vigorously to this court that Liam Rivers was a danger to the minor children, this court ruled that the overwhelming evidence presented was *neither recent nor relevant* and ordered unsupervised visitation with the minor children.

"I delivered the children to Liam Rivers faithfully for years, despite my deep belief that something like this would someday happen."

It had been my worst fear, and now my worst fear had come true.

The court declined Liam's motions.

Even so, Liam continued to keep filing more. I think half his strategy was to break me down. I went to court nineteen times in the first three months after he assaulted Grayson. You'd think at some point he'd have the decency to give us some space to heal and have some peace, right?

Wrong.

At home, the kids rarely came out of their rooms. If someone came to the door, they dove to the floor like a bomb had detonated. One time the postman was trying to deliver a package to us and I saw Grayson, huddled on the bathroom floor, hiding, with his hands over his head.

This is the legacy their father left them.

Meanwhile, Liam kept trying to negotiate a better deal with the DA. He asked for a non-assault charge. He asked for the charges to be dropped if he took some parenting classes. Eventually, when presumably his attorneys convinced him his chances weren't good, he agreed to a plea bargain. Almost one year after he assaulted Grayson, we showed up in court to hear him plea. Everyone was there but him. His attorney explained, "The good doctor is in another state, saving lives, and I am here to enter the plea on his behalf."

The injustice of it all enraged me. Here I was sitting in court while he paid someone $50,000 to show up for him. The judge set a date for sentencing. Before I even left the courthouse, one of my girlfriends texted me: *your ex is here at Rubicon.*

Rubicon is a local brew pub.

I texted back: *right now?*

She texted me a photo of him standing at the bar, then proceeded to send more photos and told me all about how he bought the whole bar Girl Scout cookies, tried to pick up her friend, recognized her from our children's school, asked about me, then proceeded to tell her how crazy I am and how I keep the children from him. All while he was supposed to be in court pleading guilty to child endangerment. I forwarded all of it to the DA, who forwarded all of it to Liam's attorney and the judge.

Two weeks later, we all showed up, including the children, to the county jail courtrooms to read our victim witness statements and watch Liam be sentenced. At that time, he withdrew his plea.

It seemed it would never end.

Finally, a month later, we went to court again. This time, he showed up and he pled out. The kids went up before the judge to read their statements. Liam turned in his chair at the table to face them.

"Sir, turn your chair around; the witnesses are directing the court, not you."

He didn't turn around.

"Sir, turn your chair around."

He didn't turn around.

"Let's let them read," said the judge.

And that's how each of the children ended up reading their victim impact statement directly to their father, less than two feet away from him, face-to-face. Avery was by then sixteen, Grayson fourteen, Aidan twelve. Avery went first.

"Hello, my name is Avery Anderson, and I am sixteen years old. I have two younger brothers, Grayson and Aidan. We have been through a lot together over the last ten years.

"NOTE: I will never use his name or anything that associates him with me, so I am using *him, he, his,* or *blank* instead of saying his name.

"About ten years ago, when we were still living in Ocean

Springs, Mississippi, things changed for the worst. After Hurricane Katrina, my ___ started drinking more and more every day and started screaming at us all the time. One night, he attacked my mom with all of us watching. We left the next morning. My mom filed for divorce, and my dad tried to take us away from her. He told us we'd never see her again. He was drunk and violent and scary. Ever since that time, I have really bad anxiety attacks whenever I see gore, violence, or people being hurt. I've even had a panic attack (I pass out cold and faint) because I was so scared he would come to my school for back-to-school night. I still have them to this day, and I'm always scared something is going to set one off. I have to tell all my teachers at school to warn them, and the kids at school have seen me faint. I've tried to prevent them, but I can't control them. This happens because of him.

"When I was in sixth grade, I got pneumonia. Even though he is a doctor, he refused to even let me stay home from school. He didn't want me to take up his free time during the day to go shopping and go to bars. I just got more and more sick. He was angry that I was sick so long. One day, he came in my room at his house. He was holding up this huge rusty saw, the kind you cut wood with. He said, 'I can cut that cough right out of you with this.' Then he held it up to me and laughed. I was terrified.

"After he attacked Grayson last summer, I had horrible nightmares about him. I had nightmares about us going back to his house, about him beating me up, about him bullying me, and about him coming to my house to try to kidnap me. With all those dreams, I would wake up in tears. Those dreams worry me and make me feel bad because the nightmares are either stuff he did that was horrible, or stuff that I'm really scared will happen.

"On the same night of July 14, 2014, I was physically abused, too. I was in too much shock about Grayson, so I didn't say anything. The police and the people at the hospital were interviewing Grayson, and I kind of got lost in the shuffle. But when it happened, he grabbed my arm, yanked me out of the closet, and

I said, "Stop, stop!" in a panic. My whole arm socket hurt terribly the next day. It felt like it was popped out of place. It makes me sad because I was abused, too.

"One summer, my brothers and I had to go have visitation with him in New Orleans, where he lives half the time. I was going into middle school, so I was twelve years old—Grayson was ten, and Aidan was eight. We were in the square in the French Quarter. He kept getting beer after beer, going from bar to bar. He even left us outside of a bar all alone so he could go inside and drink. It was dark, crowded, and there were drunk people everywhere. A man came up and kissed my hand. It was very scary. It was even scarier because he didn't take care of us; he was drunk, and we didn't know anyone else. We felt alone and scared. Events like that made me terrified of going on trips with him. I was also scared to even go to places with him here. You never know what he might do.

"At home, he used to always tell me what's wrong with me. He said that no one would love me, that I'm gross, and that I'd have to live with the homeless men in the park, that they are the only people who would ever be interested in marrying me. He made fun of how I look and told me no one will ever love me. He made me cry for hours and hours. At any time, he would come in my room just to say a mean thing. Last summer, he kept telling me how I needed to go to a therapist because I was sick in the brain and needed 'help.'

"In the end, that was one true thing he said; I did need help. I need help to be safe from him, to never be hurt by him again, and to not live in fear of seeing him. In fact, I hope I never have to see him again."

Avery came back to the bench and sat by me and gave Aidan a small squeeze on the arm as he went up to read his statement.

"Hi. My name is Aidan Anderson. I am twelve years old, and I am the youngest of our family. I am here to talk about how Liam Rivers affected my life. I don't think of him as my dad anymore.

"I don't like how he bullied me so many times. He made fun

of my hair, he called me fat so many times I lost count. He would constantly, every time I saw him, pretend to "wrestle" with me. What he was really doing was throwing me around, pinning me on the floor, pretending like I was his punching dummy. I would always tell him to stop, and he wouldn't. Instead he would laugh at me and wouldn't stop. Usually I ended up crying and hurt.

"A father should be someone who supports you, accepts you, feels proud of the person you are, and takes care of you. He didn't support me and help me, he didn't like me, and he didn't take care of me or help me in any way. He made me feel like he was ashamed that I was his son.

"When I was with him, I felt uncomfortable because he would always be very, very drunk and crazy and usually very mean. Last summer is not the first time he hurt any of us—he has hurt us a lot of times over our whole life.

"I do not want to see him again because of his actions. I feel like if I have to go see him, then he will do it again. Last summer when he attacked my brother and sister, I was hiding in a different closet. I heard crying and screaming. It made me feel so confused and scared. He told us if we called the police he would beat us up again. That is not the words he used, but I do not want to say what he said. He basically told us he would hurt us if we tried to get help.

"Even though there is a protective order, he still tries to contact me. When I see his name come up on my iPad, I feel panicked. It feels like he is creeping up on me and coming back into my life. This last year, when we didn't have to see him at all, have been the most amazing days of my life. I felt safe. I felt free."

Liam smiled through these statements as if the kids were reading book reports in school, as if he were a proud parent at a spelling bee. Aidan came and sat down and hard next to me, not catching my eye. Finally, Grayson went up and stood, facing his father. His voice was low, steady, strong.

"My name is Grayson Anderson. I stopped using the Rivers in

my name years ago because he is not a father to me. A father does not scream at you in a drunken rage. A father does not lock you in hotel hallways in the middle of the night in your underwear when you're five. A father does not leave you and your sister alone outside of bars in the French Quarter while he is inside drinking at night. A father does not tell you your mother is crazy and call her names. A father does not shove you into walls. A father does not come after your sister with a saw. More than anything, a father does not try to kill you.

"On the night that we are here for today, he took us out with him and his girlfriend to a string of bars. In one after another, we had to sit at a different table, alone, while they sat at the bar and drank. What kind of people make their kids sit at a different table? It was so bad the waiters felt sorry for us and gave us free food and drinks. I wish someone had helped us. On the way home, he was so drunk he kept falling off his bike. When we got there, we were just having fun, playing with squirt bottles. It's summer, it's hot. That's what kids do. They goof around. We squirted water off the balcony and got him wet. Most kids would laugh at that, right? Not us. We were terrified. We hid. My little brother hid in one closet, and my sister and I hid in another. We have a father we know to hide from.

"And he came up in his usual drunken rage and found us. And he pulled my sister out first. He yanked my sister out by her arm and threw her across the room and onto the bed, and that's when I came out to help her. And that's when he did it. He grabbed me and threw me down on the bed and put his hands around my neck and choked me. I thought he wouldn't stop. I thought he would kill me. He was on top of me with a red, drunk face full of rage and hate. I've seen him do this before—to my mom. This is the second time. The second time. Then he finally got off me and he started kicking me everywhere with his pointy, hard boots. Then he yelled at us to get in bed and not to call the police. That's the kind of father I have. And that's why I have no father at all.

This last year with no contact with him has been the best year of my life. Because it has meant safety and it has meant freedom. Finally, I know what it means to be safe."

The judge thanked Grayson and instructed Liam's attorney that Liam was allowed to make a statement to the court as well. Instead of issuing an apology or any remorse, Liam stood up and gave a short, inspirational speech about how the kids should do their best in school, strive for greatness, always be honest and kind, and continue to know right from wrong. He addressed each child by name, and when he got to Grayson, he said, "Grayson, you are the most like me."

What he said after that is anyone's guess, as I had blocked him out with the force of sheer blind rage.

Liam put in a new guilty plea and was sentenced on the spot.

He received not a single day of jail time.

He was, however, stripped of both physical and legal custody and given a five-year protective order that is renewable for life.

As we walked into the sunlight down the wide steps of the courthouse, Avery said, "Remember when I yelled down the stairs that night, '*Finally*'?"

"I do," I said to the kids, "and finally just arrived."

DREAM A LITTLE
DREAM

I'm second to wake up every day. Mama wakes up first, when it's
still dark outside, and—when I hear the apologetic slap of her
size 11 feet pad down the stairs to the kitchen, moving last night's
plates from rack to shelf, the coffeepot starting to bubble and
tick—I get up, too. Brother and Papa sleep in. I see her like this
every morning (hips bumped up to the counter, black hair wild
down her back, hot-pink velour zip-up robe open to her naked
body, her nipples like small saucers of raspberry punch) watching the coffee drip. When she hears me, she turns. And it's then I
see it.

The dark flower of her eye. Deep purple with veins of green,
it opens slowly, the way a cactus flower opens overnight in the movies they show at school. The morning flickers, bits of light jumping
through the room, bits of moonlight filtering in from the screen in a
thousand square beams that only I can see. The black eye is the

center of her face now, the truth of what she holds in her heart
laid bare.

Summer quarter. Forty students, only one female, fill a class of busi-
ness writing at the tech college, and we're in the criminal justice
wing. On every wall, student posters of "murder victims." There's a
guy with stab wounds; a child with a garbage sack over her head
cinched tight with a cracked vinyl belt; there's one of a suit with the
head blown off, a perfect splash of blood on the wall behind him;
one with a lady with a yellow rope around her neck; more. The stu-
dents, most of them vets on the GI Bill, work on portfolios while I
grade. My phone, upside down on the folding table, starts to buzz.
Buzz.
Buzz.
Buzz.
There's always a warning, if you know how to listen.
On the freeway, the sky full of infuriating starlight, I talk with
the dispatcher, tell her where his house is on that block, read the
texts aloud.
They're sending someone, ma'am.
When I pull up, I see Avery and Grayson: two children shapes
in a window looking out.
A police car pulls up, lights on, no siren, just as I do.
We both get out.
Stay back, ma'am.
I hide behind a palm.
The door opens, the policeman takes him down.
The road fills up with sirens.
After ten years of abuse, finally the sirens.
The forensic cop comes in, camera hanging from his neck.
Can you lift your shirt, son?
Yes, sir.
Take it off.

And that's when I see it.

Bruises like desert flowers everywhere on his body, thirteen years of skin and bone. And his neck, the mark of fingers encircling his neck, the scratches from where his own fingers tried to pry his father's off still raw, blood rising like revelation.

Grayson stands there shirtless like that, the flash popping in the room, each one sounding like a word, whispered:

Flash: pain

Flash: heart

Flash: love

Flash: hate

Flash: freedom

Flash flash flash: a boy alive

Flash: I wake; next to me in bed is Avery, and the boys are in the other bed and the ocean crashes a few floors below our open sliding door hotel window. It's the first family vacation we've been on, ever, just the four of us. Our lives have been run by the tick and hum of trials and fear and misfortune, and finally we've come to this: some ease. These nightmares come, but they are only this: dreams.

Eventually, the sweet three wake, stretching like big ridiculous cats in the too-small room, leaping over the bags everywhere from the outlet mall the day before, the boxes of Vans and the piles of shirts, soft with that smell all new clothes have now of rainy forests. Down to the car and onto the highway, music blaring the way it always is, all of us laughing, singing along, darting between cars on the way to the beach.

And then we're there. And the beach is everything it is to everyone: rescue, respite, relief. Wide and white, the water pounding against the shore the way it does in SoCal: extravagant, ornate. I watch as the kids run in and out of the cold surf, laughing. And it's then I notice it, how happy they are. How they laugh. How they don't have a care in the world. How it took me ten long years to deliver them this ease.

Grayson, who has picked up a shitty plastic football down to the Walgreens along with the bucket and castle set Avery and I chose and the mountain of snacks, magazines, drinks, and sunscreen we paid a fortune for, is trying to get the kids to throw the ball with him, but they're not biting. He holds the ball above his head, catches my eye, and shrugs his shoulders up in that motion that means, *Will ya?* So I get up and run down to the water's edge.

And despite the last eight years of fighting back from traumatic brain injury, despite being told I'd never walk without aid again, never read again, never teach again, never write again, I continue to every day find one more thing that I can do that I thought would probably never happen. Today, that thing is throw a plastic football by the Pacific with my son. And fuck if I'm not good at it. Grayson and I launch that football back and forth as the sea rushes cold and sweet over our feet again and again and again, back and forth, back and forth. The look in his eyes shows me he's as amazed as I am that I'm able to do it.

When Liam strangled me and oxygen was cut off to my brain, I developed a seizure disorder, which caused the seizure that made me fall and sustain my brain injury, a coup contrecoup with diffuse axonal shearing of the brain: you don't think about the ways domestic violence can kill you in slow motion. But recovery from traumatic brain injury is also slow motion, painstaking, but constantly moving forward the way a football arcs and spirals across a white blue sky, the way a seagull does, the way sometimes it just hangs there, standing still. But eventually it will move. And just like that, I move forward. Every year, I get better: teach a class, take a trip, write a book, take my kids to the ocean.

Things fall to pieces: things fall back together again.

The ball arcs across the sky, spinning, and Grayson is laughing and I glance left and see Avery and Aidan up to their necks, swimming, and this time my throw is a little off, but that's okay because this time Grayson's not diving into a bathroom terrified but into the ocean, free.

It turns out sometimes extraordinary things happen on very ordinary days. It was mid-August, scorching, at a public beach: there must have been a thousand people there. We had four cheap towels from the Walgreens spread out in a row, anchored with fashion magazines and a six-pack of Pepsi and a pink bucket full of sand and a pile of flip-flops dug in straight like rubber roses. Next to us, two women in their eighties with floral-skirted one-pieces sat in low-slung chairs and sipped tiny bottles of rosé from straws and held hands. There was a big family behind us that had put up a tent with a striped top, like a circus tent—they had a table to one side with food, and the men were in the middle, singing and playing guitar while the kids buried each another in dark, muddy, funeral-like mounds. Teens walked through all day, back and forth, sand kicked up from their smooth heels as they went. I imagined somewhere in the endless crowd was someone just like me, who carried the ghost of fingerprints around their neck. Somewhere was a mother who'd taken her children and run. Somewhere was a trio of siblings who knew what cruelty meant. Somewhere was a family who'd lost it all. Somewhere, maybe in the concession stand line, was someone who'd stood in court and told someone they'd loved once why they no longer existed in their heart before they watched them walk away for good. But today all we had was sun. All we had was sand. And the wild sky above holding us all there in our chapel made of scars. And all I had was music rising from a tent and waves crashing against the far back corner of my heart and my children finally laughing without being struck through with fear. And all at once, I could breathe again. Be again. Live again.

Finally.